HAUNTED ANGLESEY

Bunty Austin

ISBN: 0-86381-883-8

Cover Illustration: Bunty Austin
Cover design: Sian Parri

Published in 2005
by Gwasg Carreg Gwalch, Llanrwst.

Gwindy
(cover photograph)

The ruins of Gwindy are all that is left of a once thriving Coaching Inn – the second and last of the two staging posts on the old road between Menai and Holyhead.

It is a very haunted place, as people walking past in the dark will confirm. The bustle of coaches arriving, the clip-clop of horses on cobbles, and men shouting orders in the old courtyard can be plainly heard. People would skirt the place by leaving the road, crossing the field and rejoining the road beyond the ruined inn.

But not many people walk in these days of car travel.

Acknowledgements

I should like to offer my grateful thanks to everyone who has taken endless time and trouble in helping me to compile this book. These include:

- TOMOS ROBERTS, BA, DM, PSA (Formerly Senior Archivist, Bangor University) for his research into the records of the Anglesey Antiquarian Society
- PROFESSOR DAVID CRYSTAL (Recognised as the foremost authority on Linguistics in the world)
- Mr ANDREW DAVIDSON (Leading Archaeologist)
- Mrs JOYCE PIGGIN (Dragon Channel, Anglesey Internet)
- Ms ANNE VENABLES, BA, DM (County Archivist, Môn)
- Ms ELEN WYN-HUGHES, BA, DM (Assistant Archivist, Bangor University)
- Rev. J. AELWYN ROBERTS (Author, 'Holy Ghostbuster')
- Mr M.P. MARKWOLD (National Gardens Society)
- Mr H. BROUGH (Feature Writer, Daily Post)
- Mrs SUSIE VINCE (Kings Secretarial Services, Poole) for her expert and faultless presentation of my MSS.

The many contributors who are named in the stories and, finally, with love and gratitude, to Walt for his endless patience.

Bunty Austin
Llaneilian, Amlwch, 2005

Glossary of Welsh Place-names

Anglesey	Ynys Môn
Cardiff	Caerdydd
Newborough	Niwbwrch
Swansea	Abertawe
Holyhead	Caergybi
Red Wharf Bay	Traeth Coch
Church Bay	Porth Swtan
Menai Strait	Afon Menai
Point Lynas	Y Leinws

Words frequently used in place-names:

big	mawr/fawr
bay	bae
hill	allt/bryn
mountain	mynydd
river	afon
brook	nant
crows	brain
chapel	capel
beach	traeth
cemetery	mynwent

Contents

Foreword

I have always been fascinated by ghosts. When we came to Anglesey years ago, I was overwhelmed by the fund of stories about people and places – and the matter of fact acceptance that there really were such things. So I wrote to the Editor of the *Holyhead and Anglesey Mail* and this is what I said:

'I am compiling a book about Anglesey ghosts and hauntings, and I have come across many incidents that seemed to have slipped through the net of previous more widely based books.

Being Celts, the Islanders seem to have very strong psychic powers, having a sixth sense which most of the materialistic generations elsewhere seem to have lost.

I should be delighted to hear from your readers who have ever felt or heard anything for which there seems no rational explanation.

Some houses have resident ghosts, others have haunted lanes or nearby roads, and I am sure stories have been passed down by older members of many families.

I shall be grateful for any information, and names of contributors will be mentioned in my book, unless the sender wishes to remain anonymous, and specific addresses will be confidential if need be.

I am a published author with the Thomson Group, and have researched ghost stories for many years, so I am writing this book for future generations of Anglesey people, as, alas!, in these days of TV, video games and easy travel, families are becoming fragmented, and this immense fund of folklore will be lost forever.

I look forward to your readers' replies with eagerness.'

This letter was printed under the heading 'On the Trail of Ghosts', in the *Mail* dated February 11th, 1998.

Now, years later, I have completed the book.

As you know, by their very nebulous nature, ghosts are impossible to pin down and obtain actual facts and details of them.

The first-hand accounts were straightforward and simple to

record – it was the ones which had been handed down the generations which were the most troublesome.

Some had become embellished by the storytellers, some had portions left out, and eventually many different versions were told about the same ghost.

I took great trouble to verify the stories, it was like taking directions from one helpful adviser, and moving on happily to the next person, only to be told gently that I had been badly misinformed, and then given a completely different tale.

In the end, I had so many variations on the same theme that it was comparable to reaching a mental 'spaghetti junction'.

I tore up story after story in despair, wondering how I could possibly avoid offending those kind people who had gone to the trouble of telling me their own versions.

So, in the end, I have trodden the middle path, and written down the ones which seemed to be the most interesting and/or the most unaccountable.

If you start to read a story and you grunt – 'Huh! She's got that wrong for a start!' – please accept my sincere apologies – I have done my best with the information I was given.

I had great fun writing it (I think!) and I've met many lovely people to whom I say – Thank you!

Bunty Austin

Introduction to ghosts

To believe in ghosts most people have to see, hear or, at least, sense them. Years ago, we were staying in a very old coaching inn in Derbyshire, and we were dining one night near to a table occupied by a group of American lady tourists.

They were very impressed by the age and atmosphere of the place, and my husband, Walt, and I both pricked up our ears when one of them enquired whether the place was haunted. The waitress told her that it was, although no one had ever seen the ghost, many had smelled it.

'We call her the Lavender Lady,' she said, expertly stacking dishes, 'she seems to pass along the upstairs corridors at night, and she leaves behind a beautiful scent of lavender.'

Walt's eyes met mine – I knew he was thinking what I was – what a nice ghost, gentle and harmless, just like they should be!

I looked across at the bar tender, who looked as if he'd been here since coaching days, polishing glasses. His stolid expression never changed, but he gave me a solemn wink. We'd only known him a few days, but we got on like a house on fire.

Later that night, I was lying awake listening with envy to Walt's gentle snoring, when I heard a soft creak in the corridor outside the door, then the unmistakable aroma of lavender.

I slipped out of bed, quietly opened the door, and peered out into the dim corridor, lit only by the emergency lights. There, at the end, the old bar man was creeping along, his bald head gleaming dully, mysteriously dipping low when he came to a bedroom door.

He straightened stiffly, as he rose from the last one, a hand holding his aching back. Then he turned and saw me watching him. He paused for a moment looking very guilty, then he grinned and held up a large spray can of lavender scented air freshener. Giving me a thumbs up sign he vanished around the corner.

My grin matched his as I climbed back into bed. Oh well, that gave the American ladies something to write home about – and it didn't frighten the horses!

My ghost

My first introduction to a ghost wasn't to a gentle one. It left me with a sense of menace and fear that lasted for years. I was only seven years old.

It happened in Bootle, Liverpool, my father was then a Police Sergeant, later rising to Inspector. Both my parents came from farms in Derbyshire, Mam from Montpelier Place, in Buxton, Dad from a farming family in nearby Burbage.

Mam died in Bootle in her early forties, leaving Dad with three young daughters, of whom I was the youngest. We moved from the house that held so many memories, to a tall, narrow house in Clare Road.

Eight rooms, four up and four down, so that the large front bedroom (Dad's) was a long way from the big kitchen, which we used as a living room.

I was temporarily installed in Dad's room, with chickenpox, feeling very important and cosily reading comics with the light on, about 8.00 p.m. one windy winter's evening. Comfortingly, I could hear vague snatches of conversation and laughter from the kitchen, where my eldest sister and her boyfriend were dancing to the radio. Behind me, to my left, was the bedroom door. Facing me was the large bay window with curtains drawn, and halfway down the left wall was a big Edwardian wardrobe.

Suddenly, from the side of the wardrobe furthest from me, an elderly woman appeared, and walked quickly across the room to the foot of my bed. Laying her arms along the wooden rail at the bed-end, she looked straight at me. Or rather, she didn't look, she glared. Unsmiling.

I can see her now. Grey hair, tightly permed, spectacles perched on a thin nose, and an annoyed, resentful look on her face. She wore a grey jumper, covered by a crossover pinafore, black with small purple flowers on – which I saw later, tied at the back.

I had plenty of time to see these details, including a thick gold wedding ring on one of the hands resting on my bed, as she stood there without speaking for what seemed an age. She looked absolutely real, and I had never seen her before in my life.

What seemed hours later, and was probably only a couple of

minutes, she turned abruptly, walked away, and disappeared again around the side of the wardrobe. I lay rigid with shock.

How had she come from beside the wardrobe, and how had she gone again? There was no door there.

Fright kept me still. What if she was still hiding and jumped out at me if I got out of bed and tried to reach the door? And why was she so angry? In a wobbly voice, I started to call for my sister. I called and called, but the kitchen door was closed and the radio was still playing dance music. I shouted until I was hoarse, but no one came.

Fright turned to terror, and by the time someone opened the kitchen door to come up to the bathroom, my voice had dropped to a croak, and I was sobbing and hiccupping hysterically. My sister's boyfriend, Stan, leapt up the stairs, two at a time, and carried me down. As I gulped out my story, he ran back up and searched the room thoroughly. Nothing.

When Dad came home, reassuring and strong in his police uniform, he too searched the house and drew a blank. Everyone comforted me, telling me again and again that I'd had a nightmare.

I might have been only seven, but I knew what I had seen. That was no nightmare.

After that I hated being in that house. The stairs made my hair stand on end. I used to fly down them, shoot through the gloomy dining room, and only breathe freely when I reached the warm, bright normality of the kitchen.

The family tried to laugh me out of my fears, but children's instincts are very strong. I never saw anything again and when we left the house shortly after I gradually stopped talking about it.

Dad retired from the Force, and we went back to a pretty farm in the beautiful Goyt Valley, Derbyshire. In the fullness of time, Dad died, we girls got married, and my husband, Walt, and I came to live in Anglesey. The house in Clare Road became a distant, unpleasant memory and things may have stayed thus – but for a very curious happening.

One very cold night last winter, when the big gales were racing down the Irish Sea from the north east, and slamming against the walls of our old farmhouse with giant fists, I was lying snug and warm in bed, reading – what else but ghost stories?

This particular book was by a famous author, an ex-President of the Ghost Club, and it dealt with haunted houses in the north of England. I would dearly like to quote it chapter and verse, but as I did not want to be accused of plagiarism I wrote to his publishers for permission to include the relevant passages in this book.

They wrote back very courteously to tell me that they could not themselves give permission, but had forwarded my letter to him, and he would reply direct to me. Sadly, I have heard nothing since, which rather takes away the impact of the story's conclusion, told in my own words.

So many years after the sighting, this is the explanation of my ghost – and it made me sit bolt upright.

Apparently, in that house in Clare Road, a lady lived who was not on good terms with her family. She was a staunch Roman Catholic, who wanted to be buried in a grave that was adorned with a solid, respectable headstone. The rest of her family scoffed at this, and many times she swore that if her wishes weren't carried out when she died, she would haunt the house until they were.

Successive residents, who did not know anything at all about this lady, have met her on the stairs, in the front bedroom (which was hers) and elsewhere in the house. All their accounts of the ghost tally with the descriptions of the dead woman, not only from her family, but also people who knew her when she was alive. Her family never did honour her wishes, and Mrs F.'s grave is still without a headstone.

Late as it was – I telephoned my sisters at once. I gabbled out the paragraph from the book, proving at long last that I hadn't just had a nightmare, all those years ago. They both told me that though they had never *seen* the ghost, they had often heard unexplained footsteps, and felt areas of cold air in the house.

They too had been very frightened, but kept it from me, as I was so much younger. My sighting had brought things to a head, Dad didn't want us to be alone while he was on duty, and so we moved shortly after.

I should love to contact the author of the book, to thank him for solving my small mystery, but the only address I have was for the Savage Club, which sadly, is now defunct. If I was fortunate enough to speak to him, I should like to tell him the *number* of the

14

house in Clare Road. I'm sure he already has it on his records, but it would put the final seal on the validity of my story, should our numbers match.

So that's *my* ghost! (My first one that is . . .)

And now to other people's ghosts.

Amlwch – old man walking

Recently, we were having our central heating and Calor Gas fire serviced by an excellent workman known as 'Charlie Gas'. He knew of my interest in Anglesey ghosts and kindly gave me this story on condition that I did not name the house, as he has recently sold it, without mentioning the fact that it was already occupied by someone not living in this world!

Charlie and his wife came to the Island about thirteen years ago. They arrived in Amlwch in their caravan, Charlie got a job as a gas engineer and they started to look round for somewhere to live.

Standing above Amlwch in a commanding position, and once the home of a wealthy family, is a tall, black and white house that absolutely fascinated Charlie's wife.

'Wherever I am in Amlwch,' said Lyn, 'I look up and see that house – I have a feeling it's calling to me.'

They walked up to the house many times, and close-to they could see it was empty, shabby and uncared for, and it was no surprise to learn squatters, who had only recently been evicted, had inhabited it.

'We both felt drawn to it in some way,' said Charlie, 'We could see it had seen better days, but now it looked so run down we both felt sorry for it.'

To cut a long story short, they found out to whom it belonged and, after a brief haggle about the price, bought it.

'Our hearts sank when we inspected it thoroughly,' said Charlie, 'It was in a terrible mess, but we had the caravan, I had a regular job, and we had all the evenings and weekends to do it up. Besides, we were both young and strong, so no problem.'

Being an engineer, Charlie's first priority was to get the central heating in tip-top working order, before he even thought about decoration. Fortunately, the fabric of the house was sound, roof, doors and windows all weatherproof; it was the interior which was a shambles.

'We put the caravan in the garden,' said Charlie, 'and I started work. Right from the start, that house had a strange atmosphere – every time I let myself in – you know the feeling you get when you walk into a house and someone is already in? Well, that's what I mean – I always felt as if someone was there – especially when I was working alone.'

'One evening, I came home from work, had my tea in the caravan as usual, and went into the house to examine the painting I had been doing upstairs.

'It's a big, three storied house, I was on the middle floor, and suddenly I heard someone walking about on the top floor. I thought it was my wife, so I went onto the landing, looked upstairs and called "Lyn?"

'There was no reply and, as soon as I called, the footsteps stopped, it seemed as if they had stopped just behind the door in the room upstairs.

'I don't know why – it just seemed as if whoever (or whatever!) it was, was standing behind the bedroom door upstairs listening to me.

'All the hairs on the back of my neck stood on end, and I went down and back into the caravan, Lyn was there but she'd never been out.

'I told her what I had heard, but she just laughed and said I'd imagined it – I couldn't convince her, and in the end I felt a bit of a 'nana'!

'Another time, I was working on the top floor alone, Lyn was out shopping, and the house was silent and empty, when suddenly in the room next to the one I was working in, I heard a woman – she started to cough, a really deep racking cough, as if she had something wrong with her lungs – and she couldn't stop coughing: It gave me such a shock, I froze – couldn't move – then the next minute I was downstairs and out before you could say knife!

'When winter came on with the big gales sweeping in from the Irish Sea, the caravan rocked like mad, it was in danger of turning over, so we decided we'd be safer in the house.

'We only had the caravan furniture, so we carried the mattress in, and the bedding, and we had to sleep on the floor. Of course, we had to have the TV, so we brought it in, and stood it on two paint cans!

'Talk about spartan – but we felt safe and warm, with the heating on full blast – and the wind howling outside.

'We moved in on the second floor, using a bedroom for a lounge, and when it was time for bed, we switched off the TV, and lay down on the mattress.

'The first day we moved in, I was working on the landing outside our room, it's a big landing, and at teatime when I'd finished, I left the ladders where I'd been working, just outside the door.

'We watched TV for a bit, then we went to bed, and I fell asleep right away. It must have been much later that Lyn shook me awake, I'm a heavy sleeper and I was well away.

"Charlie, wake up," she kept saying, she was shaking me like mad.

"What?"

"I can hear the ladders moving," Lyn whispered, hanging onto me.

"What?"

"The ladders – somebody's moving them."

'I was only half awake but I remembered I'd left the ladders outside the door. So I listened, but I couldn't hear a thing – and I lay down again.'

"Can't hear anything," I muttered, "you're dreaming, go back to sleep."

'Then I fell asleep again, but in the morning she said she'd been awake for ages.

'She was quite right. Next morning I found the ladders had been moved right across the big landing, opposite the place where I'd left them. Nobody else in the house and all the doors locked.

'Next thing that happened – we found the room that we were living in was getting colder. All the heating was on, and the radiator was red hot, and when we settled down after tea, everything was cosy and warm, but slowly it got colder and colder.

'Lyn gave a shiver and said, "I think I'll put my cardigan on, I thought I'd be too hot in this thick jumper – but no way!"

'We hadn't imagined it; by bedtime the room was freezing, even though I couldn't bear my hands on the radiator. I examined the room for draughts, running my hands up and down the sides of the window and door frames, but they all fitted tightly, and nothing came in there. Lyn kept looking round and fidgeting, she said she didn't like the room much; she had a creepy feeling that she was being watched.

'Next day we moved our stuff into the next room, which was warm and seemed more normal when we went in. We settled down in that, snug as bugs. For the first few weeks it was OK and stayed warm all the time. Then the same thing started to happen – every evening the temperature dropped until we were shivering. I even bought a thermometer and stuck it on the wall – it was 70° odd at teatime and by the time we went to bed it was below 40°. Weird!

'It was when we had been in the house for a couple of weeks that we started to hear the footsteps.

'I was watching TV one night when Lyn said the programme was boring and she was going down to make a cup of tea – it was boring me too, so I turned the sound down. Then in the silence I could hear heavy footsteps slowly crossing the room above me. I could hear Lyn downstairs in the kitchen so I knew it wasn't her. I crossed the room and opened the door without making a sound and I crept upstairs.

'I could still hear the floorboards creaking as if someone was walking slowly and heavily in the room. I caught hold of the knob and suddenly threw the door open. The noise stopped instantly – the room was empty and everything was silent, but I had a funny feeling as if something had just stopped moving – as if it was still there somehow. I waited a minute, but nothing happened, so I went back downstairs to the room we were living in, and I was sitting pretending to be watching TV when Lyn brought the tea up. I didn't say anything about it to her. In fact, I wouldn't have mentioned it to her, but next night it happened again.

'We were having our tea when the footsteps started, louder than ever, and we both stopped eating, and looked up at the ceiling – listening to whoever it was, crossing and re-crossing the floor like an animal in a cage.

'Then we looked at each other – Lyn had a piece of sausage on her fork, halfway to her mouth – funny the things you remember – and she said:

"Have you heard them before?"

'I just nodded.

"So have I, lots of times, while you were at work."

'I stared at her. "Weren't you frightened – on your own?"

'She nodded. "A bit, but not as much as I was at first, they just keep crossing to and fro in that room for a bit, then they stop. They never come out."

'She must have seen something in my face, she's quick on the uptake is Lyn, because she said:

"Have you heard them anywhere else? You have – haven't you?"

"Well," I said, "I do hear them in the night and they don't stay in the room."

'I saw her eyes widen, and I put my cup down – I didn't want to frighten her, but if I told her she'd know what to expect.

"You see," I said, "In the night they cross that room above us, then I hear the knob rattle as the door is opened, the footsteps come out onto the landing, tramp right down the three flights of stairs and then they go out of the back door. I hear it open and close."

'She was silent for a minute, sitting thinking.

"Have you seen the cats?" she asked.

'I shook my head.

"Well," said Lyn, "If ever we stay up late to watch a film or anything and I go down to wash the cups, the cats go to sit in the hall about half past eleven and look up the stairs. You watch."

'So we did. We went downstairs about quarter past eleven to wash up, our two cats used to roam all over the house, but sure enough, just before half past eleven, they walked into the hall and crouched with their tails around their legs looking upstairs.

'They stayed there for about fifteen minutes staring upwards, and then they both got up at the same time and wandered into the kitchen, as if the show was over. We didn't see a thing, either then or any other time, but they were aware of something.

'Well, we finally finished renovating, decorating and painting, everything looked new and fresh and we were ready to have the place carpeted. It was going to be expensive, but a house looks nothing without carpets, and it was a big house.

'We'd had such dreams about this house, but somehow we felt very uneasy in it, as if someone resented us being there.

20

'So we decided to carpet and furnish it and, if we still felt unsettled after that, we could sell it and buy somewhere else.

'Anyway, we went to Peter Lees, the big carpet store, chose all the carpets (and what a price they came to!) then the bloke came to measure up.

'It was a big job; so he arranged for six lads to come down to do all the floors, on the following Saturday and Sunday. What a row that made! Six hammers going in different rooms, you never heard such a racket, it was enough to wake the dead!

'I was on the second floor watching them work – I enjoyed that – when a lad came tottering down from the top floor and stood hanging onto the banister.

'He was chalk-white and shaking like a leaf, and he would have fallen down if he hadn't had something to hang onto.

'I sat him down on the stairs, and gave him a drink of water, it sloshed all over the place, his hands were shaking that much.

'Finally, when he could speak, he told me he was laying the carpet in **that** room upstairs, when someone tried to open the door.

'He sang out to tell them to hang on a minute, the carpet was rolled up behind the door – but whoever it was kept trying to push the door open.

'So he put his hammer down, got up and moved the carpet away, and opened the door. No one there. No one else on that floor. All silent.

'He looked around, then went back in and shut the door, a bit shaken, but more puzzled than anything.

'He knelt down, picked up his hammer and had just started hammering again when suddenly the door flew open and crashed against the wall.

'The doorway was empty, no one there.

'He froze with fright, then after a minute he shot through the door like a bullet from a gun and straight downstairs. Nothing would persuade him to go back up – he wouldn't stay in the house even. He went outside and sat in the van, and there he stayed until they'd finished. He was a very scared young man.

'Of course the room he'd been carpeting was the room we heard the footsteps in, and whoever or whatever was in that room certainly resented being disturbed, but I didn't say anything to the lad.

'Well, after that, the noises became louder, and the funny thing was, the footsteps still sounded as if they were on bare boards, even though the floor was carpeted. Then we started to hear them very loudly tramping down the stairs late at night, they echoed on the wood too, even though the stair carpet was thick.

'The atmosphere in the house got worse too – it was almost "solid" sometimes, as if someone there was very angry and yet very despairing at the same time. Some nights we could feel the depression all over the house and, other nights, we felt as if someone was trying to push us out, they were so angry.

'Anyway, we couldn't settle, however hard we tried, so we finally decided we weren't wanted there – the only thing we could do was to sell, pack up and go.

'Which we did.

'After we left, I made a few enquiries about who had lived there. I found out that at one time, an old man had lived in that bedroom, never going out in the daytime.

'He used to walk around that room all day, and then when night came, he would tramp down all the stairs, go out of the back door, and walk around the garden.

'One night he hung himself in that bedroom. As far as I could tell, that didn't stop him.

'He's still walking.'

The cobbler of Porth Amlwch

In the early nineteenth century, before the railways came to Anglesey, each district specialised in one particular industry, according to the needs of the townsfolk.

For instance, Llannerch-y-medd, having fairs and markets, catered to the local farmers and farm labourers who thronged there, by selling them much needed boots. The trade reached its peak in the 1830's, when as many as 250 cobblers worked there.

Men came from the surrounding villages to learn the trade of boot making, while the business of clog-making flourished in Pen-y-sarn and Llaneilian, much needed by the copper miners of Mynydd Parys.

The decline came in the late nineteenth century when the big boot and shoe factories opening in Northamptonshire coincided with the railway coming to Anglesey, so that in time only a few cobblers were still plying their trade, although apprentices still came forward to learn a life-long job.

Both people and horses always needed shoes and blacksmith's forges flourished all over the island. Records show that the house which is now number 7 Llaneilian Road, Porth Amlwch, was a blacksmith's house and forge in 1834, and still a smithy in 1891, when Richard Roberts and his wife, Jane, lived there.

I cannot trace the exact date when the smithy ceased to exist, but my older friends in the district have confirmed that a cobbler was living there forty years ago. He both lived and worked there, his workshop being a lean-to building attached to the house, and here his friends and customers gathered to watch him work and swap local gossip.

To begin with, he was tall and lean, but as he grew older a weakness in his spine (probably osteoporosis) caused him to become very bent and stooped. Eventually, as his illness progressed, he was forced to give up his trade and his shop, and he moved away to Cardiff (where he had relations) and the house was sold on.

In 1971, the then owner of the property demolished the lean-to workshop and had an extension built on the site, which comprised a downstairs room and a small bedroom above.

About 1976, Mrs Pat Shearer and her husband bought the house, and had it redecorated throughout, and the small bedroom was fitted with a blue carpet, blue wallpaper and matching blue curtains.

'We loved the house right away,' Mrs Shearer said. 'It had such a friendly atmosphere, and we were thrilled with the decorating.' It took quite a time to renovate and recarpet the house right through and it was during this time that odd things started to happen.

When they moved in, in 1976, Pat's youngest son Tim was just four years old. One morning, he came yawning downstairs in his pyjamas and sleepily asked his mother who the old man was on the landing. Of course they laughed and told him he had been dreaming, there was no old man there. He said no more but looked very puzzled.

Next, various members of the family heard someone walking about upstairs. One summer evening, they were all sitting around the table when everyone distinctly heard the sound of footsteps above them.

'It was as if someone was walking about on bare boards,' Mrs Shearer told me. 'We tried to recreate the noise by one of the family walking about in the same room, but nothing could be heard downstairs, because of the fitted carpets.'

They decided that the little blue room must be haunted, but there was nothing to be afraid of, and they all got used to the footsteps.

Time moved on, her family grew up, married, and then it was the turn of the grandchildren to come to stay.

The first grandson was brought for a visit when he was just seven months old and was put to sleep in a drop-side cot in the little room over the erstwhile cobbler's workshop.

On various occasions during their stay, each time Lydia, his mother, went up to check on the sleeping baby, she found the side of the cot had been dropped, although she knew she had always left it securely fastened.

One night, the baby started crying loudly, as if in pain, and dashing upstairs, she found he had fallen out of the cot, as the side had again been lowered. She picked up the howling infant, and before carrying him down to soothe him, she spoke angrily to the invisible presence in the room.

'I don't mind you *looking* at my baby,' she said, 'but don't drop the side of the cot – it's dangerous!'

It never happened again.

* * *

William, the second grandson, was very fey. When he was two and a half, the family came to stay with his grandparents. Very often at night, after he was put to bed in the blue room, the adults downstairs would hear him talking to someone, and laughing happily. When they asked him whom he was talking to, he said casually, 'Oh, it's the little old man in the bedroom.'

The grownups looked at each other over his head.

'And where does this little old man live?' they asked.

'He lives under the bed, he comes out when I'm going to sleep,' said William. 'The family stayed for two weeks, and on the morning they were going home, as he was lifted out of the cot, he bent his back and slumped his shoulders, and shuffled slowly around the room.

'Look at me,' he cried gleefully. 'I'm the little old man who plays with my feet!'

He was in no way disturbed or frightened by his visitor, and Mrs Shearer was curious to know who the old man was and thought her friend, Mr Elias Jones, a local man who had the Post Office next door, would solve the mystery for her.

He did. 'Oh, I remember him,' he said, his face lighting up in a smile. 'He was the old cobbler who lived there. He loved children; he used to tickle their toes to make them laugh while he was fitting their clogs on. In his younger days he was quite tall, but he had a weakness in his bones that caused him to stoop, and become round-shouldered in age.'

'His name was Evan Williams, but he didn't die in the house, he went back to his childhood home in Cardiff. It's strange he haunts the house where he worked – perhaps he was very happy there.'

Mrs Shearer felt so sorry for the ghost, she went for advice to the Rev. David Redrobe, and after explaining the situation to him, he said he thought what was needed was a simple service of sacrament in the house; exorcism was not needed, as they were not dealing with an evil entity.

So the family and a few close friends gathered together around the table, the sacrament was taken, and the Rev. David Redrobe offered up prayers for the family and the cobbler. Afterwards, he spoke to the cobbler, whose presence was felt by everyone gathered there, and told him with great gentleness and sympathy, that the family and children were all very happy and assured him that he was loved by them all, but now it was time for him to go to his eternal rest and be at peace.

That was four years ago, and the cobbler has gone.

Mrs Shearer said that last year, William was looking thoughtful, and suddenly said to her:

'Grandma, did you have a ghost in this house?'

Mrs Shearer laughed and said:

'Yes, don't you remember? He used to play with your feet!'

This was absorbed in baffled silence, 'as if,' Mrs Shearer said, 'he could only recall it hazily and didn't know whether he had dreamt it and I was kidding him.'

'But there again,' she added, 'nearly all children are psychic, when they are young but it fades as they get older.'

* * *

An example of this early gift was once displayed when the boys' family were driving back home to Lincoln, after a holiday on Anglesey. Nearing home, still on the motorway, William's Mum (Lydia) drew her husband's attention to a big cloud of black smoke billowing upwards on the horizon.

'Just look at that,' she said. 'It must be a big fire somewhere.'

'It's Daddy's tyres burning,' piped up a little voice from the back seat. (To William, at four, all tyres were Daddy's.) 'And there's a little girl there too, it's all dark and she's afraid and crying.'

As they were trying to work this out, he added reassuringly: 'She's going to be all right though.' Then he lapsed back into silence.

Next day, the fire was shown on TV news, a big tyre depot,

26

blazing furiously. There were no casualties.

'*That's* what we saw then,' said Lydia.

'I told you it was Daddy's tyres burning,' William murmured.

The little girl still puzzles them, as no one had been reported missing, but they have found out that the area was full of disused coal workings, and they wondered if the little girl was one of the pitiful children, who, long ago, were forced to work down the coal mines at the tender age of six.

We shall never know.

The alcoholic ghost

Mrs Harris of Newborough told me this lovely little story about an unusual ghost.

A great friend of hers, one Mrs Jones, was married to a 'lovely old man', as Mrs Harris described him, who was an alcoholic. Subsequently, he died, and his widow went to winter in Australia, as they had done for years.

She let her house to Mrs Harris for six months, and she and her husband moved in.

The bedroom next to theirs was the one previously inhabited by Mr and Mrs Jones, and when he was alive, Mr Jones always went up to the bedroom to spruce himself up for his nightly visit to the pub.

The first night, and every succeeding one, Mrs Harris would hear the bedroom door open and close at 8.00 p.m., footsteps tramp down the stairs and the front door slam.

Later, about the time the pubs shut, the whole thing would happen in reverse. The front door banged, footsteps ascended the stairs (a little unsteadily) and re-entered the bedroom.

At first Mrs Harris was puzzled, but not disturbed, and as she grew familiar with the nightly performance, she would comment to her husband:

'There goes old John for a drink!' and later she would say, 'Pubs must be shut, here he comes back again!'

Although her husband listened intently, he never heard any of the ghostly nocturnal trips, all the time he was there.

Later, when the widow was back home, an Australian lady who was her close friend came to stay for a holiday.

After she had been in Mrs Jones' home for a week or so, she was having a cup of tea with the lady next door and said she would like to ask her a question in confidence, as she was very puzzled.

'Who else lives in the house?' she asked, 'I never see anyone during the day besides Mrs Jones, but every evening I hear someone come out of the bedroom where she sleeps, and go downstairs and out of the front door.'

28

She went on to describe exactly the activities that Mrs Harris had heard.

'Mrs Jones has never said anything, and I wondered if perhaps it is someone she doesn't want to talk about.'

The neighbour remembered Mrs Harris's story and related it to the Australian friend.

'Ah, that explains it,' she said. 'Do you know I don't think Mrs Jones hears the sounds, because, although they are pretty loud, especially the front door closing, I've looked at her but she never remarks on them, in fact she doesn't react at all.'

They both decided it would be kinder not to mention anything.

None of the ladies, who are friends of the family, have ever told the story to anyone related to the old man, in case it upset them.

Naturally, Mrs Harris wanted the characters to be anonymous and I have respected her wishes.

But one does wonder if the dear old man still goes out for his nightly tipple and, if so, has anyone ever seen him at the bar?

Come home

I am indebted to Mrs Mair Davies (RSPCA Chairperson, Môn, at the time of writing), a charming most helpful lady, for this little story told to her by her father many years ago.

Around the turn of the twentieth century, an old farmer, one John Rowlands, who lived not far from the Mermaid Inn at Brynsiencyn, was walking tiredly home one summer evening after a hard day's work in one of his outlying fields.

He was deep in thought about the tasks to be undertaken on the following day as he clambered over the last stile into his barn meadow.

As he stepped down, he was met by his faithful old collie, which greeted him joyously, wagging her tail frantically and looking rapturously happy.

John smiled and bent down stiffly to stroke her and, in the act of stretching out his hand, the dog vanished.

It was only then that he remembered with a shock that his beloved old dog had been dead for two months.

Bewildered and shaken, he went home and told his wife and they puzzled over it all evening.

That night, John died peacefully in his sleep.

Ghost on the football field

The village of Trearddur Bay is a very popular tourist destination, and caravan parks, bungalows and elegant holiday homes have proliferated.

The sea is shallow for many yards from the shore, ideal for paddling and swimming, and the golden sands have spurs of rock running down to the water, full of cracks and crevices which hold many small pools. Caravans and holiday homes are deserted for most of the year, but the villagers themselves are a close-knit community, many families having lived there for generations. Nowadays, the tourists have boosted small businesses, cafes and shops, so that little Trearddur has prospered, but it has not always been so.

Like much of rural Britain, Anglesey saw hard times at the beginning of the twentieth century, work was scarce and money even more so.

Those people who had a smallholding and a few acres of land were the fortunate ones. A house-cow, a pig fattening for winter, a few hens and maybe a duck or two were the source of their meat, milk, butter and eggs, whilst the garden was carefully tended to produce vegetables and fruit, eaten fresh in the season and pickled for winter.

Every penny was needed and the women, as well as coping with the back-breaking housework, baking and gardening, spent the long winter nights knitting socks that were sold for a few pence.

One of these tiny homesteads stood where the football field is now and, in 1915, was inhabited by Mr and Mrs Owen Jones-Bennett and their twin sons.

Like most young lads in their early teens, they were growing rapidly and their appetites were huge. It was all Mrs Jones-Bennett could do to keep them filled.

There was no work to be had on the Island, the few jobs that came up were applied for by ten times as many men as there were vacancies, and Mr Jones-Bennett tried in vain to get jobs for his sons.

The Great War, and the need for many men in the services, was seen as a boon to some. Those that were too young to be in the Army or Navy were asked to go to southern Wales, both as munitions factory workers or to replace the many miners who had been enlisted.

The Bennett twins were now strapping lads of fifteen, bored and restless, with no prospects of work. One day they learned that a group of their friends, also unemployed, had volunteered to go to work in the mines.

Many were taken from Holyhead by sea to Swansea and from there to different destinations in southern Wales.

The twins were excited at the idea of venturing off the Island and told their parents that they wanted to leave home and go and get a job in southern Wales.

At first their parents said no, they loved the boys, and were anxious about their future, but they began to reluctantly realise that it was the only thing to do – there was no work for them here and it was hard to make ends meet with the meagre amount of money coming in.

So in the end they agreed, Owen reassuring his wife that they would still be in Wales and would come home as often as possible.

The wheels were set in motion and by early November the boys were instructed to be at a certain spot in Trearddur with a few other young locals who had volunteered. There they would be picked up and transported to Holyhead, then put aboard a ship to Swansea.

The day of their departure dawned, grey and miserable, with a bitter wind blowing.

Mrs Jones-Bennett was up very early after a sleepless night, and busied herself in the kitchen, making a hearty breakfast for the boys and a pile of sandwiches for their journey. Her husband gave the boys what money he could spare, warning them solemnly about the world they were about to enter.

So they set off – nervous and excited, half-dreading leaving home, yet looking forward to a future that held jobs and money.

Mrs Bennett looked pale and troubled, dreading their departure and, when they left, she walked with them along to the beach wall and stood waving until they were out of sight. Her heart heavy as lead, she stood alone, weeping in the bitter November wind, unable to return to the house that had always been noisy with boys. So she left the wall and wandered desolately along the shore, half-blinded with tears, and stumbling amongst the rocky outcrops.

Suddenly, the gusting wind caught her between one faltering step and another and catching her off-balance – threw her heavily down – smashing her head against the rocks. It was hours before she came to, dusk was gathering, and she was sick and dizzy, her hair matted with blood. Painfully, she crawled across the rocks, over the shore to the seawall and, after many stops, managed to make her way home.

Owen had been out looking for her, was nearly frantic with worry, and he gasped with relief when she half-fell into the house. He was immensely shocked when he saw the amount of blood on her clothes and the great wound in her head. Catching her, he laid her on the couch and ran for help. Eventually, she was taken to the nearest place that offered medical treatment, the workhouse in Valley that was used as a hospital.

But she was so severely injured that she slipped into a coma, and died within a few days – so she never had to face life without her beloved boys.

Whether the boys ever knew of their mother's death is not recorded, but what is known is the fact that they hated the claustrophobic life in the darkness of the mines so much, that they enlisted in the Army and were sent to France, where they were killed in action in 1917 – just as they celebrated their seventeenth birthdays.

Mr Owen Jones-Bennett received the official letter from the War Department, informing him of their deaths and he never really got over the triple tragedies, dying in 1924 in his early forties.

This sad little tale may well have been forgotten as time passed, staying only in a few local minds, until, in November 2000, something strange happened.

A statement was published in the *Holyhead and Anglesey Mail* (at the beginning of November) from an 'Anonymous Eye-Witness' and compiled into an article, written by Mr Richard Rowlands, a staff reporter on the *Mail*.

I quote Mr Rowlands:

There have been a number of reported sightings recently of a ghostly apparition of a woman in a flowing dress appearing near the edge of the football field in Trearddur Bay, but a witness told the *Mail* that many were keeping tight-lipped about their experiences for fear of being ridiculed.'

The witness, who did not want to be identified, said:

'I have heard a few different versions of this story over the years but never took much notice of them really.

'I was walking my dog on the coastal side of the football field about two weeks ago at dusk and was enjoying the fresh air and my mind was far away.

'I noticed about twenty five yards to my right what appeared to be a woman in a dark flowing dress (wind-blown?) which struck me as rather strange since it was a very calm day.

'She appeared to have simply come over the wall from the beach, then over the road and onto the football pitch and moved quickly down the side of the field.'

She added that the woman then suddenly turned around and headed back towards the same spot near the seawall and appeared to fall back into the sea.

Both Lady, my pet poodle, and I were rooted to the spot and I had to carry her back home. It took her several hours to settle down.'

This narrative was followed by a plea by the Mail to anyone who had seen the ghostly figure or knew anything about the history behind this tale to contact the Mail office.

The following week, Mr Wm. Paul McDermott, of Holyhead, wrote to say that the late Mr George Jones of Bryn-y-Môr, a local historian, told the sad story of the Jones-Bennett family to him about five years ago. With the kind permission of Mr McDermott, and the Mail, I have reproduced the tale, which has left me wondering again whether violent feelings of anguish and despair leave lasting impressions on the atmosphere, resulting in their re-enactment for many years to come?

The mystery of the burning mini

Mr Owen Hughes, a pleasant and courteous man, came to install a new television aerial at Eilianfa, and told me this very curious tale.

About 5.30 p.m. one autumn evening, Mr Hughes had been for petrol to Dulas Garage, which lies on the main Bangor road and was returning up the hill towards Pen-y-sarn. The particular stretch of road he was using is now three-lane but in the 1960's when this incident took place, it had not been widened, it was only two-lane.

Although it was nearly dark, and a cloudy evening, Mr Hughes said it was light enough to see on-coming traffic and he saw, coming down the hill towards him, a white mini. This caught his attention, because Minis had not been long on the market and this one was brand new.

He watched it pass with great interest and then looked out of his rear mirror to see its progress. As he did so, something happened that filled him with horror.

In his own words:

It had just gone past down the hill, I was going up, and I watched it through my rear mirror.

Suddenly, just in front of it, the figure of a man appeared on the side of the road, threw down what appeared to be a big sack and set fire to it. It immediately blazed up fiercely, right in the path of the oncoming Mini.

I only had time to think 'That's dangerous', when the Mini passed over it and burst into flames. It didn't slacken speed, just carried on down the hill, round the bend and out of my sight.

It was horrifying – I thought it would crash and the occupants burn to death, so I slapped my brakes on, and turned around fast, putting my foot down hard as I followed. I raced after it down the hill and around the bend, thinking any minute I would come across the burning wreck. But I didn't, I went on and on and the road was absolutely empty.

So I turned and came back, wondering if the Mini had crashed through the hedge into a field, but I couldn't find a thing, I must have spent a good five minutes searching. I was very shocked and decided to go for help, so I went to my friend's house, told him what had happened and asked him to come quick and help me. We both tumbled into my car and went back as fast as we could.

We searched and searched, because usually if a car has burnt out on the road, it leaves some signs, even if there is only a patch of melted tar, but we found absolutely nothing.

I was shocked and bewildered and I listened to the Welsh news for days after, but nothing was reported. I asked all the people who used that road regularly, but they just looked blank.

It took me a long time to get over that and I can still see that blazing Mini to this day.

The man who set fire to the sack just disappeared and so did the burning sack. I can find no reports in the papers regarding a car being burnt out on that particular stretch of road any time in the 1960's and I am just as baffled as Mr Hughes. No one else has ever recorded seeing it, but the sincerity of Mr Hughes is beyond doubt.

It is only one of the many strange happenings recorded on that stretch of the Bangor Road. At least three of these included fires and I shall go into them all in other chapters.

Phantom horseman

Mr Owen Thomas Hughes, who saw the burning Mini, also told me this, a ghost story that over the years has become inextricably mixed with legend.

The story is that at Parciau Mansion, in Cromwell's time, there was one John Bodwell, who became a 'turn-coat' and as this was regarded as a criminal act, he had to be suitably punished.

Now here is where the truth becomes merged into folklore. Whatever his punishment may have been in reality (and in those cruel days it would have been meted out with customary savagery) the tale told around many a cottage fire over the years was, that he was condemned to count the grains of sand on Lligwy beach. Legend has it that he is still there, and will be for all eternity.

Mr Hughes was told this story one winter's evening as a boy and, as it made a deep impression on him, he told his school friends the next day. Word got around the school and, as boys are always looking for adventure, three of them and Wil announced that they were going to walk all the way to Lligwy beach, to see if John Bodwell was still there.

The dire predictions and warnings from the other boys secretly undermined their resolve, but the admiring looks from the girls (who squeaked and shivered when they heard the story) caused them to swagger a little and adopt an air of great bravado. They announced their intentions of setting off straight after school.

It was a dark January day, cold and windy and, as Mr Hughes said:

We were cold, and we wanted our tea, but as all the boys and girls were watching, we were determined to go. It was a long way and, before we were halfway there, I think, we were all wondering why we were doing it.

Anyway, we finally went down the lane that leads to the beach and, at last, we were there. There is a little bridge there that spans the stream where it leaves the fields and flows onto the beach, well, we crossed that and we were halfway down the beach when my mate and I stopped at the same instant. We were side by side and we both saw a man standing by a horse.

I can't remember exactly how he was dressed, but I do remember it was very old fashioned. He was holding the reins in his hand and he seemed to be looking at us.

Although they both looked solid and alive, the strange thing was, we could see the body of the horse, but not the legs.

We had stopped dead and the other two lads cannoned into us.

'What's the matter? What are you staring at?' one asked us.

We both pointed at the man and the horse, but even though they stared hard, they couldn't see anything, only Huw and I could. If Huw felt as scared as I was, then he certainly was scared.

'It's a trick,' I said, 'someone's trying to frighten us – let's get him!'

So we charged forward, the two of us, and left the others standing there.

We had nearly reached him, only two or three yards away, I could see his eyes looking at me, and the horse seemed to be looking down at the sand – when suddenly, man and horse vanished. One minute they were there, as large as life, and the next second – Mr Hughes clicked his fingers – they were gone.

It was a terrible shock – Huw and I stared at each other and then we turned and flew back up the beach, over the bridge, and we didn't stop running until we were well up the lane and didn't have any breath left.

The other two came pelting after us, they hadn't seen anything, and they were wondering what it was all about, but when they saw the look on our faces, they must have been infected by our fear; they didn't stop to find out, they ran as fast as us.

We were too shaken to talk much about it, we were sure somehow that it was a live man and a horse, and we couldn't understand why we couldn't see its legs – but when they vanished we realised we had seen two ghosts.

I don't know who he was or why he was there, we didn't stop to find out – and I can tell you I've never been back there on a January afternoon.

I'm still wondering why the horse had no legs and why only Huw and I could see them.

In answer to my question Mr Hughes told me that since his experience, he has heard many times that the beach is haunted, and not only by the phantom horseman.

The voice from the sea

My friend Mr Ted Hughes, Bryn Alaw, told me that he had never seen a ghost, but something once happened to him which he has never been able to explain.

During the war, when I was in the navy, a group of us were on guard at night on a small island called Burnt Island, under the Forth Bridge. It was a vital spot to watch for mines, flares from ships in distress, submarines etc.

I was detailed about 3.00 a.m., middle watch, shaken awake in my hammock and told to get dressed. It was the middle of winter, very cold, and with rifle and full kit. I climbed into the back of the jeep which took me down to the guard hut, from where we used to patrol. The guard hut had a telephone and, occasionally, the guard commander would ring to check we were alert and hadn't gone to sleep. Apart from that, the man on guard was completely alone.

Well, this night, *said Mr Hughes, settling back on the Chesterfield and stretching his feet to the fire,* it was rough, very rough indeed, blowing a full gale and so dark you couldn't see your hand in front of your face.

There was a long concrete slip, going out to sea, which we had to patrol, watching keenly, as I said, for flares, mines etc. and it was very narrow, so I picked my way carefully along it, for one false step and I would be in the water.

I couldn't see a thing and the only noise was the sea roaring in the gale. I was about halfway along the slip when suddenly I heard something.

I stopped and listened. It was a voice coming from the sea – but the odd thing was, sometimes it was faint and sounded as if it was far away, next it sounded right near my feet.

'Help! it shouted, and after a bit, 'Help!' it went again, and kept on.

Now it seemed to be right in front of me and I remember thinking if it was light I would be able to see him and I thrust my rifle towards the voice and said,

'Here! Get hold of that!'

It was the only thing I had, you see, and it stretched further than my arms. But nothing grasped it and I couldn't even see the water, it was so dark. There was just the roar of the wind and the sea and this voice crying for help.

One minute it was right in front of me, to the left of the slip and, as I held my rifle there and shouted, it would come from behind me on the other side. It confused me, how could it get from one side of the slip to the other?

I did my best, holding out my rifle to wherever the voice was calling. It went on for three or four minutes, me turning from side to side, and completely bewildered by the dark and the gale.

Then it stopped, just as suddenly as it had begun. It didn't get weaker and weaker as it would if someone was drowning, but just as strong as I first heard it. I stood there in the blackness and the uproar, and I suddenly started to think how unnatural it was. Wrong somehow. So I groped my way back along the slip to the guard hut and telephoned my guard commander.

I told him what had happened, about the voice sounding from here and there, and changing position every minute. I was a bit wary when I was telling him, I thought he'd burst out laughing – you can imagine what a Navy man would say! But, he didn't say a word, never asked me one question. He listened in absolute silence and I had a very strong feeling that he had heard it all before.

I asked him if anything had happened – a U-boat or a plane crash, but he said no, everything was OK. We would have been alerted at once if anything had happened, so I knew really that nothing was wrong.

I told him about the voice again – I knew there was something queer and waited for him to say something, but he didn't, not one question, just said right, get back on patrol.

He wouldn't have told me if he knew anything anyway, in case it got back to the others – things like that go round a camp like wildfire, but I could tell he knew something – but he wasn't going to tell me. I never did find out. I've puzzled about it ever since. But one thing I do know, whatever called to me out of the sea that night, it was nothing living.

The haunted farm

Ted Hughes told me this story:

During the war, I was home (Anglesey) on leave from the Navy, and went for a drink to the local pub.

Four Land Army girls came in and sat down at a nearby table with their drinks, chattering and laughing. They were pretty and lively and, as in most pubs, they were being closely studied (as strangers always are) by the regulars.

The four girls had been split into two pairs that day, working on different local farms, and one pair had spent the day threshing on a large farm that had intrigued them.

'It's so old,' the tall blonde said, 'I think it's Elizabethan, full of panelling and antique furniture, absolutely beautiful!'

Of course, everyone was listening intently, politely appearing to be disinterested, but one old farm labourer, sitting in his work clothes and clogs, removed his pipe from his mouth and muttered to his neighbour.

'They wouldn't be going on about it so much if they'd seen the ghost!'

When he said that, something clicked in my mind and I remembered another ghost at a farm. I'll tell you about it but I won't name the farm, because people still live there, and wouldn't want the publicity.

It was at my mother-in-law's. She was always a truthful woman and this is what she told me.

When she was a young married woman, she and her husband moved into a big farm in the Rhos-goch area. Actually, it was built like a mansion, with a big garden, glasshouses, ornamental trees and a grand pillared porch. The house belonged to a businessman in Liverpool, a Mr Jones, who also had other farms on the Island.

Mr Griffiths had the position of farm foreman and Mrs Griffiths looked after the large house, which was furnished, and she also acted as cook/housekeeper for Mr Jones, when he made his infrequent visits.

One night in winter, Mr Griffiths had been round his stock as usual and, coming back in, he took his work boots off at the front door and, as he straightened up and turned to lock the door, he saw, standing near a porch pillar, clearly outlined by the full moon, the figure of a beautiful woman. She was tall and slender, dressed in a long white gown, with golden hair which fell about her shoulders.

He blinked in surprise and, in that instant, she vanished. He opened the door and looked around but there was no one about. Puzzled, he went in for his supper and told his wife about it, but she laughed and told him he was seeing things.

Two weeks later, Mr Jones arrived, the first time he had come down since they moved in. Mrs Griffiths bustled about, making his room ready and had a sumptuous evening meal waiting for him on his arrival.

He ate heartily, congratulating Mrs Griffiths on her cooking and, when he had finished, he pushed his plate away, leant back and looked at them quizzically.

'Well!' he said abruptly, 'have you seen her yet?'

They knew immediately what he meant.

'Yes, William has,' said Mrs Griffiths. At the same time William nodded.

'Yes, I have.'

They then discussed the lady ghost and Mr Jones said he had seen no reason to tell them. She had been seen many times, but had done no harm.

In answer to their questions, he said he hadn't got the faintest idea who she was or why she was haunting the house. The house had been built about 1700, she might have been there since then – he neither knew nor cared and (being the hard-headed business man that he was) had no intention of finding out – it was of no importance. With that they had to be content. Nothing else was seen of her and life ran normally for months, with everything going smoothly in their busy lives until a certain evening in summer.

The day's work was done, tea was finished and the dishes washed and put away. Mrs Griffiths was writing a letter to her mother, on the deep sill of the kitchen window, catching the last rays of the setting sun, and her husband was peacefully smoking his pipe by the fire.

Suddenly, they heard the ornate front door open and close and the steady tramp of a man's footsteps coming along the wide, stone-flagged hall. They looked up and stared at each other in surprise – who could be so bold as to enter the house and walk down the hall without knocking or calling?

Even as the thought flashed through their minds, the footsteps came to the door, and *something* walked straight through the kitchen between them, across the scullery and descended the stone steps of the cellar. Then silence.

For a moment they were paralysed with shock, then Mr Griffiths leapt from his chair, shot across the kitchen and scullery, and she heard him bound down the cellar steps. All was quiet.

He came back in slowly and stared at his wife.

'Did you hear it?'

She nodded speechlessly.

'Did you *see* it?'

Still silent, she shook her head.

'There *was* someone,' he said bewilderedly, 'but I've searched the cellar, there's nothing there. I'll try upstairs,' he said, and she heard him going through all the upper rooms one by one. They were all empty.

The half-written letter lay forgotten as she drew nearer to her husband. Eventually, they went to bed, still sorely puzzled. That was the start.

A few nights later, they were both gently wakened by a soft tapping on the wall above their bed head, seemingly coming from the bedroom behind theirs. As they froze, and listened, the soft tapping became more insistent and louder. It gradually increased in volume until it became a crescendo, becoming so thunderous that it filled the room, the whole wall behind them vibrating so much they leapt out of bed, expecting to see it bulging – ready to explode.

They couldn't hear themselves speak – the row deafened them. Suddenly it stopped. Not a tapering off, but abruptly, as if someone had clicked a switch. The silence that followed was unearthly. As soon as he could get his limbs to move, Mr Griffiths groped for the matches and lit the bedside candle. He went into the next room quite fearlessly, leaving his wife quaking in the dark. A few minutes later, he returned and gave his wife a baffled look.

'Nothing,' he said shortly, and climbed back into bed.

Hardly had they settled down when, from the same room, noises began. Heavy footsteps crossed the floor; there were loud knocks at the bedroom door and noises of chairs being dragged about. To his great credit – Mr Griffiths felt more anger than fear – once more he rushed into the next bedroom and, once more, found nothing amiss.

They passed the rest of the night sleeping very spasmodically. The next day Mrs Griffiths was pale and nervous and told her husband that she wanted to leave, but he was a brave man, my father-in-law, and he reassured his wife by saying they were only noises, and he would lose his job, it was part of the contract that they should live there. Besides, he also had his own animals on the land, living free, the house was very comfortable and they were both enjoying life.

So, reluctantly, Mrs Griffiths agreed to stay and, although their nights became disrupted frequently, she tried not to listen to the crashes and the footsteps in the bedrooms, but lay with her hands clenched, muttering her prayers rapidly.

After a time, Mr Griffiths gave up searching for the source of the noises, every time he laid his hand on the door knob of the room, everything would cease instantly and, if he looked into the room, every item of furniture stood undisturbed in its allotted place.

Mrs Griffiths' mother was coming for a holiday and the bedroom they were using was the nicest in the house – apart from Mr Jones's private quarters. They had decided they would give her their bedroom with its solid oak furniture and beautiful views from the big windows. But my mother-in-law was very reluctant to move into the haunted bedroom, which was the only other bedroom fully furnished.

After a lot of discussion, and persuasion by her husband, she agreed to the move and busied herself spring-cleaning their bedroom, putting up fresh curtains, polishing the furniture and generally making the room cosy. To calm her fears of sleeping in the haunted chamber, her husband sensibly pointed out to her that when anyone was in the room, nothing happened.

So they moved in a few nights before their visitor was due and, no sooner had they settled down in bed and blown out the candle, when all hell broke loose in the room they had just vacated.

First, they heard the wardrobe door crashing open and closed repeatedly. Next, the sound of the linen sheets being roughly torn apart and, finally, to add to the cacophony, all the ornaments and mirrors were hurled against the walls, to fall in tinkling fragments to the floor.

The din was so loud they were convinced someone was smashing up the room. Mr Griffiths was out of bed in a trice and raced down the landing, fully expecting to see the room in ruins. Again, as soon as he touched the door handle, the racket ceased, and plunging into the room, he found everything intact.

He went back to bed and found his wife in tears, and quite unnerved, saying she couldn't possibly ask her mother to stay, the place would frighten her to death. They agreed to make up an excuse and put their visitor off for a while, to see if things settled down.

This was done the next day.

The tenor of the hauntings now seemed to change, for beside the crashing, banging and general noise, a new manifestation took place.

Lying in bed one night, they heard the sound of the now familiar footsteps enter the front door, move down the hall and into the kitchen where they stopped. A chair was dragged noisily from the kitchen table, then back again, as if someone had moved it to sit down. Listening intently, they both heard the sound of coins being poured onto the table, as if someone was emptying a bag of money. Then it was the noise of coins being counted separately and, slowly sliding across the table, audibly chinking into a cloth bag, every sound loud and clear.

Creeping quietly downstairs, Mr Griffiths flung open the door, only to find the kitchen empty and quiet, barely lit by the glow from the dying fire.

They must have been a very brave couple to have lived in such a badly haunted house, particularly Mrs Griffiths who moved around the big house, opening bedroom windows to air the rooms, climbing the stairs and walking along the upstairs corridors to close them again at dusk.

One night, Mr Griffiths had been out to the fields, tending to his lambing ewes, and he came back again about two o'clock in the morning. As he got close to the house, he saw, standing in the portico, a tall woman.

His first thought was, 'Why, what is the matter with Nellie?' The woman seemed to be waiting for him, so he hastened his steps. He was looking at the woman and, just as he opened his mouth to speak – she vanished.

There one minute – gone the next. As he stood dumbstruck, he realised that it was the ghostly woman he had seen once before. When he got upstairs, Nellie was lying asleep. He never mentioned it to her next day, she was nervous enough as it was.

There was another man working at the farm living with his wife in the lodge at the bottom of the drive.

One bright, moonlit night, the worker's wife thought she would stroll along and meet her husband coming home from working in the yard. She was about halfway up the drive when, to her surprise, she saw a woman walking slowly towards her. It was unusual to see anyone there, particularly a woman in a long white dress. 'Goodness me,' the woman thought, 'it must be Mrs Griffiths dressed up to go to a party or something.' She smiled and was just going to speak as she drew nearer, when the woman vanished into thin air – and she was alone on the drive.

She was shocked to the core – frozen to the spot and, when she could move, she ran home as fast as she could, looking over her shoulder constantly to see if whatever it was following her. When she finally got to the lodge, she flew in and slammed the door, locking and bolting it tight. She collapsed shaking into a chair and, when her husband arrived and tried the door, she called out fearfully,

'Who's there?'

'Why me –' he said shortly, 'who did you expect – open this door and let me in.'

Flinging open the door, she threw her arms around his neck crying: 'Oh, I've seen a ghost – I've seen a ghost!'

Well, he was tired and hungry and thought she was being hysterical and, when she blurted out her story – he was angry with her.

'Don't be so silly woman – there's no such thing as ghosts, pull yourself together!'

Anyway, the more he scoffed, the more she tried to tell him details, which only made him madder. So much so, it was the first thing he said when he went to work next morning – relations with his wife had been strained all night, his disbelief had made her sulky and withdrawn.

He told Mr Griffiths that he had lost his temper with his wife the night before, told her not to be a fool.

'Why?' asked Mr Griffiths. 'What had she done?'

The farm labourer laughed and said she maintained that she had seen a woman in a long white dress.

'She saw her coming down the drive and thought it was Mrs Griffiths going to a party – and then dammit, she said the woman vanished in front of her eyes and that it must have been a ghost!'

He gave another scornful laugh, looking at Mr Griffiths to see if he was amused by the foolishness of women, but Mr Griffiths was looking very grave.

'Don't you blame her – don't you quarrel with your wife,' he said slowly and sternly. 'She is quite right, I've seen the white lady too, at the front door, I know very well what she looks like. Your wife is telling the truth.'

Then he impressed upon the farm labourer the need to keep quiet about it, and his wife too, as he didn't want Mrs Griffiths to know.

There were quite a lot of uncanny happenings that he never told his wife about, until years later when they had left the farm.

For instance, she never got to know about the gate to the big garden, with its exotic plants, ornamental trees, glasshouses, tool shed etc. which were always locked every evening by Mr Griffiths after the gardener had finished work.

Large ornamental gates led into the garden and Mr Griffiths would close them together, thread a chain through both gates and secure them with a padlock which he snapped shut and locked with a key that he always carried with the rest of the house keys.

He did this for a period of time with no trouble whatsoever, until one evening at dusk, he closed and locked the gates, and was just turning away when the gates started to shake violently, as if someone was behind them demanding to be let out.

As he turned back in surprise, there was a loud click, the padlock fell open, and the chain swung loose. The shaking stopped.

Mr Griffiths picked up the open padlock, puzzled how it could have fallen off when he was certain that he had locked it, and pushed open the gates to make sure no one was playing tricks on him, but there was no one inside the garden so, after pondering for a while, he stepped back again, and relocked the gate, this time tugging on the chain to make sure it was properly fastened.

Satisfied, he pocketed the key, and turned for home. At once, the gates started to vibrate, as if something was furious that they had been relocked. Nothing could be seen, but they were being shaken so hard, tiny flakes of rust fell off and lay on the path.

William Griffiths was a brave, sensible man and did not take to his heels as many less phlegmatic souls would. He stood still and watched until once more the padlock fell off and the gates became still again.

Next time it happened, he retested the chain, and stood back to watch.

Nothing happened.

After a minute or two, he turned to go. As soon as his back was turned, the racket began again and the padlock fell.

He found out after trial and error that if he watched the gates, nothing happened, but as soon as he stopped looking, *something* expressed fury at being locked in and shook the gates in real anger.

After a time, he removed the lock and chain and put them away in the tool shed, leaving the gates closed to, but always unlocked. There was no further trouble for the rest of his stay in that job.

Nellie Griffiths was not told this until years later when they had left and William also told her about something else he had kept secret and, which (in my opinion) was the eeriest thing of all.

Being a big house, the cellars were very spacious, and my father-in-law kept his handyman tools in the first room at the bottom of the stone steps that led down from the back kitchen. This cellar door was very solid and, because the steps it opened onto were very steep and dark, it was always kept locked.

Dim light filtered through a small window high on the wall

(which outside was at ground level) nearly obscured by grass. As in most subterranean rooms, the floor was always slightly damp; it was clay, packed tight with years of use.

An old table under the long, narrow window came in handy as a workbench for repairing, oiling or sharpening pieces of farm machinery and household utensils and there was always an assortment of things waiting to be mended. The cellar also contained lots of household junk – broken furniture, discarded pictures, and the usual assortment of household clutter.

One evening, after tea, Mr Griffiths made a determined attack on the piles, making things much tidier by throwing out everything that was useless, stacking the broken furniture in the next room and generally having a good clear out. The result was an almost empty room, which would make an ideal workshop for him.

When everything was neat and shipshape, Mr Griffiths went for a yard brush, and swept up all the rubbish, until the room was clean and bare. He cast a satisfied look around, working out in his head just where he would hang implements and tools on the walls and then left the cellar, locking the door after him.

A couple of days later, he went back down again, carrying a small vice that he was going to set up on the table. As he put it down, he noticed the marks his hob-nailed boots had left on the swept, damp floor, leading from the cellar steps.

Something else there made him stoop down and gaze intently at the floor. His boot marks, plain to see, had crossed over other tracks that were certainly not made by him. At first, he couldn't make them out in the gloom but a ray of the setting sun shone diagonally through the window and lit up the cellar. There, plain to see, deeply imprinted in the damp clay, were the marks of a child's footprints.

Small bare footprints, with fine little round toe-marks plainly visible in each print, traced a distinct circle all around the edge of the room and, as he stared, he could see that they completely encircled the cellar not once, but repeatedly. *Something* had walked around and around countless times, so that some tracks almost obliterated others and, the pitiful thing was the *smallness* of the bare feet-marks.

After everything that had been happening, Mr Griffiths was not easily shaken, but even he said the hairs on the back of his neck 'stood up like a dog's.'

Grimly, he picked up the stiff brush and swept the marks away, until they were completely erased, leaving only the traces left by the brush, which had the effect of making the damp clay look as if it had been combed. He had no desire now to set up the vice, but went back upstairs and locked the door.

Next day, he returned again in curiosity. Again, plain to see, childish bare prints marked many circles around the cellar.

He erased them again, but they re-appeared as often as he swept them away, although the only key to the cellar was always kept in his pocket and, of course, there was no child about.

After a time, he ceased using the cellar and kept its secret to himself.

Mr Hughes was (understandably) reluctant to tell me the name of the farm, saying that all this happened a long time ago, when Mr and Mrs Griffiths were young, and they have been dead for at least forty years. He did add that a few years ago, the son of the family living at the farm instructed his girlfriend not to come through the garden at night, so Mr Hughes said he thinks that 'there is still something there'.

Reappearance of a ghost

This story, more than many others, invoked for me the atmosphere of a fire lit room years ago, with children sitting big-eyed, listening to this tale told to them by their grandfather. I could almost hear his voice solemnly repeating the story, as Ted Hughes, of Bryn Alaw, recounted it to me.

Richard Roberts, my grandfather, was the foreman on a farm at Rhosbeirio. He was a big strong man, patient and gentle and not easily frightened. The old people used to tell me how straight he was and that he never told a lie in his life.

On the farm was a great bull, short tempered and very fierce and, it was always looking for a chance to kill a small man who worked there, because he kept beating it with his stick when he knew it couldn't reach him. A cruel man.

With my Grandfather it was as meek as a lamb. He talked softly to it all the time and it followed him about like a dog.

Very early one winter morning, when it was still very dark, he coupled two horses to a big cart to go for a load of lime for the land. They got it in those days from the Swaith hills near Cemaes.

There were three carts going at the same time from three different farms, Bodewryd Farm, Felin Wen and Rhosbeirio Farm. They all went together, because when they were coming back loaded, they had to unhitch the horses, make them into a team to get the heavy wagons up the hills. They did it one wagon at a time, leaving them at the top of hills, and bringing the horses back to the other carts, as it would have been too much for just two horses.

So they met together, and set off, with the Rhosbeirio cart at the rear.

As he was driving along the dark road that goes from Four Crosses to Cemaes, which was deserted at that hour, he was just passing the field that had the lonely Standing Stone in it, when suddenly a man jumped into the cart without making a sound and sat beside him. He couldn't see what the man looked like in the dark, but Grandfather said he brought a terrible atmosphere of great cold, and Grandfather said he was filled with a sense of dread.

The horses instantly stopped dead and stood trembling.

Grandfather dared not look at the silent figure sitting beside him, it was all he could do to urge on the horses, who eventually started to move forward very slowly. He could hear the Bodewryd cart going, and the Felin Wen cart going, clopping along normally, but his horses were hardly moving, as if they were dragging a great load, although the cart was empty.

He looked straight ahead, and the frightened horses stumbled on, until they came level with the gate of Bodewryd Church, when the man suddenly jumped down from the cart and vanished silently through the *closed* gates of the churchyard.

When he did so, the horses both snorted and shook their heads, then set off at a brisk walk, just as normal.

Grandfather was not a fearful man, but he always said that whatever rode with him that night, was not of this world.

*   *   *

There is a sequel to this story, which happened many years later. The late Lieutenant Commander Lewis, who has just passed away in Llanfair PG, was a very intelligent man who married the daughter of Mr Pritchard of Plas Bodewryd. Mr Pritchard taught him everything he knew about farming and, in due course, when Mr Pritchard died, his son-in-law took over the farm when he came out of the services.

One night, returning home to Plas Bodewryd after a long journey, Mr Lewis was just opposite Bodewryd churchyard, when a man stepped into the road about two yards in front of him and walked deliberately into the path of the car, looking directly at him. Mr Lewis stamped on the brakes so hard that the car stopped with a tremendous jerk, causing the contents of the back seat to fly forward – but it was too late, and to his horror, he hit the man head-on.

He immediately jumped out and ran to the front of the car, expecting to see a body on the road.

'I must have hit him,' he said afterwards, 'he was looking right at me, and there wasn't time for me to pull up before I ran him down, but there was no one there. I looked all round the car, got my torch out and looked under it, then I searched both sides of the road, but there was no one lying anywhere. Just nothing. I was shaking so much I could hardly get back in the car, so I sat there for a minute until the shock wore off a bit, then I pulled myself together and drove slowly home.'

And that happened in exactly the same spot as the thing that befell my grandfather all those years before.

The pale dog

This is another story Mr Hughes told me.

Not so very long ago farm labourers led a very hard life. Everything was manual labour then, no luxuries like sitting in a heated tractor cab, protected from the elements and all the hard work done by moving a few levers. They had their meals at the farms where they worked and usually slept in the outbuildings.

Such a one was young Wil Pritchard, a cheerful hardworking lad who was employed at Gwredog farm, Rhos-goch, and slept with the other men in a loft at Four Crosses.

One summer evening, after having supper at Gwredog, Wil and two older men were walking back to their sleeping quarters at Four Crosses. This loft (which is a ruin now) had a flight of stone steps leading up to it, which can still be seen.

About halfway there, a big whitish dog joined them and walked alongside Wil.

'Where did you come from, old man?' asked Wil in surprise. The dog looked up at him in a friendly way and Wil saw that it had its mouth open, panting with its tongue lolling.

He clicked his tongue at it and smiled as it trotted at his side.

'Duw,' said Wil admiringly, 'you're a *big* dog.'

The two men walking just in front of him, turned to look.

'Talking to yourself now, Wil?' asked one.

'No,' Wil answered, 'I'm talking to this feller.' He bent down to pat the dog's head.

His two companions looked at Wil curiously and, at that moment, he lifted his head, looking puzzled.

He stopped dead, and the dog stopped too, looking up at him and slowly wagging its tail.

'That's funny,' Wil said. 'I can't feel anything.'

Bending down again, he gently stroked the dog's back, but his hand didn't feel fur or a backbone, but went right through the dog itself.

The two men watching saw nothing but Wil, bending down in the road, stroking thin air. They were tired after a day's hard work and wanted to get to bed.

'Oh, stop fooling about, boy,' said one, and they strode on. Wil wasn't afraid, but he was mystified about the dog's lack of substance and he hurried after them, looking at the dog all the time, as it trotted beside him.

'Can't you see it?' he asked disbelievingly, 'It's here, as large as life, just look, will you?'

By this time the two older men clearly believed that Wil was trying some stupid joke on them and they became more irritable as he tried to prove the dog was there.

Wil was excited, and curious, so he went on talking to the dog and trying to stroke it, but to no avail.

'Don't tell me you can't see it,' he said, 'it's big enough, and cream coloured, but I can't feel it – just *look* will you?'

The two men, who were senior to Wil in work as well as years, were really angry now, believing Wil's playacting to be a form of cheek, so they swore at him roundly, threatening him with a thick ear if he didn't stop.

By now, they had reached the loft and the senior man with the key went up first, closely followed by his mate. Wil put his foot on the bottom step and looked round for the dog.

It had vanished. The straight road was empty, as were the fields on either side. Baffled, Wil started to climb the steps, just as the man with the key flung open the door.

As they moved inside – both gave a yell of fear. One started to buckle at the knees with shock, and falling, clutched out for support from the other, who was trying to back out of the door behind him. They both crashed painfully to the floor, one hitting the doorpost with his face.

Immediately they scrambled up, dashing past Wil and nearly knocking him over in their haste to get back down the steps. Wil stared down at them in amazement then turned to look in the loft. There was nothing to be seen.

The men were speechless and shocked and sank down on the grass as if their legs were too weak to hold them up. One of them wiped his sleeve across his bloody nose, where he had hit the doorpost, and the other felt the large bump that was rising on his forehead.

When Wil demanded what the matter was, the older man

stared dazedly up at him, shaking his head and muttering – '*What* a dog! *What* a dog!

'It was as big as *that* Wil,' the other said, struggling to his feet and drawing a four feet high shape in the air, 'big as a calf'! Then together, they told him what had happened. As they had opened the door to the loft, inside stood a huge, pale-coloured dog barring the way. It stared menacingly at them, lips pulled back, showing its teeth in a ferocious snarl.

They refused to enter the loft again, until Wil had been up and searched it. This Wil did quite happily, the dog had not frightened him, indeed he had tried to stroke it, and it had wagged its tail in a very friendly way.

The loft was quite empty, and they never saw it again, but Wil grinned to himself that they had been forced to believe him. He always swore later that the dog had frightened them on purpose!

The Ladi Wen of Bryn C

Throughout the ages, Anglesey men hav
invaders. Only a tiny island, it has alwa
fearless fighting men, peaceful farmers a
working hard at their trades during the
together to make formidable enemies wh

Long before the Vikings appeared, raide
Scotland would land in the quiet coves and bays, r
cattle, sheep and pigs nearby, burning farms and crops in light
raids and be away again before the alarm had spread.

So sea-robbers have been around for many centuries and, one
of the most famous pirates of all time was Francis Drake, who was
rewarded with a knighthood by Elizabeth I for filling the nation's
coffers with gold and silver he had seized from the Spanish
treasure ships. Piracy was rife.

Wreckers came later, when beacons and lights were lit to warn
mariners of dangerous reefs. This gave wreckers the chance to alter
the position of the lights, thus leading vessels onto rocks where
they would founder, their crews murdered and their cargoes
instantly spirited away.

There were three types of sea-faring outlaws, pirates, wreckers
and finally smugglers.

Smuggling did not begin in the British Isles until goods became
taxed when customs was introduced. When trade was free,
smuggling was unknown, but the state or the king, always
required money and one of the simplest ways was to collect it from
a trading vessel before giving him permission to come and sell his
goods ashore. In medieval times, cash was rare, so it used to be
extracted in kind from the cargo.

Levies rose higher and honest traders were forced to pay far
more than they thought was reasonable so, as people do today,
they resorted to subterfuge.

By the eighteenth century, smuggling had become a very
efficient, highly organized business. Many 'free-traders' had their
own vessels plying between the British Isles and the Continent.
Others met merchant vessels out at sea, usually by night, and
transferred the cargoes into smaller sailing ships to head for

the isolated coves and beaches, the fine tendrils of a
rk ran across the British Isles, transporting the goods by
e and wagon.

toms Board officials were appointed all around the coasts
eir riding officers patrolled the lonely cliff paths. Sometimes
y rode in pairs, but many were alone, riding by night in all sorts
weather around the shores and cliffs.

If they did come across a 'run', one or even two men on
horseback were not much use, being outnumbered and easily
captured.

A favourite trick of the contraband runners was to securely
bind an officer's feet together and tie his hands behind his back.
Then he was laid on top of a seaward sloping cliff, with his head
hanging in space over the edge and left there until discovered. He
dare not wriggle, as each movement would thrust his body
forward and he risked falling to his death on the rocks below.

One officer on patrol down south came across loaded
smugglers travelling inland and demanded them to surrender their
goods, but he was greatly outnumbered and they jeered and pelted
him and his horse with stones. When he charged them, they beat
him up with clubs. A brave man, he staggered up in a daze and
drew his sword – but they took it off him with ease and promptly
cut off his nose with it.

Articles that can now enter freely were subject to heavy duty in
previous centuries – jewels, silks, velvets and lace etc. and in the
seventeen hundreds they entered the country very craftily, hidden
and disguised.

Lace, carefully and tightly wrapped, was hidden in hollowed
out hams and in small wooden boxes carved and painted to
resemble apples. Jewellery and watches were hidden in loaves of
bread and pies. Liquor was found in all sorts of places aboard ship,
from false hulls to hollowed out oars and masts, some even found
in hollow broom handles.

So numerous and so well armed did the sea-robbers and
smugglers become, that it got to the stage where the riding officers
dare not apprehend them, unless assisted by the dragoons.

Windmills, lonely farmhouses and barns near the coast made
good storage places, where the contraband would change hands

and travel inland. Hardly a house on a lonely coast did not, at some time or another, give shelter to smugglers or goods – a very lucrative business for their accommodating owners.

Churches and their towers were often used, with the full knowledge of the parson (who liked his brandy and tobacco), and most of the gentry were party to the smuggling, even providing men and money to assist the cause.

In Anglesey also, smugglers and sea-robbers thrived, and I was told of a curious incident in the eighteenth century (when law and order was striving for ascendancy during the turbulent years), which has resulted in a very well documented haunting.

Though most people in power were turning a blind eye to how their supplies of spirits, tobacco and finery for their ladies were obtained, there was a strong element of honest, upright men, who were determined to enforce the laws of the country.

One of these was Squire Pritchard of Treysgawen, who was a well-known man in the mid-eighteenth century. A man of honour, great wealth and property, he had absolutely no sympathy for pirates, wreckers or smugglers, nor for anyone who had dealings with them.

Being a man of power and influence, and whole-heartedly on the side of the Customs Board, he came down heavily on the lawless ones, who knew that if they were captured by the Squire's men, and found guilty, they would be imprisoned or hanged.

But the sea-robbers always lived dangerously and, in those days, people were hanged for stealing a sheep; life was cheap.

They made sure that people with whom they dealt, using their houses or buildings for storage before the goods were moved along the network, kept their mouths firmly shut. Hiding places were very ingenious – false walls, tunnels, secret rooms – some taking years to perfect, were all made with elaborate care, as were the hidey-holes for anyone on the 'run' and staying in the house.

Just below City Dulas on the north east coast of Anglesey, lies Dulas Bay, its firm isolated beaches making it a prime spot for landing illicit cargoes and used constantly over the years by the sea-robbers.

Approximately a mile inland rises Allt Jenni, one of the foothills of Mynydd Bodafon. A bare, inhospitable rocky place, it was very isolated and lonely and on it was a run-down farm, used as the local depot for the goods before they went onto the next stage of the network. This farm was always guarded by a lookout man and avoided by the law-abiding locals.

Not far from Capel Coch, stands the mansion of Bryn Golau, a very ancient place, and the home of the Squire of Treysgawen in the eighteenth century.

A mile or so north of Bryn Golau lies the grand house named Plas Llanfihangel and living there at this time was a gentleman named Lewis. He had a daughter (name unknown) whom he idolized. She was tall, with the strength of a man, a vicious temper and a tendency to lash out with her fists at the slightest provocation.

Although in her father's eyes, she could do no wrong, she was hated and feared by her servants and the local people, who constantly felt the lash of her tongue and whip. Many deep grudges were harboured against her and no one, other than her close family, would have grieved if she had died. Wealthy, with plenty of money to indulge her whims, she paid her way into the gang of sea-robbers and their hangers-on and, after seeing her guineas, they were more than willing to supply her with the jewellery, laces and finery which she desired. Like most unpleasant people, she was arrogant, greedy and vain, flaunting herself in her rich clothes, on a beautiful milk white horse.

Her go-between always informed her when the pirates had landed and she impatiently had to wait until dark before she went to the farm and chose her purchases.

Squire Treysgawen knew of her dealings and was determined to catch her, as he had caught others, who went to gaol at Beaumaris, some to serve long prison sentences, others to hang. He also had knowledge of the landings and, when he was told that the robbers had landed, he knew the daughter of Llanfihangel would go there as soon as dusk fell, so he sent a group of his best law-enforcing men to Allt Jenni.

They rode to the foot of the hill under cover of darkness and there they hid, knowing she would have to return that way. The Squire had instructed them to apprehend her as she came down the hill and, if she was carrying illicit articles, these would be proof of her guilt and she would be arrested.

The men had dismounted a short distance away, leaving one of their numbers in charge of the horses, to keep them from whinnying and betraying their presence. Then they had moved silently into position and waited.

The night was still and overcast, the cloud-covered sky making the darkness even thicker and the men grew colder as time stretched on.

Eventually, they were rewarded by the clink of metal on stone, the faint sounds of a horse's hooves drawing nearer. The sound of a woman's muffled cough made them tense and fade even further into the undergrowth. Peering into the darkness, they saw the shimmering shape of the white horse, bearing the daughter of Plas Llanfihangel, and bulging panniers, down the final slope of Allt Jenni.

As she passed, they sprang into action. One grabbed the reins and halted the startled horse, another threw his arm around her waist and dragged her from the saddle, preventing her from bolting, at the same time clamping his other hand across her mouth.

After the first shock, she struggled so fiercely she knocked him to the ground and fell on top of him, but he did not let go. The other two rushed to help him, her great strength took their combined weight to pin her to the ground. Fighting like a tigress, she used her nails to rake their faces and bit the hand across her mouth so savagely the man grunted in pain.

As she fought, tooth and nail, she opened her mouth to scream, but before she could, she was tightly gagged and her wrists lashed together. She was pulled roughly to her feet, but using her bound wrists like a club, she lashed out sideways and landed a blow on one man's head that sent him reeling. The only way to subdue her was to thread a rope between her arms at the back, then truss her like a chicken. That left her flailing and kicking like a mule, until one man sat on her legs while they tied her ankles together and left her lying on the ground.

The panniers, on examination, were bulging with fine Spanish lace and beautifully wrought foreign jewels in gold settings, the spoils from some merchant ship raided by the pirates.

Dishevelled and panting, the Squire's men squinted at these treasures in the dark, then one man leading, another riding each side of her, they made their way back to Bryn Golau, the daughter of Plas Llanfihangel slung helplessly across her white horse.

When they arrived, her ankles were untied so she could walk, but they kept tight hold of her. Still she fought like a mad woman, kicking out with her feet, convulsing her body into a dead weight and even using her head as a battering ram into their faces.

She was dragged across the courtyard, through the rear door to the cellars, glaring and struggling all the way.

Below the cellars, lay the well-used dungeon and, here, the story divides.

One tale says she was thrown down into it from the top of the steps; another version is that in her struggles she fell.

The third, most generally believed, is that she was stabbed and murdered by one of her captors.

Whatever the truth, when Squire Treysgawen reached the dungeon, the daughter of Plas Llanfihangel lay dead.

Thus started one of the best-known hauntings in Anglesey.

* * *

The next time Mr John Roberts, Bryn Teg, came to see me, we discussed the death of the daughter of Plas Llanfihangel and the stories that arose then about her ghost and are still talked about today.

As usual, I went to make some tea and scones and when I came back, Mr Roberts was sitting quietly looking into the fire and, as I poured the tea, he said, thoughtfully:

I remember an old man who worked at Bryn Golau for years. He lived in Amlwch and he told me that one winter's night he set off to walk back home and he had only just left Bryn Golau when he heard a horse's hooves coming along the road behind him. As it got nearer, he could hear the chinking noise of the harness as it drew parallel with him.

He peered all around him in the dark, then the moon sailed out from behind a cloud and, all he saw was the empty road, shining in the bright moonlight, although the sound was right next to him, then it seemed to pass him and gradually faded into the distance.

He heard it many times after that, he never did see the horse, but said as the noise of the hooves got louder and went past him, the air around him grew very cold and only returned to normal as the hoof-beats died away.

Talking about it to the other servants at Bryn Golau, he learned that some had heard and *seen* it – a lady rode it in old-fashioned clothes and both horse and rider were enveloped in a white glow. Her gaze always seemed to be fixed straight ahead and she made no sign that she had seen them.

One old lady who had spent her life in service at Bryn Golau, told him that her mother, who had worked there before her, said the apparition was the ghost of the daughter of Plas Llanfihangel, and was often to be seen on that stretch of road just outside Bryn Golau; she was known as the Ladi Wen (The Lady in White).

He avoided this part of the road as often as he could by cutting across the fields and then rejoining the road.

In years gone by, farm labourers had very hard lives. They usually worked and ate at the farm where they were employed and slept in the lofts. Usually the farmers allowed them to keep a beast or two on the farm and they were sold to supplement the worker's meagre wages.

It was in the days when there was a big Christmas Cattle Fair at Llangefni and a lot of good-natured rivalry went on between the farm-labourers as to who could present the best beasts at the Fair.

As they usually didn't have the land to grow crops, it was the custom to go around the neighbouring fields at night, when the corn was ready for cutting, armed with sacks and sickles. The best corn would be cut and stolen to fatten up their bullocks; it was an accepted way of life and an open secret.

One evening in late August, sitting quietly in his local pub, the man who worked at Bryn Golau was enjoying his pipe and a pint of ale and listening to the talk and banter.

As usual at that time of year, the talk was about the fattening of their beasts for the Fair, as it was very close to harvest time. There was a lot of bragging about their own beasts, and jeering about others, but the Bryn Golau man didn't join in as usual, but sat listening to the others, saying nothing about his own beasts.

Then he broke his silence. Taking his pipe out of his mouth, and pointing it at them to emphasize his words, he said solemnly: 'Whatever you do – whenever you go for your grain, *don't* go along the road that turns the corner at Bryn Golau granary when it is dark.'

Then he stuck his pipe back in his mouth and said no more, just shaking his head at their questions.

In reality, he was giving them a friendly warning, as he knew that part of the road was badly haunted, but they were all astute countrymen and, immediately, jumped to the conclusion that the wheat field behind the granary was prime grain and they thought – well, he should know, he works there – he wants the grain for his own beasts. Nothing more was said, but one of his listeners was determined that he would have a share too.

So he went to bed early that night, as soon as he had eaten his supper and got up again in the wee small hours. He picked up an empty sack, a sickle and a hurricane lamp, and quietly left the sleeping loft.

It was a very dark night, no moon and being of country stock yourself, you know what a dim light a hurricane lamp gives – hardly enough to see your next step, but even so, he wasn't going to light it until he got to Bryn Golau.

He approached Bryn Golau as silently as a poacher and felt his way around the granary, where the corner abutted onto the bend in the road, groping along in the pitch darkness.

As he turned, he was immediately almost blinded by a dazzling white light, as suddenly as if he'd opened a door.

It hadn't shown itself on the road until he'd turned. It had no source, seeming to come from nowhere and, as he said days later, it was so bright 'you could have picked up a half crown.'

As he stood staring in bewilderment, a vague figure began to take shape, growing in the centre of the light. It was the form of a woman and, when she had become opaque, she started to sway slowly towards him, at least a foot above the surface of the road.

A very tough man, he managed to stay his ground, even though what was happening was completely beyond his comprehension. He stood and stared as the ghost approached him, surrounded by the luminous white mist, and he saw that it was indeed a woman with long dark hair that swung in ringlets about her face.

Then he saw a most horrible thing. Although her face was fully fleshed as a living woman, where her eyes should have been there were two hollow sockets.

He went stiff with shock, quite unable to move and, as she drew nearer, she exuded a paralysing coldness and an all-pervading rage.

She stopped not a foot away from him, and went like this,

(Here Mr Roberts clenched his fists close to his chest and made angry, outward pushing movements with them.)

... and she made a deep, growling noise like this:
'Nnnn-nnnnn-nnnnn –'
He told me he was suddenly galvanised into action – he dropped the sack and lantern, turned tail and ran all the way home, and how he got up the stone stairs to his sleeping loft he doesn't know, he was shaking so much.

But this is what I can't understand, he lived around there for years and years and he never saw anything before or since.

Since I first transcribed Mr Roberts's tape, I have puzzled many times about the unusual, if not unique, actions. Then not long ago, the possible solution dawned on me.

If the daughter of Plas Llanfihangel, described as tall and strong, with a vicious temper, was bound and gagged to stop her fighting so fiercely, this would explain the feeling of fury that emanated from the ghost.

Also the description – 'her fists close to her chest, making short angry, outward pushing movements with them' and again 'and she made deep growling noises like this,
'Nnnn-nnnn-nnnn'.
The incoherent noises of someone furiously trying to speak through a gag and the struggle to get her arms free and fight –
Was this an image of the woman as she was captured?
Or was it the moment before she was murdered?

*   *   *

There's one thing about the ghost of the White Lady.

I remember talking to Frank Jenkins, he was quite psychic and, if there were anything to be seen in the ghost line, Frank would see it, but there was one time when he didn't.

Treysgawen Hall had been restored in 1989, and it was a beautiful place. Frank had a niece who lived in Rhyl, and she had come on holiday to help them with the haymaking.

She told Frank that she would love to see the Hall and the alterations so, when they had finished a field about tea-time one day, they set off; it was a hot, sunny day, not a cloud in the sky. It wasn't far, down a horseshoe shaped lane that runs past the mansion and rejoins the main road again after passing Bryn Golau.

They were walking past the mansion, Frank pointing out the big new windows and grand entrance, when the girl suddenly went rigid and gripped Frank's arm very tightly, almost pinching it.

'Don't grip me so hard,' said Frank in surprise, but she never answered, but walked on as stiff and silent as a piece of wood.

He tried again to show her the alterations to the Hall by pointing, but she wouldn't look round or answer his questions, it was as if she had gone deaf and blind and, he was virtually talking to himself, so he gave up.

Finally, in silence, they reached the main road again and she suddenly went limp and fell against him.

'Oh – thank God for that – thank God for that,' she muttered, and let out a huge sigh of relief.

'Thank God for what?' Frank asked blankly.

'Didn't you see her? The lady in white – she never left me – she kept by my side right past the mansion and when we got back to the road she suddenly vanished.'

She was shaking so much her legs would hardly hold her up and Frank had to support her back home, where her aunt put her straight to bed.

She was so terrified, she begged her aunt not to leave her alone and so distressed that Frank had to call for the doctor in the middle of the night. He gave her a sleeping draught and advised them to keep her quietly in bed, as the shock had badly affected her nerves. Her aunt slept with her for the remainder of her stay.

And so that is another one who will bear witness to the fact that The Lady in White still walks and, yet, not everyone can see her – some just hear her.

I used to know a Miss Jones who lived at Bryn Golau – had done all her life – and she used to visit two sisters at Tŷ Lawr – a very remote place – late in the evening, winter and summer, and she would leave Tŷ Lawr at one o'clock in the morning to walk back alone to Bryn Golau.

I asked her whether she had been afraid.

She looked at me in surprise.

'No indeed,' she said, 'I was going home wasn't I?'

'Have you ever seen anything?' I asked. She shook her head.

'Have you ever heard anything? Any noises?'

She nodded immediately.

'Things like chinking metal or creaking noises like leather?'

'Oh yes, I often heard *that*,' she answered, 'but I always thought it was a dog that had got loose.'

* * *

Frank and I had two friends who bought Bryn Golau a few years ago. Owenna had just graduated and her husband was a Professor of Geology.

We asked if we could visit them and, they said yes, of course, come any time. On the day we went, another friend was there, who was also a teacher.

The five of us were sitting relaxed with cups of tea, when I heard a man coming along the passage from the front door with a brisk tread.

I looked up and said,

'There's someone in the passage!'

Owenna went on stirring her tea – then shrugged her shoulders at me and said:

'Oh don't take any notice of that, we hear it every night. At first we used to go and look, but although the footsteps would go right past us as we stood in the doorway of the room, we never saw anyone. Now we just accept it.'

Nevertheless, I had to go and open the door and look, but the footsteps had ceased. No one was there.

Owenna and her husband bought Bryn Golau about ten years ago and the house needed a lot of restoration.

'We found that the window frames were all rotten,' said Owenna, 'so we engaged a very experienced joiner to make new ones.'

He brought the new frames and Owenna was talking to him when he lifted a new frame to put in place. It was inches too big and it wouldn't fit into the aperture.

'You measured it wrong,' said Owenna, a bit tactlessly.

The joiner was both baffled and annoyed.

'No way,' he said hotly, 'I got the measurements exactly right. I learned my trade from a master joiner. He always said – *measure* a *hundred* times – and cut *once* – and so I do.'

He tried all the other frames and every one was too big. He stared at them and scratched his head.

'There's something funny here,' he said, 'there's absolutely no reason for them not to fit,' then reluctantly, 'anyway – I'll fetch my saw – you just hold the frame there.'

When he came back, he took hold of the frame to see where to cut, held it against the aperture and the frame slid in, nice and snug. So did all the others, each a really tight fit, one after the other, and the joiner and Owenna stood and stared at each other, speechless.

'It seemed as if the frames had got longer or the window holes smaller,' Owenna said, 'and suddenly they fitted perfectly. It was as if someone resented us changing the house.'

*   *   *

Bryn Golau is a very old building, which has always belonged to powerful men, changed structurally over the years, but the cellars have remained much the same from medieval times.

Below the cellars is a dungeon, where criminals or law-breakers were taken and, usually, manacled to the walls. Today, in old castles or fortified buildings they can still be seen, with evidence of their long usage visible on the floor near the manacles, the stone of which has been worn away in tight circles, where the poor wretches incarcerated there have shuffled around in a small circumference for months or even years.

I thought about this as Mr Roberts went on.

While Frank and I were there, we asked if we could have a look round and Owenna said, of course, so we wandered all over the old place, beginning with the upstairs rooms and going down floor by floor, until we found ourselves in the cellars.

As far as I could see, they were extensive cellars, quite ordinary, with stone shelves like they used to have years ago.

Then we suddenly came to what seemed to be a deep square pit, not covered or anything, just stone steps going down one side.

So I started down, I wanted to explore, but as I went down the first few steps, Frank grabbed my arm and dragged me back.

'Don't go down there,' he said in a very urgent voice, 'don't go down there, whatever you do.' And he pulled me up. I was very disappointed – I wanted to explore – but he hustled me out of the cellars and upstairs without any explanation.

Anyway, on our way back home, Frank, who is sometimes very psychic, said in a quiet voice:

'Do you know why I didn't want you to go down that deep cellar?'

'No,' I said, very curious.

'Well, as you started down, I suddenly got the feeling that it was a bad place. A very bad place. Then I realised that it was where the daughter of Plas Llanfihangel was murdered. I just *had* to stop you going down there.'

He was quiet for a little while, and then he said:

'She is not at rest you know, the daughter of Plas Llanfihangel, not at rest.'

We walked the rest of the way in silence.

Llanallgo Rectory

Above the pretty fishing village of Moelfre, on the east coast of Anglesey stands the small but beautiful church of Llanallgo, built on the site of the church of the Celtic Christian St Gallgo, who erected it in the seventh century. Over the years, the church has been rebuilt and restored and, the present structure is mainly medieval, although it was enlarged late in the nineteenth century.

The tranquil life of Llanallgo church, with its eternal cycle of births, marriages and deaths, came to a sudden end one awful day in October 1859, when it was catapulted into horrendous publicity by the effects of the worst hurricane of the nineteenth century, which swept northwards over Britain, leaving a trail of death and destruction throughout the country.

The October day began calmly enough, but as afternoon drew on, the light south-westerly wind grew stronger and then came the rain, sweeping over Anglesey and blotting out the mountains of Snowdonia with a grey curtain of driving rain. During the afternoon, the wind swung to east-north-east and gradually increased to gale force, while the glass was falling rapidly.

Beating up close to the coast of Anglesey, homeward bound for Liverpool, was the magnificent clipper ship, *Royal Charter*, carrying four hundred people back from Australia and a cargo of gold bullion. The passengers were nearly all miners from Britain who had joined the gold rush to Australia and were returning home in triumph, each with their own personal fortune of golden guineas or bullion. Some wore their money in body belts, others in pockets or purses, and gold coins and ingots lying in the strong room came to £330,440 – a vast fortune in 1859.

All the passengers were happy and excited, coming to the end of their two months' journey and, expecting to dock in Liverpool next morning, but as the wind started to thrum in the rigging, and the seas became more turbulent, more than one stared up nervously at the scudding clouds.

Darkness fell early, the night was thick and black and, at 10.00 p.m. the wind increased until it was a force ten gale and, gradually to the consternation of the crew, the Charter started to balk and refused to answer her helm.

The waves were now mountainous, their tops sheered cleanly off by the wind and the noise was so colossal, even shouted orders could not be heard. Struggling mightily as they did, the crew could not stop the clipper drifting towards the granite teeth of the Moelfre rocks.

Now a force twelve, with gusts of 150 mph, the hurricane was screaming in the rigging and thirty foot waves towered over the doomed ship.

Sometime after 3.00 a.m., the remaining anchor cable parted and the Charter was driven bows onto the granite reefs, which she struck with a violent juddering crash, repeated again and again as the giant waves alternatively sucked her away then hurled her against the rocks with thunderous force.

Most of the women and children were below decks, sheltering in the warm and cosy saloons, but the passengers and crew on deck were thrown overboard in a tangled mass of spars and rigging, surging up and down as each wave hammered in.

Some were drowned by the weight of the gold they were carrying, others by the heavy and cumbersome Victorian clothes; the majority were killed by being smashed repeatedly against the rocks and the wreckage.

One survivor who was saved by clutching at a light spar and, miraculously avoiding the plunging wreckage, said he saw, in the huge walls of water which made up the waves, mutilated bodies without limbs, some headless, swirling about in the flotsam.

Then the helpless, once beautiful clipper snapped in the middle like a dry twig, the two halves of the hull turning to face the on-coming sea, the waves sweeping along inside the exposed body of the ship, washing out and drowning the terrified women and their children trapped inside.

Not a woman or a child survived that night.

There were nearly five hundred people aboard the *Royal Charter* and only about forty people survived. By the great courage and humanity of the people of Moelfre, they were snatched from the boiling sea by a chain of extremely brave men, roped together and standing waist-deep in the tide, who dragged them ashore.

They were carried over the wet, slippery rocks and up the steep paths to the cottages. The villagers put them in their own beds, tended the injured, fed them and did everything in their power to help.

The dead were carried to Llanallgo church.

For days the tide threw up mutilated bodies, limbs and severed heads, all of which were taken to the church and placed in the care of the Rev. Stephen Roose Hughes. They were all gently laid in rows on the floor of the church near the pulpit and must have made a scene of unbelievable horror.

When the news broke, relatives of the missing trekked from all over the country and, for weeks, Moelfre was crammed with grieving people. The church became the focal point for those searching for loved ones and, those who couldn't travel, wrote urgently to the Vicar for news, giving details of each person or child, eye-colour, hair-length, clothes, tattoos etc. and the Rev. Roose Hughes moved quietly amongst the pitiful remains, trying to perform the nearly impossible task of identifying crushed and partial bodies, before he carefully numbered them, prior to numbering the graves in which they were solemnly buried.

Charles Dickens visited Moelfre at the end of December that year and was immensely impressed by the courtesy, courage and selfless dedication of the Vicar. He was told that a hundred and forty bodies were buried at Llanallgo, another thirty four in the churchyard of his brother (also a Vicar) and many more in churchyards along the coast, as the tides washed up the dead.

The force of the waves had been so strong that a large gold ingot had been driven deeply into an iron plate of the ship's hull. When it was removed, it was found that a number of sovereigns had been driven before it into the same plate, as solidly as if they had been welded there.

Hundreds of people visited the little church and vicarage of Llanallgo, and the Rev. Hughes took on the task of comforting them, which he did with great gentleness and fortitude, his faith and courage the only things he had to sustain him through this colossal disaster. He received over one thousand letters, and answered every one in detail, even sending money from his meagre stipend to those who had lost their breadwinner.

With every letter and, each word of comfort, Rev. Hughes gave something of himself both physically and spiritually, until he was completely worn out and, just over two years later, this good man died quietly in his fireside chair at the Rectory, at the age of forty seven.

* * *

The rocky coast, church and vicarage and, ultimately the graveyard, was the epicentre of much raw grief and suffering, and it would be most unusual if such concentrated horror did not leave any echoes behind it.

My enquiries about ghosts only yielded stories of a silent figure (seen many times at night in the headlights of passing cars) of a tall man moving slowly amongst the graves, who vanished at once if the car slowed down or stopped for the occupants to get a closer look. Sometimes he was seen moving from the church into the yard and, sometimes between the graves near the boundary wall, but no one ever observed him long enough to describe him.

I was intrigued with the vague story of the Llanallgo ghost, so next time I spoke to my old friend, Mr Roberts, I asked him if he knew anything about the haunting.

This was on the phone and, to my delight, he said cheerfully: 'Oh yes, I'll come up soon and tell you about it.'

He was as good as his word, but before he did, I had the luck to talk to Mr Paul Johnson, of Matlock, Derbyshire, about his experience in Moelfre. This is what he told me.

I was on Anglesey in October 1977, during my son's half term holiday. One evening I went for a stroll along the cliffs near Moelfre. There was no wind, it was calm and dull, with a slight drizzle in the air.

I was alone, it was just before dark, and I had gone past a small cove or inlet, when I saw a group of men crossing the path before me.

They were coming up from the shore, about ten or fifteen yards in front of me. I thought they were local fishermen, about half a dozen of them, carrying a hurdle or something between them – it had a bundle on it that seemed very heavy.

They all seemed to be straining and out of breath and their boots were slipping a bit, as if they were tired. I didn't think anything of it just then, as they climbed up into the field, until it dawned on me how silent they all were. I don't mean not speaking – I mean everything about them. I couldn't hear their boots on the stones, I couldn't hear them breathing and although I was ready to call 'Good Evening' they didn't look my way – or even seem aware of me. They looked ordinary and real enough, but it was like watching a silent film, you know where you see people moving but no sound and nobody looks at you.

They stepped off the path into the field going up the hill, when suddenly the whole scene vanished.

One minute there was this grim group of men struggling with a load, next – puff! Nothing. It was so *weird!*

I was so shocked I just stood there wondering if I was going mad. Then I turned and legged it back to the cottage as quick as I could and told my wife – she didn't believe me at first, and said I'd been in the Kinmel (the local pub). Finally, I managed to convince her. I've never believed in ghosts, but I can't explain that at all. It still gives me the shivers whenever I think of it. It was the eeriest thing that has ever happened to me.

I told some of the local men in the pub that night. I was expecting them to laugh at me, but they just nodded and didn't say anything, I still don't know whether they believed me or were just being polite! I don't know, perhaps they knew more than I did!

When I questioned him, Mr Johnson said he'd heard about the sinking of the Charter, but didn't know anything much about the rescue.

Apart from Mr Johnson's story, I haven't heard of any more sightings, if anyone has, I should be very pleased if they would kindly get in touch with me.

Mr John Roberts duly arrived and we settled in front of a big fire, with a tray of tea and a dish of homemade scones. We chatted over tea, then when Mr Roberts sat back in his chair and cleared his throat, I knew he was ready to begin, so I switched on the tape.

He started with the story of the Rectory hauntings, which were quite unknown to me.

The Haunting of the Rectory

The Rectory at Llanallgo used to have a servant girl, who stayed in service until she was a certain age, then she would leave and a younger one would come to take her place. There were three sisters who lived locally and each, in her turn, went to work at the Rectory when she left school. These girls were well known to me, as their Auntie Margaret lived nearby, and I heard this story from her.

Now the staircase at the Rectory, I think it was eighteenth century, was wide and beautiful, but the girls learned to dread it.

The eldest girl, Mair, had been working there happily for a time and, one evening she was carrying a hot water bottle upstairs to the Vicar's bed. Halfway upstairs, she came to an abrupt stop. There was a great weight pressing against her chest. She looked down, nothing to see, the starched ruffles of her white apron undisturbed. Yet, lying heavily against her breast, she could feel the weight of a man's head and, in the shocked silence, she could hear slow, tortured breathing all around her.

Nothing was visible, just the weight of the heavy head against her bosom.

For a long moment she was paralysed with fear, then she bolted upstairs to the bedroom and thrust the water bottle into the bed.

Back at the top of the stairs, she listened and looked down. Nothing to see, nothing to hear, except the hammering of her own heart. Everything was still and normal, so taking a deep breath, she slid rapidly down the wall, keeping well away from the centre.

This terrifying experience happened again and again that week, but Mair kept it secret until she went home on her precious half-day. Then she told her mother, talking quietly as she helped to hang out the washing, her voice earnest and troubled.

Mair had learned to keep close to the wall, going upstairs or down, keeping well away from the centre and running as fast as she could. That way she seemed to avoid the haunting, unless it didn't happen every day.

She described the awful weight of the man's head and the slow, agonized breathing that filled the air around her, and her mother listened worriedly.

When Mair had finished, her mother declared her intention of going back to the Rectory with her, to explain to the Vicar's wife why Mair could not continue working there, but Mair, knowing how precious her small wages were to the family, shook her head and said she would go back and continue with her job.

So no more was said, as they both knew that the two younger girls would follow in their turn and it wasn't fair to frighten them or put ideas into their heads.

Courageously, Mair went back, grimly sticking to her daily tasks and, although she felt and heard the ghost many times, it did no harm, apart from the nervous dread it instilled.

Time went on, she left Llanallgo rectory and, in their turn, her two sisters took her place. In their turn also, they were visited by the same haunting on the stairs, but were reassured by Mair that it would not harm them. The Vicar and his wife always seemed totally unaware that their house was haunted.

Here Mr Roberts seemed to become lost in his memories, so I stirred up the fire to a cheerful blaze, as Mr Roberts looked at me and said:

'Do you know Evan Owen, who used to be a mechanic on the Moelfre lifeboat?'

I nodded.

'Yes, we used to see him sometimes when we went to the 'Pilot Boat' for lunch.'

'Well, his wife had been there in Mr Parry's time and, in those days, the Rector used to go and visit his parishioners in the evening.'

Here Mr Roberts looked at me and sadly shook his head.

'They don't now-a-days do they? But they did then. Anyway, the house rule was that as soon as the Reverend came back from his evening visits, the maid must prepare his supper at once.

Well, one night Evan's future wife was standing in the front garden calling the cat. A bright moon was shining and, as she stood there, she saw the figure of a man walk up the back path, alongside the churchyard wall, and enter the house by the back door. So immediately she went to the dining room and started to lay the table for supper and, just as she finished, Mrs Parry walked in.

'What on earth are you doing?' she asked in surprise. 'Mr Parry won't be back for another hour.'

'Oh yes,' said Nia, 'I've just seen him coming in the back door.'

Mrs Parry went into the hall and called his name. No reply. She shouted upstairs, still no answer.

Nia was adamant about seeing a man come in, she was so convincing that when she finished, they looked at each other nervously, and both worried about burglars.

When Mr Parry came home at his usual time, an hour later, Nia repeated her story and, was so positive she had seen a man enter the Rectory, that a puzzled Mr Parry searched every room.

Except for the three of them, the Rectory was empty.

* * *

A few years later, Canon Wooding, a bachelor who lived with his sister, became the incumbent at Llanallgo. As part of his duties, he had to spend one month in every twelve living at Bangor Cathedral.

One very dark and windy night in winter, his sister waved him off at the front door then returned thankfully to the warm fire, not in the least upset about being left on her own. She read until bedtime, then got up and started her usual round of the house, locking doors and making sure the windows were tightly fastened against the howling gale.

Switching out the downstairs lights, she started upstairs.

She was about halfway up when this ghost took over. She felt the heavy weight of his head against her breast and the sound of his slow breathing was loud in her ears.

The shock paralysed her, as she stood with one foot on the next stair, her hand grasping the banister. After a horrified second, looking down to see if the heavy head was real, she turned and fled downstairs, across the hall and shot into the front room, slamming and locking the door behind her.

She stood listening, but all she could hear was the sound of her own heart hammering in her ears, as she picked up the phone with shaking hands.

When she heard her brother's voice, she gabbled at him: 'Oh, come and get me – I can't stay here – I can't stay all night in this house!'

Canon Wooding was flabbergasted.

'Why – what's wrong?'

'Oh, I've had the most awful experience – ' and she gasped out her story, which he found difficult to understand, as she was almost incoherent with fright. She begged him again and again to come and fetch her.

'Stay just where you are, in that room,' said the Canon, 'I'm coming right now.'

He was there within the hour and took his sister (who was half fainting with fright) away. She swore she would never stay another night in that house, and she never did.

After that, he resigned.

At the Committee meeting, which was held to decide who the next Vicar of Llanallgo should be, Canon Wooding stood up and declared:

'No way' (and he gazed sternly around the assembly), 'no way must Llanallgo be a rectory again.'

Then, he told them about his sister's experience and how she had lost the power of speech for three weeks, due to the shock. He also told them that he had heard the previous maid's stories from their own lips and believed them implicitly.

The Committee was stunned into silence when he finished speaking, wondering how to tackle the problem. It was impressed by the Canon's earnestness and knew Miss Wooding to be an intelligent, well-balanced woman, not given to hysteria.

After much discussion and, as (sadly) the congregations in the local churches were dwindling, it was finally decided to combine two parishes into one and put the rectory up for sale.

Before this could be put under way, however, a Rev. Hughes and his family occupied it briefly. Eventually the parishes of Parciau, Bodafon and Llanallgo were combined and the Rev. Hughes chose to live at Bodafon Vicarage. So Llanallgo Vicarage was put up for sale, empty except for its ghostly resident.

Then Mr Roberts remembered something else about Llanallgo.

Many years before the *Royal Charter* made Llanallgo Church famous, another Rev. Parry was the incumbent there. The church needed restoration and enlarging and, during the alterations, the altar, which had occupied the same site for centuries, was moved. Below it, the builders found an ancient decayed coffin and, in it, was a skeleton, which, from its length, must have been the remains of a very tall man.

Now, if someone had been buried there, that must have been his wish, and the bones should have been covered over again and left alone, but Mr Parry took them away and had them buried elsewhere and, do you know, that man was haunted for the rest of his life?

He wouldn't go out alone in the dark, he always thought someone was following him and he was always looking over his shoulder. Gradually he grew very morose and nervy and he died a very young man.

* * *

I remember when they were renovating and enlarging Llaneugrad Church, you know, just by the Parciau estate, very nice little church. In those days, the practice was, when they made a church bigger, they built right over the nearest graves, which they did at Llaneugrad.

When the man was digging the foundations for the extension, he came across a lot of bones.

'Look here,' he said to the Rector, 'all these bones – what should I do with them?'

And the Rector said:

'Leave them exactly where they are, don't disturb them in any way, whatever you do, if you want to stay free of being haunted. They must be left in peace.'

Anyway, they laid the concrete over them and, now, they are there forever – at rest. It's very dangerous to play with those sort of things.

* * *

After hearing about Llanallgo, I was eager to find out about this beautiful eighteenth century vicarage, which seems to dwarf the little church behind it.

So, after a lot of enquiries, I was able to pick up its story from when it was abandoned as a Vicarage and put up for sale thirty nine years ago. It stood empty all that winter and spring, from November until June, when Mr Clarke, a Manchester businessman, came on holiday to Anglesey with his wife. They both fell in love with Llanallgo Rectory and bought it.

Mrs Clarke (sadly now a widow) still lives there and, she cheerfully and kindly, brought me up to date.

I live here with my married daughter and grandchildren and, none of us have either seen or felt anything odd, but the house is so full of children, all noisy and busy with computers and TV, I'm sure no self-respecting ghost would be seen dead here!

They sound a very happy lot, much too involved with life to even consider that they may be sharing the house with someone from another age. It made me wonder whether these days' ghosts are becoming an endangered species!

The only story that Mrs Jones has heard (and local people confirmed) is that the garden is haunted by the sad ghost of a small pony, who years ago got his head jammed in the fork of a low tree branch, was unable to free himself and, by the time he was found, he was dead.

Mrs Clarke also told me something else very interesting. Apparently the 'cannon' from the Royal Charter is in the Rectory garden.

I was curious as to how it got there and I asked Mr Tomos Roberts (BA, DAA, FSA), Archivist at Bangor University, and he went to a great deal of trouble to furnish me with the facts.

In a letter, he told me that the signal gun from the *Royal Charter* was removed from Bangor City Museum and set up in the garden of Llanallgo Rectory in 1937. He also enclosed a photocopy taken from the 'Transactions of the Antiquarian Society for 1937' which states: 'The signal gun from the *Royal Charter* has been removed from Bangor, by the kind permission of the Mayor and Corporation, and has been set up on a new gun-carriage in the grounds of Llanallgo Rectory, close to the high road.

The total cost of removal, stone platform, and gun carriage was £9 8s 5d.

Towards this sum, £1 was given by Mr Farrar Roberts, who obtained permission for the removal of the gun to Llanallgo and £3 7s 0d (the cost of the new gun carriage) by Col. Lawrence Williams.

Your Committee has voted the £4 4s 0d towards the balance of the expenses.'

So – there is the story of the Royal Charter and its deep connection with Llanallgo Church and Rectory.

The identity of the ghost on the stairs has never been established but it seems to be that of someone in desperate need of comfort. (Dickens, in his report on the wreck of the Charter, says that every room in the house had been the scene of unassuaged grief and weeping.) Whether the ghost is that of one of the sorrow-stricken relatives or poor Rev. Roose Hughes, who witnessed such unbelievable horrors and comforted over a thousand bereaved people, thereby wearing himself out and dying within two years of the sea tragedy, we may never find out.

In passing, I wonder whether the skeleton of the tall man, in the decayed coffin under the altar, and 'buried elsewhere', could possibly have been the remains of Saint Gallgo, who built the original church?

'Deryn Corff and the haunted church

One day Mr Roberts came to see me. It was a miserable, cold afternoon and he was glad to get into the warmth of the house. Once he had settled down and he saw I was ready he began.

'Have you ever heard about 'Deryn Corff – The Bird of Death?' he asked. 'Well, I'll tell you a story now.'

There was a mechanic, who worked at Llangefni a few years ago, and he was motorbike mad. He lived for his bikes and he was a superb motorcyclist. One day he went for an outing to Rhyl on his bike and hit a car that was reversing out of a drive. The driver couldn't see him coming and there was a bad smash.

The young man was very badly injured and, although the doctors said his life was not in danger, he knew that he would never ride again because his legs were so severely damaged. He was in hospital for a long time and he became very depressed and seemed to lose the will to live.

His uncle had been out shooting one day with the young man's friend and they were sitting by the fire that night talking about him. The uncle was very fond of his nephew, and was worried about him and the way he had lost interest in everything.

A great tree grew at the gable end of the house where they were sitting and an owl came into it. She was a screech owl, and she started calling and calling, she was going *mad*, she made such a noise they couldn't hear each other speak – screeching like anything she was.

So finally the uncle said, 'Look here, just go out and give a bang into that tree – she's a nuisance.' So he did, and fired into the air and frightened the bird away, but two minutes later she was back, screeching like mad, she just wouldn't go away.

They gave up then – the friend went home and the uncle went to bed. Halfway upstairs – the owl suddenly stopped in the middle of a screech and all was still. The grandfather clock had just finished striking eleven.

Next morning, there was a knock at his door, and the local policeman asked if he could come inside as he had some bad news. It was to tell him that his favourite nephew was dead. He was dying just at the time the owl was shrieking and she had stopped calling the moment he died, at eleven o'clock.

Mr Roberts stared pensively into the fire for a moment.

My mother used to attend confinements and lay people out when they died and, if someone was gravely ill, almost invariably the owl would come close to the house and call. Mother would look very serious and say, 'Oh, so-and-so is going to die tonight'. And they would too – it's something that's been recognised for hundreds and hundreds of years.

Another sign is the Cannwyll Corff, the Death Candle. Not many years ago, a little boy who lived at Llanbedrog had to have an operation, not a serious one, just for appendicitis, but something went wrong.

While he was in hospital, a neighbour was coming home late from work in the dark and he suddenly saw something flickering. It was the Cannwyll Corff. It came out of the little boy's house, right in front of the man, and moved slowly and steadily just above ground level, straight along the road before him, then turned into Llanbedrog churchyard, and disappeared amongst the graves. That was the night the little boy died.

That church is haunted you know – I shouldn't have told you the name in case the congregation gets frightened and stops going – I don't want to get into trouble with the Vicar!'

Seriously though, five boys went out lamping one night to catch rabbits. (Lamping is going out in the dark with dogs and powerful torches.)

There is a huge field, which rises high above the church, plenty of rabbits there. So the boys stood in this field in the pitch dark, at the side of the church, and the dogs were all eager to work.

They shone the lights, rabbits galore, and they thought the dogs would dash in straight away. But they wouldn't move, they got behind the boys and cowered down shivering. As the lads were urging them on, one pointed downwards at the church and said:

'Look – there are lights on in the church.'

They all looked now and saw the church was brightly lit inside – so they quickly switched off the torches, and stood in the dark, making no noise. It was then they heard, through the silence, the sound of the church organ playing. Slow, mournful music, with long drawn out base notes echoing eerily in the night air.

'Someone practising for a service,' muttered one boy.

'Must be keen,' said another, 'practising at half-past one in the morning – anyway, we'd better clear off, in case they see us.'

The gang melted away into the night.

A couple of weeks later, they sallied forth again and went quietly into the field through the gate at the top. Making sure the coast was clear, they were about to start activities, when one suddenly clutched his mate's sleeve and pointed down at the church. Although it was 2.00 a.m., cold and dark, once more the church was alight, and faintly, above the rustle of the wind in the trees, they could hear the dolorous notes of the organ music.

'Let's go down and see who it is,' said Wil and they scrambled down the steep slope of the field, to the church gate at the bottom.

The churchyard was dark, but as they drew near the building, the lights inside showed them the way through the gravestones. Although they circled round the little church, they couldn't see inside as the windows were too high, and eventually they came back to the main door.

The music was louder now, booming in their ears, so Wil twisted the ring of metal that lifted the latch inside, and the big door creaked slowly open.

Instantly, the music stopped. Not with the notes dying slowly away as most organ music does, but abruptly, as if someone had switched off a recording. No one sat at the organ and the church was empty, but lit.

'It's a trick,' Wil said, breaking the silence, but the little group of boys drew closer together.

'Who's there?' Wil called bravely, but his voice set up hollow echoes, which washed about the building.

'Anyone there?'

The only noise was the wind sighing around the church and there was a queer feeling of expectancy in the air, a feeling of waiting.

In the heavy silence, the boys could feel the hair on their necks bristling, goose pimples on their arms and more than one was secretly wishing himself safe back in his bed.

'Let's go,' Wil said, his voice now a small whisper, and the boys huddling in the doorway all tried to bundle out at once.

Outside, Wil, the leader, bravely put his arm back in and switched off the lights. He shut the door smartly and it made a deep booming noise in the eerie silence. They tried not to run down the path, fearing they might miss it and go blundering amongst the graves in the thick darkness, but their strides became longer and quicker as fear lent wings to their feet.

The dogs had absolutely refused to enter the grounds and were anxiously waiting for them at the gate. After the briefest of relieved tail wagging, they all turned and trotted firmly homewards occasionally glancing over their shoulders to see if their owners followed.

With great relief, the boys passed out of the graveyard and Wil turned to close the gate.

'Look,' he whispered in disbelief. Once more the church was flooded with lights and they could hear the organ music mourning through the night air.

They never went there again.

Nant Orman

Ghosts and their stories are by their very nature difficult to pin down. Promising beginnings become lost in a maze of blank ends, sheer speculation and folklore, and the maze becomes denser with the passage of time.

So it was with Nant Orman, a charming, sturdily built dwelling in Cemaes. My friend, Sheila Tell, told me it was a haunted house and gave me the telephone number of Mr and Mrs Wright, who were currently living there. Now here begins one of those tales which contain a tenuous thread – tenuous threads often leading to jolly interesting stories, so they have to be patiently unravelled.

Mr Wright, a retired lecturer in horticulture, supervised the superb grounds of Cestyll, which had been built by the Right Honourable Violet Vivian, Lady in Waiting to Princess Victoria, and aunt to Lady Astor. Cestyll gardens became famous; they included hot houses, water gardens, rock gardens and thousands of tropical plants and trees. Also, in a special place in the gardens was a pets' cemetery, containing the graves of all the dogs she had in her life, each with its small headstone and the name of the dog inscribed in the stone. Lady Astor inherited Cestyll from her aunt and she too added her own dogs in the course of time and kept up the gardens splendidly.

When the plans for Wylfa Power Station were mooted, Lady Astor was faced with a compulsory purchasing order. Cestyll had to be demolished. She resisted very fiercely, and fought a hard battle, but at last she had to give way to progress and bow to the inevitable – but only on the stipulation that the now mature, beautiful gardens, were kept up and thrown open to the public on bank holidays, at a small charge, the proceeds to go to the RNLI. This was done – hence the presence of Mr Wright supervising the garden.

(The tenuous thread which linked the Wrights to the haunting at Nant Orman were the dog graves at Cestyll – or so I was told – if *you* think these facts are confusing, imagine how *I* felt sifting through them!)

The Wrights had a much loved little dog called Fog, who became very ill and eventually died. The Wrights were devastated, and Mr Wright often paused sadly by the small graves at Cestyll, reflecting on the grief of their owner when each dog had died.

It was at this time that Mrs Wright complained that she frequently heard a woman singing in the house when she was alone. She was scared and when Mr Wright tried to laugh her out of it, saying it was her imagination, she became very cross. When the locals heard of it, they wondered whether the owner of the ghostly voice had anything to do with the dogs of Cestyll, and knowing how sad the Wrights were about the death of Fog, was trying to comfort Mrs Wright.

Mr and Mrs Wright were discussing this one evening when the singing had been heard two or three times in one day and Mr Wright made a surprising confession. He stated that he had *seen* the ghost. Not just once, but on a number of occasions, and always in the same place. She was a beautiful young lady, he said, with her hair piled up on her head. She wore a Victorian dress and always came down the servants' small staircase, before vanishing at the bottom.

Their daughter-in-law was present, and she exclaimed in surprise. They both looked at her, and she admitted that she also had seen the ghost, several times, in the same place, but hadn't mentioned it to the others, as she didn't want to frighten them.

Mr Wright was quite excited and they compared notes, both assuring Mrs Wright that the lady had a sweet and gentle face, and they were sure she was quite incapable of doing any harm. They both agreed that the atmosphere was tranquil when she appeared and also that they felt most peaceful afterwards.

Mrs Wright was horrified. She told them that she would be terrified of seeing the phantom and she would never be at ease when she was alone in the house, in case she saw it. It must go. She was quite adamant about it and proceeded to make arrangements to have it banished. The other two protested, pointing out that it was doing no harm, but she wouldn't listen.

Eventually, she got in touch with the Church dignitaries, who put the wheels in motion, finally sending a Canon of Bangor Cathedral to officiate at the ceremony.

As the ghost was by no means evil, exorcism was unnecessary, and the gentler rite of sacrament was performed, whereby the earthbound soul is shown how to pass on in its journey. This was done.

When the Canon had left, Mrs Wright gave orders that the servants' stairs must be ripped out and the entrance blocked off.

The ghost was seen and heard no more. This left me with a question. Who was she? What was the history of the haunting?

I made more enquiries about Nant Orman and tried to piece the jigsaw together.

Finally, after yards of tape from my trusty tape-recorder, and hundreds of questions, I came up with a pretty likely story.

This is what I was told.

Nant Orman was built in the 1800's by one Ishmael Jones, a wealthy ship owner who, besides building the harbour at Cemaes, shipped slate from Wales to Liverpool. He built the house for his young bride, Mary, complete with a staircase built like the bows of a ship, in solid timber. Halfway up is a small half-landing, with a circular window like a large porthole, which looked out to sea.

But Mary died young and Ishmael spent many lonely hours in his chair on the half-landing, gazing morosely through his telescope at the shipping, which passed the window.

Shortly after, he sold the house, moved away and was heard of no more. So that was the story I heard and still was no nearer to a solution.

Then Mr and Mrs Wright left Nant Orman, so my last connection was gone. Glumly, I was ready to abandon the tale, until Sheila Tell came to my rescue.

'You need to get in touch with John Hughes, Tregof farm,' she said, 'he knows a lot about Nant Orman.'

So I phoned him, and he was a mine of information!

He is Anglesey through and through, kind, courteous and diffident, with a lovely sense of humour. He loves the old ways of farming, which are fast dying out – he still hangs a gate the way his grandfather taught him and makes his fences expertly, as they have been done for generations.

On his land is a bog that is known throughout Wales for its rare plants and mosses, and has been labelled SSI – Special Scientific Interest – and so it will remain. This is the tape I made of his story, verbatim – and here it is.

First of all, I told him my struggles with the Nant Orman story, and he listened keenly, with great interest. When I had finished, there was a short silence while he digested it all, then he said quietly, 'Well, I think you have been given a lot of misinformation.'

I groaned and asked him if he could give me the right information – and would he mind if I put the telephone call on tape?

He didn't mind in the least – and this is what he said:

'Nant Orman was built for my great-great aunt in 1843 by Ishmael Jones. He was a local builder who built Cemaes pier, Bethesda chapel and the village hall for the Hughes' who were at Wylfa at the time.

I still own the outbuildings at Nant Orman, and his signature, written in beautiful copperplate handwriting, and dated Aug. 29th 1843, is still on one of the inside walls.

My great-great auntie never married, she was a spinster all her life, but she had many friends, a lot from abroad, and many ships' captains came to visit her. The house was full of pictures of ships, and Ishmael Jones built the fine staircase like the bows of a ship, with a little circular window like a porthole, halfway up.

After she died, the house was eventually passed on to my father, who rented it out to a family called Evans and, after that, to the Gibbons.

I'm fifty-six now, I was born in 1945, and the two Miss Gibbons had been there for a few years then. I think they came from Manchester, perhaps to escape the bombing, because another sister and brother, Freddie and Ida, would come down to visit them.

All my childhood, I remember them riding round the village on bikes, they rode them right into their nineties – I think it was the well-water at Nant Orman that kept them so fit – beautiful, it was, cold and crystal clear.

They started the Swimming Gala here in Cemaes. It went on for many, many years, probably between thirty and forty, and the sister and brother came down to help.

When I was a child, between ten and twelve years old, I used to carry the coal into the house and the firewood to start the fire for them. In the evenings we used to play cards around the table, with the oil-lamp turned up, and a few candles in the corners and a big roaring fire.

We used to open the pack and shuffle the cards and put pennies and ha'pennies in the middle for the kitty. High stakes in those days – the old pennies and ha'pennies you know!' Then, in a completely matter of fact tone, Mr Hughes said something that took my breath away:

'We used to deal the cards for four – one for Auntie Jessie, one for Auntie Meg, one for me, and one for the ghost.'

Me:	The ghost! Who is she – or who was she?
Mr Hughes:	*(thinking deeply)* Er – she was between twenty and thirty I should say, I've only got a young boy's memory of her.
Me:	*(interrupting)* What did she look like?

There was a pause; I could almost hear him searching back. Then he said slowly:

	She used to have beautiful long hair, all done up like, beautifully done up it was – Oh Duw! (God!) How can I – it wasn't white, it was more like cream golden hair.
Me:	Was she pretty?
Mr Hughes:	*(gravely)* Yes.
Me:	Why – who – how long had she been dead? I've got so many questions to ask you.

Mr Hughes was still casting his mind back to how he remembered what the ghost looked like, and he went on as if he had not heard me:

	And the design of her clothes was unbelievable, like crochet what do you call it – crochet?
Me:	Yes, crochet or lace.
Mr Hughes:	Round it all everywhere, especially round the collar.
Me:	Oh – lace?

Mr Hughes:	Yes, lace – around the collar and around the bottom of it like.
Me:	Was it high-necked, like Victorian?'
Mr Hughes:	Yes, very high-necked.
Me:	And did she just appear – in the chair?
Mr Hughes:	*(Once more back in his memories)*
	I hate people touching my hair – always have, but she used to brush her hand over my hair every time she came and I didn't mind.
Me:	How did she appear? Did she used to just be suddenly there?
Mr Hughes:	She used to come from – there were two staircases in Nant Orman in the old days, the main one for the people of the house and a small one for the servants. She used to come down the servants' stairs.
Me:	Did you always know when she was going to appear?
Mr Hughes:	She used to open the door and come in, she would walk over to me and put me at ease, and stroke my hair for a while, then she used to come round the table, and you could see the chair move backward and forward like, then she was sitting down.
Me:	And you could see her then, could you?
Mr Hughes:	Oh yes, we could see her properly, we could see her all the way through. She never frightened me because I was brought up with her from an early age.
Me:	When did she start coming? Had you begun to play cards on a Sunday night or whatever?
Mr Hughes:	We used to play cards about three times a week.
Me:	And when did she first appear – did it stick out in your memory?
Mr Hughes:	Well, I was brought up with her you see, so – er, I just took it for granted, I didn't think anything of it – it was just that I was brought up with it, I never worried about it.

Me: And did she actually move the cards, could you see the –

Mr Hughes: Oh yes.

(Then he said with mock indignation)

She used to cheat and everything!

Me: Oh did she – that's lovely! How did she cheat?

Mr Hughes: She used to lead sometimes, then my Aunt would, whoever was supposed to but she usually liked to start, she liked to lead you see. You could see her lifting up the cards and placing them where they should go. Whist was the game we played and when it was time to cut the cards, she would cut the cards – she just used to play proper cards with us, like.

When Jessie had won a few games and Meg had won a few games, she used to make sure I won one or two and she won one or two. I think it was just to make sure things were even all round.

Me: What did she do – swap the cards?

Mr Hughes: Oh yes, when my two Aunties had been winning, she used to look at my cards, and if she didn't like what I had been dealt, she swapped them – you could see them floating.

Me: I think that's lovely! And did you say anything to her when she did that?

Mr Hughes: Oh yes, I used to say thank you, when the cards landed in front of me. I was glad that she helped me to try and win.

Me: And how did she – when did she go – when the card game was over, did she just get up, push her chair back and go upstairs or did she just vanish in front of you? What happened?

Mr Hughes: Oh, she used to stay with us. After we'd played cards for an hour or so, we used to have a cup of tea, Jessie, Meg and myself, then we'd go and sit round the fire, Jessie and Meg in single chairs, one each side, and there was a two-seater settle in the middle, I used to sit on that and she used to sit

92

beside me. We never heard her voice, but she used to smile at me, we knew she was there, and we never thought anything of it.

She was a very kind lady.

Me: Why on earth did Mrs Wright have her exorcised? She belonged there, didn't she?

Mr Hughes: She belonged there.

Me: They had no right to get rid of her, did they?

Mr Hughes: *(sadly)* I don't think I will ever be able to forgive Pat for that.

Me: I don't think I could either, I mean they exorcise evil ghosts but if it was someone who belonged in the house and was there before them.

Mr Hughes: Well, I asked her – did she do any harm? And Pat said, oh no.

Me: But they saw her, didn't they? The Wrights saw her?

Mr Hughes: Yes, oh yes, they saw her.
(Then he hesitated and said diffidently)
The thing was you see ladies don't like other ladies in the house, do they?

Me: I wouldn't mind if she was a ghost – I mean she belonged to the house. There are still so many of them around in houses where they used to be. Who did they call in to exorcise her?

Mr Hughes: A Canon from Bangor.

Me: Oh, did they. And how long ago Mr Hughes – how long is it?

Mr Hughes: Oh, about halfway through their time there – about six years ago.

Me: And you never found out who she was – or her name?

Mr Hughes: I never bothered; I just took her for granted, because I was brought up with her. After the Gibbons left, Auntie Jessie and Auntie Meg, I never bothered with Nant Orman house. I was just in the buildings at Nant Orman, busy with the sheep. I was always happy when I was there; I think she used to help

	me with the sheep.
Me:	I bet she did – she was very fond of you.
Mr Hughes:	Yes, there have been one or two fortune tellers and they say there is always a lady with me, round the farm like.
Me:	Really? And can you feel her yourself sometimes?
Mr Hughes:	I can feel her, yes, but I don't see her anymore – I could see her all right in Nant Orman.
Me:	Yes, but not outside?
Mr Hughes:	Not outside – no.
Me:	I'm so sorry they got rid of her.
Mr Hughes:	*(sadly)* Yes, I've lost a good dear friend – if that makes any sense.
Me:	It makes a lot of sense!
	I know Mr Wright saw her on the landing and his daughter-in-law did too.
Mr Hughes:	Yes, she was always on the landing, quite often looking out to sea through the round window. She would come out of the door leading to the servants' quarters; it was a very small door, only about four feet six high. It has been blocked off since and the little staircase pulled down from it. Mr and Mrs Wright did that and, once they did that, the ghost didn't come again.
Me:	What a shame. Can you tell me, how did she die and when?
Mr Hughes:	I really don't know, I've never bothered.
Me:	Also, did she sing? Mrs Wright said she often heard her singing – did you?
Mr Hughes:	Yes, she didn't sing words like – she just hummed, happy sounds, there was always a nice feeling around the lady, she was always happy.
Me:	I wonder who she was?
Mr Hughes:	I dunno.
Me:	You didn't even know her name?
Mr Hughes:	No.

I then asked about Ishmael Jones, if he had ever lived in the house.

Mr Hughes: I don't know – I don't think so, I've got the deeds of Nant Orman outbuildings in the bank, perhaps there are some details in them.

The old buildings consisted of a stable for the horse and a cart shed and, next to it was the feed store, where the hay was kept for the horse and the barley and things and, the upper storey was where the men workers slept, the big open fireplace is still there. There are holes in the wall of the building, where they used to shovel the food through for the pigs in the yard.

My auntie used to rent the place out as a holiday home – Nant Orman that is – not the outbuildings. It was £1 10s 0d for the house each month and 10/- for the horse. That was in years gone by, and then she left it to my sister when she died.

My sister sold it to Mr and Mrs Evans and, when they moved the Wrights bought it. They in turn sold it to a Mr and Mrs Albrecht, who are there now – a very nice couple indeed.

*   *   *

So that is the story of Nant Orman and the charming ghost who lived there.

She was obviously very fond of the little boy and had a great sense of fair play – or was it a sense of humour?

First hand ghost stories are quite rare, but the image Mr Hughes conjured up in his matter of fact way, of the pretty, transparent ghost with her high lace collar and beautifully dressed hair left me with so many unanswered questions:

Where did she come from when she appeared on the servants' staircase – and where did she go when she left them? And above all, why did she stay in that house where she obviously belonged – and *who was she?*

I don't suppose we will ever know.

Phantom dogs of the river

Mr Hugh Owen told me that his father, as a young man, lived at Rhosneigr, and used to go to work on a pushbike.

One dreary November day, coming home, he was crossing Afon Crugyll and, as he reached the middle of the bridge, he looked down at the water below him and saw it beginning to bubble and become very disturbed, as if something was rising from the bottom.

He stopped, rested his foot on the ground, and stared. As he did so, he saw two huge black dogs emerging from the water and looking fixedly at him. Imagine the shock he got when he realised, as they came into view, that they were perfectly dry, their jet-black coats shining and smooth.

The whole thing was so uncanny that he started to cycle off the bridge as fast as he could. To his horror, as he did so, they came up and loped along the road, one on each side of his bike. Their size was not the only fearful thing about them because they seemed to be the centre of an area of freezing cold, which also enveloped Mr Owen. They moved in absolute silence and, although the hissing of his tyres on the tarmac seemed unnaturally loud, the feet of the dogs made no sound, no clicking of claws on the road, neither could he hear them panting, although their mouths were open and tongues lolling.

Greatly unnerved by their sudden appearance and soundless movement, Mr Owen leaned hard onto his handlebars and sprinted forwards, pedalling faster and faster, but in no way could he out-distance the dogs, who effortlessly kept station each side of him. It was then that he realised that his bike wheels had become luminous, with an eerie green light.

Hugh said his father had told him that the road seemed endless, he was sweating hard and out of breath before he, at last, saw his house in the distance.

When he reached home he leapt off the bike, letting it crash to the ground, and flew through the front door in a blind panic, because as he said, he thought the hounds of hell were at his heels.

As he slammed the door behind him, he gave a terrified look back.

The dogs had vanished.

Dulas beach

Walt and I were in Gwynedd Office Supplies in Menai Bridge recently, buying a stack of A4 writing pads. We were chatting to Mrs Katherine Thomas, the owner, a charming and hardworking lady, who, with her son, Adrian, first started the now successful and very flourishing business.

She told me this short and tantalizingly unfinished story:

I have a friend called John. When he was young he lived with his family at their home in Dulas.

The house is right on the beach, and is called Glan Morfa. When he was about twenty, he had been fishing with a friend on the beach, and at dusk, they decided to go home, so they packed up their gear and started to plod back up through the sand.

As they were cutting diagonally across to the house, they both saw something approaching off the sea, which looked definitely weird. It was coming inshore, and was floating at least a foot above the surface of the water.

As John said:

'We stopped to watch. It reached the edge of the sea, and started to move up the sand. It didn't leave any trail, as it was still floating in the air, and it crossed in front of us.

I couldn't believe what I saw. It was a large white cylindrical thing, longer than it was high; I should guess about four feet by three. We stared, because we couldn't make out what it was. It was white and quite opaque, and blurred or furry around the edges, that's the only way I can describe it. No head or legs or anything, just floating steadily past us.

I said to my mate:

'Are you seeing what I'm seeing?'

He just said: 'Yes'.

He sounded as baffled as I felt.

I can't give you any details about it, because it didn't have any. It wasn't just drifting around either, it had come in from over the sea, how far out it was when it started, and where it started from is a mystery to me. All we saw was this white thing coming towards us. When it got ashore, it was still moving forward steadily, and it made a straight line over the sand and up to the bushes.

It wasn't going very fast, and we started to follow it, but my dog ran away from it, and stopped and stared from a distance, with all his hairs bristling.

Then this white thing disappeared into the bushes. We tried to send the dog in after it, saying things like 'Find!' or 'Fetch!' as if it was a rabbit and we wanted him to chase, but he wasn't having any. He backed off down the shore, and just stood there looking at us.

So we went in ourselves, and searched everywhere, but whatever it was had vanished.

The spot where it had gone into the undergrowth was where an old pub used to stand, but it had fallen into the sea many years before.

Apparently, there had been a great storm and a very high tide, and the pub was swallowed into the water.

Old locals said there was furniture and barrels floating about, but I don't know any details.

The haunting of Wylfa Power Station

Of all the hauntings I have researched on Anglesey, the ghosts on the nuclear power station seem to be the most complex.

Wylfa Head is a small promontory at the western end of Cemaes Bay. There was at one time a house standing there, called Glan Dŵr (*glan* : bank; *dŵr* : water). In the 1930's a famous opera singer from New Zealand bought it for a summer residence.

This lady was Rosina Buckman, who sang with Melba at Covent Garden and, also, with Sir Thomas Beecham's Opera Company. She sang with, fell in love with and, finally, married Maurice d'Oisley, a leading tenor.

As her career had begun in the early 1900's, by the 1930's she was past her singing peak, so she started to teach music at the London Royal Academy. To get away from the noise and bustle of London, she and her husband bought Glan Dŵr and spent their summers there, taking with them Maurice's mother, Emma. She also took many students from the Academy to train at Glan Dŵr, a beautiful peaceful spot overlooking the sea.

It is said locally that Rosina had a favourite rock on the cliff edge, where she used to sit, singing arias. Her voice was so perfect, anyone within hearing would listen entranced.

In 1935, old Emma d'Oisley died and, in her will, she requested that she should be cremated and that the urn containing her ashes should be placed in a niche in a rock in the garden at Glan Dŵr, and sealed, remaining there forever. This was done.

Rosina and Maurice still spent their summers on Anglesey and, during the war, her students gave concerts in Cemaes Village Hall, in aid of war charities.

But Glan Dŵr was in a prime spot and during the war the RAF decided to commandeer it for a radio location station, and Rosina and Maurice had no choice but to move out.

Whether the RAF later sold Glan Dŵr is not known, but after the War it had become derelict and the d'Oisleys were not heard of again on the Island, as they had returned to London and, presumably, that is where Rosina died.

Then, the CEGB purchased Wylfa Head to build a Nuclear Power Station and the derelict old house had to be demolished as it came within the perimeter fence.

It was not fitting that someone's ashes should be left on what would be a busy industrial site, so although Emma had stated specifically in her will that her ashes must be left in the rock forever, they were quietly and reverently removed to Llanbadrig church, Cemaes, and re-interred.

So much for the facts, very kindly supplied to me by Mrs Ann Farrell, who used to work in the planning office at Wylfa.

It was about this time that rumours started to spread around that the site was haunted.

After Glan Dŵr had been demolished, Reactor Two was built on the exact spot. A local electrician, employed at Wylfa (now a milkman in Cemaes), was working in 'the vessel ('like a big ball it is' fisherman Jack Longman told me) on his own, when he heard a woman some distance away singing, a haunting melody in a lovely voice.

He stopped work to listen and, as he did so, the voice drew nearer, and the closer it came, the colder the air became in the vessel. The man knew he was the only worker in that area and when the atmosphere dropped like a stone and the woman seemed to be singing close beside him, the frightened man dropped his tools and ran out of the vessel.

Mr Brian Shearer, a security guard at Wylfa for fourteen years, told his wife that many times when he was doing his rounds at night, he would find all the lights blazing in the securely locked Reception Centre, then he would enter, switch them all off again and relock the doors.

His next round was approximately three hours later and, once again, the lights would all be on, the Reception Centre still locked and empty.

One warm summer night, going on his usual patrol around the back of the building, he stepped from the warmth of a night breeze into an area of air so still and icy-cold it was like walking into a freezer room.

As he told his wife later: 'all the hairs on the back of my neck stood up, I went stiff – just froze and I couldn't move on for the life of me.'

A colleague of Mr Shearer's, another security man, was doing the same round the following week. He heard footsteps behind him and, automatically assuming it was his partner, he began a conversation along the lines of a subject they had been discussing earlier, but his amiable bantering came to an abrupt end when his partner appeared from the opposite direction. Swinging round to see who had been walking behind him – he was amazed to find himself alone. He never did find out who his companion in the dark was.

Mrs Ann Farrell also sent me a very interesting article published in the 'Nuclear Times' (Nov. 1991) in which she states she is almost certain that the ghost most frequently seen is that of Rosina Buckman. She says that in 1991, a man on night shift at the station, was alone in the small canteen, drinking a cup of tea, and idly looking out of the window, when he saw, about twenty yards away, a lady in a white evening dress, with long blonde hair over one shoulder, standing at the side of the road looking steadily at him.

'He told me that he had heard the legend of the Wylfa ghost, but had no idea until I told him, that she always appears in a long white dress,' she stated.

Mrs Ann Farrell, who then worked in the planning office, did a lot of valuable research, digging out all the information she could find on Rosina.

As she writes in her article:

'Miss Buckman always looked very grand; she dressed in long white dresses and looked like old Queen Mary.'

Apparently the old road outside the small canteen (in which the man was standing) was re-routed to make way for a new building and Mr Farrell wonders if the ghost he saw standing on the corner was confused by this change. I have found this occurs in many cases, where familiar things are altered.

In 1964, four workers on the night shift told of sighting a lady in white, who was softly singing a melody.

The first time they saw her they thought it was a girl dressed in a long towelling robe going for a midnight swim. They were only about twenty yards away and they called to her. She seemed unaware of them and, to their horror, she appeared to walk right over the cliff edge, staying in the air beyond for at least two yards, then she faded from sight.

They knew nothing of any ghost.

A further three refused to work the night shift, having had the same experience.

In August of the same year, a group of Irishmen, known as the 'black gang', working on the tunnel that would eventually be the outflow from Wylfa, asked for work in another part of the site, after seeing a ghostly lady wandering about. Stories began to spread about the site that the area around the tunnel was haunted. Workers who were willing to dig the tunnel on night-shift became very scarce indeed and, the management, desperate to have the job finished on time, offered to pay a gang of six Irishmen nearly double the going rate, if they would carry on at night.

The Irishmen agreed on one condition, that the ghost would first be laid to rest by the local Roman Catholic priest. This was kindly, well-respected Father Taff, who came with other clergy to 'cleanse' the site.

The workmen called it an exorcism, a service used by the church if the entity is evil, but as this wasn't the case, Father Taff performed a simple service of sacrament and, when he had finished, declared the site cleansed.

The deeply religious Irishmen regarded Father Taff with reverence and, were greatly re-assured, returning to work immediately, to the great relief of the management.

All went well that day, until the night shift came on. They hadn't been down the tunnel for more than a few minutes, when the surface workers heard horrified yells, a stampede of feet, and the terrified Irishmen rushed out in a body, dropping their tools where they were, and popping out of the tunnel mouth like corks out of a bottle.

To a man, they swore they had seen and heard the ghost. They refused point blank to go back down – instead they left the site and they all went home, very shaken. That stopped the job. Next day they were all summoned to the personnel office, where the management tried to make sense of the incident.

They all told exactly the same story to the Personnel Manager. As they entered the tunnel and, prepared to start work, they began to hear faint strains of beautiful music, which slowly swelled until

102

it filled the tunnel and the men who were furthest along the tunnel swore they had seen a figure dressed in white, standing in a dim corner.

Mrs Ann Walton was personnel secretary at that time and both, she and the Manager, listened closely to the stories. Then she asked the men if they knew what the melody was. One immediately declared stoutly that it was 'Red Sails in the Sunset'.

As Mrs Walton said, 'It wasn't exactly high opera, was it? The Personnel Manager and I looked at each other – we had both smelt a very large rat.'

They made enquiries around the site. Far from being awed or scared other workers grinned broadly when news of the latest haunting spread and Mrs Walton felt that they all knew something she didn't.

After some detective work, she found out the truth. Apparently, one of the tea-boys, a local lad, had the ingenious idea of re-establishing the haunting by sneaking his tape recorder into the tunnel, draping himself in a white sheet and, as the night-shift moved in, he slowly turned up the volume on the tape-recorder, swaying gently from side to side in a dim corner of the tunnel to the 'haunting' strains of Red Sails in the Sunset!

The resulting stampede of men to get out of the tunnel made him helpless with laughter.

But it had stopped the job once again. When the exasperated management found out the truth, the boy was sacked. It was the only thing the Personnel Manager could do, the lad had cost the firm a lot of time and money – but personally I think he showed a lot of initiative – misguided as it was!

This though, was not the last of the ghost, as it was in 1991 the man on night shift saw her from the small canteen window.

To say 'her' does not necessarily mean that the figure was Rosina, as this story is extremely involved, and Mr Ian Clare, of the Reception Centre, helped me to untangle it by giving me a telephone interview, which made certain points clear, but also introduced some more ghostly characters!

The conversation begins on a question and answer note, until Ian got into his stride and built up for me a very lucid and colourful account, which I give in full.

He begins:	As far as I know the story, the lady in white who is seen, is Rosina's mother-in-law in old age.
Me:	Well I have been given many descriptions, one by a man standing in the canteen at night, who saw a *young* woman in a white dress, with golden hair hanging over one shoulder, so *I* don't know whether I'm writing about Rosina or her mother-in-law!
Ian:	I don't think anyone is sure to be quite honest – I've not seen either of them personally, although I've heard both descriptions seen by other people, but I'm aware that some parts of the power station are – well – haunted is probably the wrong word, but there is *something* there. The figure most frequently seen is definitely a woman in a white dress, some people have seen an old woman with white hair and some have seen a young woman with blonde hair.

Whether it is the same person at different ages, I have no idea, or whether it is Rosina *and* old Emma, I don't know.

But it is a fact that old Emma d'Oisley's ashes were removed from the garden and placed in Llanbadrig church – I believe there's a small memorial there. Whoever the ghost is, she is not alone at Wylfa. Two or three years ago, a film crew came down, they were doing a series called the 'Y' files, I think, not in old abbeys or castles, but unlikely places like industrial sites. They brought a medium down with them, they walked all over the site, and he kept stopping to tell them what he saw or felt.

When they'd finished, I got talking to him, nice chap he was, very unassuming, and asked him what he'd found.

He said he couldn't find any trace of a woman on the spots he'd covered – then he said a surprising thing.

'There's a poor feller there in his thirties, with a very badly damaged arm – I think he was killed somehow, anyway he died a very painful death.'

I suddenly remembered a story I'd been told, by a feller called John Williams, who was the site first-aider for many years, he was the first-aider to one of the constructing companies, it was a consortium – and at the time I was an emergency first-aider also.

He was talking about how many accidents there are at construction jobs, usually through faulty tackle or over-familiarity by the men who got a bit careless about safety matters. We were doing a training session at the time and he told me about a worker who got caught in the winch, he'd actually been dragged into the winch by his arm and was killed.

I told the medium this story, and he listened very carefully, then he nodded and said: 'That sounds about right.'

Me: Can you tell me what the other haunting is at the Reception Centre?

Ian: *(laughing)* Oh yes, that's far more sinister, I've actually *seen* him.

Me: Oh good, tell me, who was he? What was he like?

Ian: *(thinking slowly)* He was a tallish man, very dark-haired, with a very dark complexion. Unusually tall, because the local Welsh, being Celts, aren't particularly tall, but he was and he was wearing a white shirt, a waistcoat that was either black or dark grey and a pair of buff-coloured breeches.

Me: What time was it? Was it daylight when you saw him?

Ian: It was just going dark and was inside the – do you know the Reception Centre at Wylfa?

Me: No, I'm afraid I don't.

Ian: Well, it has an entrance foyer, squarish, about twelve feet square, with full length glass doors and windows.

105

Now, I was inside making a call on the phone that's in there and I suddenly, became aware that I was being watched.

I looked around and he was staring at me through the glass window at the side of the door.

Me: And did he look weird or unreal?

Ian: He looked quite normal, but as you do, I looked away and, a second later, I looked back and he was gone. What I did notice – half my attention was on the phone call, but when I'd finished that, I thought again about the man and what he was wearing – it struck me that he had a pair of black riding boots on, you know, the old-fashioned ones they used to wear like gaiters, it struck me who he was right away.

You see, I was the day services foreman for many years, looking after the cleaners etc. and two of the girls, who were in my team and worked for me, were detailed to look after the Reception Centre.

One of them was quite a young woman, middle to late thirties I expect Christine was, and she always did a good job when she cleaned Reception. She had no connections with the place, didn't know anything of its history – she wasn't a local girl. I think she came from Pwllheli, but she lived in Porth Amlwch.

Christine said that as soon as she started working there, she had a very strong feeling that someone was watching her, someone peering at her through the window. She kept turning around very quickly, but she never saw anyone, and she began to get a very creepy feeling when it was about to start.

She told me that she had owned a pub before, and that was haunted, so she was aware of ghosts and it wasn't something that fazed her really. But this one was different, it certainly wasn't friendly and, when it was around, the whole atmosphere changed. Usually, it was quiet and calm, and then when he was around, it became very unpleasant, because he was so – well – aggressive is probably the wrong term really, but it was – er –

Me: Resentful?

Ian: Yes, that's it!

Also, one or two people had described an odd noise in there, a sort of swishing sound, followed by a **thwack** – have you ever heard anyone slapping a riding boot with a riding crop? That.

Now I've heard it quite often, and Christine said that to begin with, the noise followed her about, as if someone was walking behind her, but she couldn't see anything.

Then one night, she turned around and saw him standing there. It gave her such a shock, she couldn't move for a minute and he just stood there glaring at her. She said he looked very angry, savage like – and he gave her very unpleasant sensations – so much so that she became quite frightened.

So she asked me one day if she could be moved and work somewhere else – I could see she was in a bit of a state, her hands were shaking, so I said yes, of course, but why?

Then she told me – I knew she lived in Porth Amlwch, she had a flat there, where she lived with her teenage daughter.

She started to hear this same noise, when she was at home at night. It sounded very far away and faint at first, and not very often, so she thought she was imagining things, and then it started getting closer and louder, and more frequent, as if it was coming nearer, and she felt as if it was looking for her.

One night, when she was in bed, she heard this swish and thwack in the corridor and she knew it had followed her home. It happened every night after that and, she was terrified when she heard it outside the bedroom door, she prayed it wouldn't get in to her.

She never said a word to her teenage daughter, she didn't want to frighten her, but one morning at breakfast, the girl said –

'Mam, I keep hearing a funny noise at night, sounds as if it's just outside my bedroom door – what is it Mam?'

Well, she put the daughter off by saying it was just noises the old house made at night, but now she was really frightened.

That's when she asked to see me. Of course I had her moved right away, to another part of the site, and as soon as she broke the contact – it stopped. Anyhow, the story got round and, I had an older feller, he'd retired a couple of years before, Tom Williams, and as soon as he heard it he said:

'Oh! I know who *that* is!'

Then he told me the story.

Years ago, the Club house was a farm called 'Simdda Wen' (White Chimney) and when Tom was a boy between twelve and thirteen, he had gone to work for the family who lived there.

I say family, but there were only two old ladies then, and they were quite elderly when he started work there about sixty five years ago.

He said the ghost was their father – he was dead when Tom started work, but there was a full-length portrait of him that Tom always saw on the few occasions he was allowed into the house – but the portrait of the man and, how he was dressed, exactly fitted the description of the ghost.

This man was a very fond and loving father to his two daughters, but there was something sinister in the background. The story was told by Tom, and corroborated by one of the other ladies (a bit younger than Tom by about ten years) who worked with me. She'd also started work in the house when she left school (a long time after Tom) and the two ladies were very old when she started there.

She knew about the picture and she was frightened of it, and she hated it, because she said it used to watch her all the time she was working in the room, wherever she was, it stared at her.

Then the story came out.

Our Club house was once the farm, as I've said, and the Reception Centre, which isn't very far from the Club House, stands on the site of the stables, which had a clock tower over it.

Quite a posh place, they were a wealthy family, gentlemen farmers. They had a lot of staff, indoor and outdoor, when suddenly, one of the pretty maids who worked in the house went missing.

Well, of course, everybody made a big search for her and, eventually she was found dead, hanging in the clock tower.

As I said, she was a pretty little thing and, ostensibly, she had killed herself because she was pregnant.

Everybody found it hard to believe that she had committed suicide, because she was so full of life, and happy, always singing as she went about her work. The men who gently got her body down were convinced she had been strangled, because of the bruises on her throat and, whoever had murdered her, had hidden his crime by stringing her up to make it look like suicide. Rumours about her master flew around, all the staff were aware of the notice he had taken of her, but nothing could be proved and as he was rich and influential, he lived on and died a natural death some years later.

Me: And would that be in mid-Victorian time?

Ian: Probably, because his daughters, the two old ladies, were well into their eighties by the time Maggie went to work for them, so that puts the maid's death in the 1850's-1860's, somewhere like that.

As I said, the Reception Centre is right on the spot where the stables were and, often probably when he's about, you can feel the atmosphere begin to thicken, become oppressive, really unpleasant.

The lights in Reception have spells of switching themselves on and off, they do so quite frequently.

I was in there last week and there is an upstairs storage area at one end of the building with a door and a vertical steel ladder inside the door, leading upstairs.

Now I know I switched the lights off as I came out and shut the door behind me – five minutes later, the door was open, and the lights were on, and nobody had been up there.

It happens quite often, that sort of thing, and a lot of the security staff report that the lights had been left on and, whoever had locked up, knew for certain that he had switched them off.

It's still going on, it still happens, you can go in there sometimes and it's like walking into a fridge.

Me: So is it the same ghost that the security men feel is following them when they are on their rounds at night?

Ian: Might have been – but there again, it could have been another one.

Me: *Another* one? Seems to me you have more people in there that are not on the payroll than there are on!

Ian: *(laughing)* There are quite a few people who said they have heard and seen another young lass who sings softly in Welsh – not Rosina, this one doesn't sing opera – but she does sing, whether she is the one who was strung up, I don't know.

That's not the end of the story either. The old house 'Simdda Wen' or 'White Chimney' in English, it has tall white chimneys, and it's still there, used as our club-house, but it's in the last

110

stages of being used, it'll be taken down shortly, as the structure is quite hazardous.

From the outside, it hasn't the appearance of being much changed, except for part of the roof being messed about, there's been an extension put on the back for toilets, and that's about all.

It really is an odd place. About twenty years ago I was on the Club committee and we had to take over the running of the club when the Steward left just before Christmas.

I was in there one night locking up and, once again, I was aware of someone watching me and I swung round and saw an old woman, in a long black dress, just disappearing.

Me: So that's another one!

Ian: Yep. She's been seen by quite a few people, not unpleasant, she's quite a pleasant one – she's been seen looking out of the upstairs windows by people. The Steward and his family, who had left, knew the place was haunted, but he was very close-mouthed about it, he told his family not to say anything, but I do know that one of the boys talked about seeing things quite often, he was very scared.

Now the couple that came in afterwards, you would think they were the most unlikely people to see ghosts.

But the lady, Mrs Breckell, was unable to sleep one night, and she was sitting up in bed reading a book with the bedside light on. Pitch black, about three o'clock on a winter's morning and she could hear children playing in the walled garden outside. Calling and laughing. I remember her telling me. Another time, she was reading, sitting up in bed, it was just coming light, when the bedroom door opened and an old gentleman in a frock coat came in, walked past the end of the bed to the window, then turned around and walked out again.

111

When I asked Ian's opinion on ghosts, he said that if manifestations or sounds could have been pre-recorded on the atmosphere years ago and, if conditions were favourable, and a 'receiver' was on the spot, they could re-run like a film or a recording. We both agreed that this does not explain the ghosts who seem aware of us or have information to impart.

Neither does it explain those that are seen to have pleasant or unpleasant personalities or any of the myriad forms they take.

As Ian concluded cheerfully:

'Well, it's nice to have some mysteries left – like the Loch Ness monster – if everything had an explanation the world would be a much duller place!'

Melin Treban

Taped interview with Mrs Clare Mead (Melin Treban).

After a preliminary chat, I started with the following question:

Me: Can you tell me about your experiences at Melin Treban, please Clare?

Clare: Yes, of course, it's just knowing where to start! Well then, I've always been interested in ghosts, but I thought I would be terrified if ever I saw one! I've been in this house for thirty-four years and, about twenty-five years ago, I gradually became aware that there was somebody beside me a lot of the time – but whenever I looked at whoever it was, full faced, I couldn't see them, but out of the side of my eye, I could see this dark figure, a tiny bit taller than me, and I always had the impression that it was a man.

It was a definite shape, you know? I might not be even thinking about it and then, suddenly – Oh, there you are again sort of thing.

Anyway, several weeks went by, and I just took it for granted, because sometimes when I was in bed at night – (the bottom of the bedroom doors don't fit) and I always left the landing light on for the children – I would see this dark shape moving between me and the door.

Me: Weren't you frightened?

Clare: Not even remotely, I'd just go to sleep. This is what I can't understand about myself. Anyway, I decided – you see I'm a Catholic and we dedicate different months to different intentions.

In November we remember the people who are in Purgatory, a place in which souls after death are purified from sins. We have Masses and say special prayers for the dead, to assist them on their way to heaven.

113

So I started to wonder if my ghost was someone who was still lingering and needed help to find their way.

Anyway, I put a request in an envelope for a Mass to be said for him, whoever it was.

Me: How can you do that? I mean how can you do it if you don't know who the Mass is for?

Clare: Well, I told the priest that this Mass was for a special intention and I knew, in **my** mind, what the intention was.

Anyway, one very dull November afternoon, I was standing at the kitchen sink at dusk, preparing vegetables for the evening meal.

Then suddenly 'my friend' materialised beside me and, for the first time ever, I spoke out loud to him and I said:

'Oh, you should be alright now, because I'm having a Mass said for you.'

Me: Did you see what he looked like then?

Clare: No, it was a man's dark shape –

Me: And you couldn't tell the clothes or anything?

Clare: No-no-no, it was just a man's dark shape as I said I didn't bother to look fully at him, because I knew if I did, he would just disappear. I just was positive he was there, because he would appear when I wasn't even thinking about him – it wasn't like a wish to see somebody.

Then all of a sudden, for the first and only time, I felt utter terror – I was completely frozen – I couldn't move – whether or not it was because I had spoken out very positively to my friend, I don't know, but quite literally I couldn't move!

Me: And was he still there then – was he still with you?

Clare: I don't know – it took me ages to come round, I just stood rigid at the sink – but when I came out of my terror, he was gone. I stood and looked and listened for a moment, then I sensed an enormous peace come flooding in, a great feeling of happiness and

114

calm, and I have never seen him since.

That was twenty-five years ago, but there are other presences in this house too, because another strange thing happened.

I was involved in a major Court case to do with the dissolving of a trust. It's been going on for years and, finally, came to the Court hearing about three and a half years ago. I was totally dreading it and, as it drew near to the time, I became very worried and tense.

A couple of weeks before the case, I kept finding lights on in rooms I had not been in – bathrooms, bedrooms, kitchen etc. at all times of the day and night. I had two sons living with me then, and one who lived away, but came home at weekends and, of course, brought his washing with him.

On this particular Saturday, one of the boys (who are all grown up) told me they were all going to a party and staying there overnight, so they could have a drink and would I be all right on my own?

So I said of course I would, I wanted to get his washing done overnight, so it would be dry by morning and I could get it ironed for him to take back. Anyway, when they'd gone I got busy. I put the washing in the machine and the doorknob of the washer came off in my hand. There were two springs sticking out of it and, I tried and tried and tried to put it back, but I couldn't, so I put the knob on the work-surface above the washer.

As I was alone in the house that night, I carefully locked and bolted all the doors before I went to bed. Nobody could have got into the house at all. When I got up in the morning, the knob was back on and the washer was mended! I was delighted and I stood in the empty kitchen and said,

'Whoever you are – thank you very much!

Anyway – at lunchtime that day, I was sitting at

the table with the boys and I said to them:

'I've got something really interesting to tell you about this house now . . .'

And Ben, that's one of my sons, said,

'Is it anything to do with lights coming on?'

And I said, 'Oh – have you seen it too?'

'Yes,' said Ben, 'but I didn't say anything in case anyone was nervous.'

So we compared notes and I found out that there had been many more incidents regarding lights than I was aware of. Then I told them about the knob on the washer, hoping I wouldn't scare them – but they thought it was great – and they started to think of all sorts of things they could leave out to be mended.

Then, I rang my friend, Lyn, who lives at Holyhead – she knew there were presences in my house, she had often felt them – and I value her opinion, as she is a genuine Spiritualist and has helped many people and I said, what do you make of this?

She told me that she knew I was going through a very stressful time at the minute and she said she had heard of things being mended and it was a gesture of support, like saying we're here for you.

'Lyn,' I said, 'I'm really glad they're here, but I don't want too many manifestations – because I don't know, I might get a bit uneasy when I'm here on my own.'

So Lyn said, 'Well, go to a part of the house where you know they are and tell them what you've just told me.'

That seemed like a good idea. I went to the kitchen, because that was where I had always felt them and, I said:

'Thank you very much for all you have done – I love you being here and I don't want you to move out of the house at all, but I'd be happier if you didn't manifest quite so much.'

I haven't seen anything startling since then, but last February I had the flu (this is what I was telling Mair), I was alone in the house except for my three dogs, so I dosed myself up and went to bed.

One of my three dogs sleeps with me and she always wants to go to the loo in the middle of the night.

After the medicine, I fell fast asleep and then, at three o'clock in the morning, she wanted to go out. You can imagine how I felt!

I dragged myself up and started to go downstairs. I have an Aga and the house is always very warm, and it was then, but all of a sudden, as I went down, it started to get very cold and it went icier and icier and icier the further downstairs I went.

Rosie, the dog, wasn't at all concerned; none of the dogs have ever been concerned.

Me: That's amazing, it's usually the other way round, dogs seem to sense and see things humans don't and they get very scared.

Clare: Yes, that's what makes me think they must all be friends. Anyway, by the time I'd got downstairs, I was absolutely frozen.

The living room door and the kitchen door were both closed, but once I'd opened the kitchen door, the feeling of cold went immediately, so I let all the dogs out and sat down to wait for them.

As I sat there, I thought 'Oh God, I've got to walk through that all over again. Shall I stay here for the night?' Then, I thought, 'don't be so stupid woman, a ghost would never harm you.'

Me: It's just being on your own, isn't it?

Clare: That's it, that's what it was, a queer prickling feeling at the back of my neck, I wasn't frightened, just this feeling I could swear to, that there was somebody or something there.

Me: I know, it's a feeling of awareness.

Clare: Oh, very much aware. That's just it! Anyway, the dogs came back then, and Rosie wanted to stay downstairs, so I shut and locked the outside door and did the procedure in reverse. I opened the door and stepped out of that lovely warm kitchen and immediately – icy, icy cold and that weird prickly feeling stronger than ever. I **did** make a rush upstairs and the higher I got, the less icy the air was, until at the top everything was just warm and normal.

Then I went into my bedroom and got my holy water. I'm a great believer in holy water, so I got a little handful and threw it over the banister onto the stairs just for a safe measure. Then I jumped into bed and fell fast asleep. In the morning everything was quiet and calm.

Me: And has it happened since?

Clare: Not as violently as that, but in that particular spot, most of my family have felt a presence there. Even now I sometimes feel that there is someone there, but never as strongly as that time, three a.m. on that February morning.

Me: It sounds as if there are two lots – two contingents as it were, one lot helpful, the other producing the cold spots.

Clare: Yes, maybe. Really, I'd like to get a couple of mediums here, not tell them anything, but see if they can explain who it is.

I feel strongly that there is a woman here, not a flight of fancy on my part when I say that, because very often when I go past the most haunted spot at the bottom of the stairs and, I might be thinking of anything under the sun, when suddenly into my mind flashes the picture of a woman's face.

Not unlike my relatives and me, dark wavy hair and dark eyes, about fortyish. She looks a bit sad and troubled and she only comes into my mind at

	the bottom of the stairs, as if she is looking out of the little window there.
Me:	You know, when Mair was telling me about you and your house, she said that you had told her there was a cold spot at the bottom of the stairs – well, she stood there for a long time and nothing happened, she couldn't feel anything, but – and she said – Clare doesn't know this -when you all went into the kitchen, which was very warm, she stood in a certain place and she gradually got colder and colder until she was absolutely frozen and, as soon as she moved away from there, everything was warm and cosy again.
	She didn't say anything to you, in case you were apprehensive.
Clare:	Oh no, not at all, I mean it's their home isn't it?
Me:	Do you know anything of the history of the house?
Clare:	Well, I had a lot of grant-work done two years ago and when the workmen chipped away the rendering, they found the back wall of the house, that's the wall that runs right along the kitchen, the passageway (which was here when we came) to the dairy, which is now the larder, past the bottom of the stairs and the living room. A long wall and, all of it, up to about nine feet high, is made of river stones and mud. The stones are rounded and had been brought up from the river, which is just in front of the house.

It's medieval really, because the Davidsons, who live across the fields, are archaeologists, and I asked them to come down and they said it was definitely medieval.

On the old map, you know the original Ordnance Survey map, of which you can buy copies? Well, I bought one a few years ago in London, and this house was called Tŷ Melin, which is Mill House, but is now called Melin Treban. It stands in four and half acres, the mill itself is on the other side of the river, so every day the miller walked across to the mill and back again at night.

The court case gave the house itself to my children and I, it was a test case, very complicated.

They also gave me all the old deeds written on parchment, back to the early 1700's, but obviously it goes back much further. It was a very important mill, being in the middle of the island and, reading them with my very inexpert eyes, it seems to have belonged to the Bulkeleys and the Meyricks, who are both mentioned.

One Shadrach Williams bought it off them in 17 something, but it doesn't say much about him.

Going back to the little window set into the wall at the bottom of the stairs – when the builders knocked the rendering off the wall around it outside, they found a huge stone lintel set into the wall, where a door had been blocked off. The archaeologists said it was a very ancient part and, even suggested, it might have been a 'long-house' it is so old.

We then had a discussion on the myriads of ghosts which seem to inhabit Anglesey and I put forward an idea that because the Island consists of mainly pre-Cambrian rocks – it is indeed very ancient – and has a great quantity of silica bearing granite (a belt runs south of Llannerch-y-medd) which may have the facility to retain images from the past, just as a tape recorder does. No one has ever proved this, of course, I only offer it as a theory.

Mrs Meade (Clare) said maybe it was right because that would explain something that keeps recurring while she is gardening.

'Over the years – I can't remember when it first began, but whenever I was busy in the garden, I would have a very, very strong impression of a small plane crashing just the other side of the river.

I never said anything to anyone at all, because I was afraid it was going to happen. I always kept it to myself, because I didn't want to alarm my children or my grandchildren. Mostly, I wouldn't think of it at all, and then I'd be gardening and I'd suddenly see it.

I can describe it to you very vividly. It was a small plane, with a double cockpit, and a man's terrified face looking out. He had a leather helmety thing on his head, and I saw that, and then the plane would crash.

Anyway, I changed to gas-heating about four years ago and the inspector came to check everything was correct and, he said: 'I was born in this house, fifty years ago.'

I was quite excited, and said: 'Oh really – tell me all about it!'

So he told me he was one of six children and his sister had died in hospital. He gave me a lot of details, six families had lived here and they drew water from the well – he was going on like this when he suddenly said:

'And the plane crashed over there – across the river.'

I was so excited, I thought – My God – *it's happened* – it isn't *going* to happen – it already has. So after that I started telling people and asked around.

Me: Was he killed? Was the pilot killed?
Clare: No, he wasn't killed – this was the weird thing. So I rang Valley Council and asked if there was any record of the crash. They said no, but a gentleman in Llangefni was researching all the plane crashes in Anglesey, for a book he was writing. I can't remember his name, but I rang him and told him the location, and the time was just after the war.

He very kindly found out some information for me, but it was the wrong crash.

I asked the local farmers, and Owen Thomas, who lives just a mile up the road, confirmed what I had mentally seen. He said it was just after the war, and he was working on a tractor nearby, and the plane came down, just skimming the wall and landing nose-down in the field. The pilot wasn't badly hurt, but there was very tight security at the crash-site by the RAF, until the wreckage was taken away.

It might have been something very important, but there was nothing on the news or in the papers, so no one could find out any details, so it remains a mystery to this day.

Lady on the landing

Mr Markwold, a member of the National Gardens Society, lives at 'Haul-a-Gwynt' (Sun and Wind) Cemaes Bay. His beautiful three quarter acre walled garden boasts over two hundred varieties of flowering shrubs, climbers and trees, and is open to the public for two days per year.

Mr and Mr Markwold used to live at Tyn-y-Maes, a very gracious old farmhouse, but they now live in a bungalow in the grounds, although it is the Tyn-y-Maes garden which thrives under his loving care.

About ten years ago, one autumn day about five o'clock in the afternoon, he was alone upstairs and, was just coming out of the bedroom to walk along the landing, when he stopped short.

'The landing is a long one,' Mr Markwold said, 'and standing at the far end was the figure of a young woman. She looked as if she was going about her normal duties, as she was carrying a wooden pail.'

In answer to my questions Mr Markwold said he knew she was not a living person, as she did not look solid.

'She looked ethereal,' he said. 'No, I didn't feel afraid, but I certainly felt interested. I looked very keenly at her and saw that, although she wasn't transparent, she did look other-worldly somehow, even though every detail of her was sharp.

Her dress was very clear, she was wearing a high-waisted dress. It was light coloured, with a very full skirt which came to the ground. I've seen pictures since of the Empress Josephine – and it was that sort of fashion – known as the Empire style.'

This seems to date the ghost to the late eighteenth century.

Although she was carrying a pail, she was not wearing an apron, as a servant girl would do, so perhaps she was the lady of the house.

During the time that Mr Markwold watched her, she did not seem to be aware of him, she seemed to be looking at the windows, standing still.

After about a minute, she gradually faded from view. Intrigued, Mr Markwold discussed the happening with other people in the house, but no one else had ever seen her nor were there any stories locally about the house being haunted.

Although Mr Markwold has 'kept his eyes open' the lady has not re-appeared, at least, not while there was anyone around to see her.

I should be most interested to hear if there have been any more sightings in the farmhouse.

Red Wharf Bay 1 – Min-y-don and 'The onions'

At the extreme seaward end of Red Wharf Bay, the great rock of Castell Mawr was once a part of a very busy quarry exporting limestone to Liverpool from the local wharf.

Just behind the quarry stood the old local pub, known as 'The Onions' and very popular with the quarry workers, who went there to slake the limestone dust from their dry throats. It was also the haunt of smugglers, nowadays regarded as a romantic lot, but at that time accepted as run-of-the-mill people, trying to evade crippling taxes.

Trade declined drastically when the quarry closed and, eventually, the licence was taken over by a local hotel and 'The Onions' became a private residence known as Gwiningar House. Sadly, it was destroyed by fire in the late 1940's. The ruins can still be seen in what is known as the 'secret garden' of nearby Sea-Garth House, owned by a lady who wishes to be called Mrs Hughes.

These ruins are haunted by 'a desolate lady in a white shift type dress' (Mrs Hughes's description) wandering sadly amongst the ruins, drifting across the garden and disappearing through the wall of a modern bungalow built nearby. The sightings of her are quite frequent – people who have seen her say she seems to be searching for someone.

No one knows who she is or why she haunts this spot, but folktales tell of a young woman who was murdered in 'The Onions' over a hundred years ago.

The licence of 'The Onions' (as far as I have been told) was almost certainly taken over by 'The Min-y-Don Hotel' on the front. The Min-y-Don was a lively, busy, holiday hotel and it is definitely haunted.

The previous owner said they had MANY (her capitals) complaints from guests about noises and things being moved. 'Room 15 was the site of most disturbances,' Mrs Hughes told me. 'One of my manageresses, who was very psychic, regularly saw an old sea captain who had died in that room years ago.

She saw him sometimes in the room or on the landing outside. He was a kindly old man in a white roll-necked sweater, who always smiled at her and once put his arm on her shoulder, before becoming transparent and gradually fading away.

We had a regular customer who was sleeping in No.15, who was awakened by a bang in the middle of the night and sat up to see his wardrobe door fly open and all the clothes simultaneously dropping off their hangers. He always made sure after that he never stayed in that room again.'

Another family also complained about the same thing happening to them. Perhaps the old sea captain didn't like them?

At the Min-y-Don there is also a ghost with a different character.

It is believed to be the ghost of a bad-tempered barman who fell to his death down the stone steps leading into the original below ground cellar. He was a relative of the landlady and was only young when he died. Perhaps the violent, unexpected end to his life may be the reason for his presence, which is still strongly felt? Nearly all the bar staff over the years have complained of a brooding, angry atmosphere in the beer cellar.

Nowadays, the modern beer cellar is on ground level, the entrance to the old cellar is blocked, but can still be seen. The hotel was put up for sale in the 1990's and, as Mrs Hughes wrote, the cellar ghost was *not pleased* and demonstrated its displeasure in no uncertain way.

The first thing happened on the day Mrs Hughes informed her staff that the hotel was up for sale, after being in the ownership of the same family since 1942.

That night, a water tap was turned on in the cellar and found in the morning to be running at full spate.

None of the bar-staff had turned it on and, as Mrs Hughes said, anyone leaving the cellar after closing time would have heard it splashing, so it must have happened after everyone had left.

That was the start. The next thing was the gas taps on the cylinders were turned on, when the barman swore he had turned them off and Mrs Hughes had no reason to disbelieve him – he had been with her for years and nothing had gone wrong in all that time.

Sale negotiations started and the ghostly activities increased. From a single water tap or gas tap – it became a regular occurrence to find beer kegs, gas taps, water and lights all on in the mornings, when at least two members of staff had made a nightly inspection to confirm that everything had been definitely turned off.

The cellar atmosphere now became absolutely charged with the feeling of an 'irate presence' (as Mrs Hughes said) and it became so menacing that the female staff were too frightened to be alone there.

Mrs Hughes tells me that the ghost must have known that after the sale the hotel would be closed (which it was) and he would be lonely!

I would be most interested to know whether any previous guests at the now defunct Min-y-Don Hotel had any experience of the ghosts during their visits.

Red Wharf Bay 2 – The flat iron murder

My husband, Walt, and I were exploring the area around the ruins of the building which once had been 'The Onions', when we fell into conversation with a Mr Rowlands, who had lived nearly all his life in Llanbedrog, not far from Red Wharf Bay.

I asked him if he could give me any more details about the ghost of the young woman who was murdered long ago at the old pub, but apart from the well-known story that the ruins were haunted, he had no details to add.

He did however tell me that, over recent years, holidaymakers taking an evening stroll along the sands in the direction of Castell Mawr, particularly in autumn, have been frightened by the figure of a youngish woman, who vanishes inexplicably.

'One couple was walking along at the water's edge,' said Mr Rowlands, 'when their attention was drawn to a woman in front of them, walking very slowly. As they drew nearer, they saw she was wearing a longish dress and walking with her head down. But although she seemed quite real, she gradually grew more and more indistinct, until she had disappeared altogether. There was nowhere she could hide and they were the only ones on the beach.'

Mr Rowlands grinned. 'They lost no time in getting back to their car, I can tell you!'

Later, talking to a local lady who does not wish to be named, I was told that last year, when she and her sister were taking their dogs as usual for their evening stroll on the beach, they saw a woman standing below them on the sands, with her back to them, looking out to sea.

'At first, we didn't take much notice, we just thought she was a holidaymaker, and then she started to move forward.

She didn't walk deliberately, like you do in wet sand, she just drifted, or floated, over the sand towards the sea. When she got to the edge, about a yard from it, she just vanished. She didn't dive in or anything – she just vanished. One minute she was there, looking as solid as you – next minute she'd gone. My sister and I looked at each other – then we turned and *ran*! Did we move! The dogs thought it was a game, they flew after us. We were shaken, I can tell you – we don't usually drink, but we both had a Scotch when we got home.

When we talked about it afterwards, my sister said she thought at the time that it must be some weird woman in a nightie and she was just wondering if she was a bit dotty, wandering about in a nightie – when all of a sudden she'd gone!'

In answer to my question, I was told that they still went along the beach – but only in broad daylight, and they still keep a weather eye open for the mysterious lady – but they haven't seen her since. They both wondered if it might be the ghost in the 'Flat Iron Case'. This made me prick up my ears, but when I pressed for further details, I was told it was something that happened in the 1940's and, she was only a baby in Manchester then, so she didn't know any details.

I was intrigued by the thought of another young woman haunting the area, so I consulted the newspapers of the 1940's and found what *may* be the solution to the identity of the ghost.

Apparently, in 1945, a Mr and Mrs Nettleton from the Manchester area were staying for the winter in a cottage near the Ship Inn at Red Wharf Bay. Both in their thirties, the wife was five or six years older than her husband, neurotic, jealous and domineering, she nagged her husband endlessly.

Their marriage was a tempestuous one and very unhappy. Her husband Albert, an ex-army sergeant, was a quiet, good-natured man, who had put up with his wife's (quite unfounded) jealous accusations for years. She would cross-question him endlessly whenever he returned home from an innocent shopping trip, accusing him of flirting with any woman he happened to meet.

In early October she had been in a terrible temper, brooding, sulking and staring at him for hours on end without speaking. Nothing worked that he tried to please her with and his nerves by the end of the week were on edge.

So, on this fateful autumn morning, Albert took her breakfast tray upstairs as usual and found her to be still in a foul mood. As soon as she saw him she started again, berating him for the same trivial argument that had been going on for days.

Albert ignored her and quietly put the tray down at the side of the bed, before turning to leave the room. This infuriated her even more and she shrieked at him to stay where he was and listen to her when she was talking.

Instead, he went back downstairs and returned to his normal household chores, which happened to be the ironing on that particular morning. His wife, still shouting, got out of bed, rushed down the stairs and burst into the kitchen, face scarlet with rage.

Had she realised how close he was to the edge, how near to losing self-control, the tragedy might not have happened. She picked up the bread knife and brandished it in his face. As she did so – he lifted the iron and dealt her a tremendous blow to the head – years of pent up emotion finding sudden release, as he hit her again and again.

When the madness had drained away, he was shaking violently and, Ivy, her harsh voice silenced forever, was motionless and covered in blood lying on the kitchen floor.

He staggered across the kitchen and sank into a chair gazing horrified at what he had done. In the silent house, as he recovered, he started to panic. What if someone came to the door?

Eventually he managed to pick her body up and carry it into the bathroom, where he laid her in the bath, then, still dazed with shock, he returned to the blood spattered kitchen and tried to clear up the mess.

He sat in that house all day, his head in his hands, thinking frantically of the best way to dispose of the body.

In the middle of the night, it was nearly 3.00 a.m., he looked out of the door into the blackness of the October night. Then with great difficulty he got Ivy's body out of the bath, wrapped her in a dark coat and, heaving her onto his shoulder, he carried her and a spade, down to the shore.

Walking along the water's edge, towards Castell Mawr, until his burden grew too much to carry, he laid it down and started to dig in the wet sand, like the children who made sandcastles, but his spadefuls were made with grim determination.

The grave was only half-dug when to his horror, the shore before him was suddenly lit up by a rectangle of light. It came from the window of the big house called 'Sea-Garth' (which, once a chapel, had been converted in the 1920's by a businessman from Manchester) and, as he stared up at it, he could see someone moving about. Possibly, if whoever it was had looked out, they might have seen him digging.

Unnerved, Albert rolled his wife's body into the unfinished grave and, hastily replaced the sand, knowing that the incoming tide would wash away all traces of digging.

What his state of mind was, and how he explained his wife's absence during the next few weeks can only be imagined, history does not say.

On the 26th October, two ladies who had rented horses while on holiday were galloping along the beach when they saw something sticking up out of the sand. At first they thought it was a piece of wood then found, to their horror, that it was a woman's arm, lifted beseechingly skyward. Cutting the story short, when she was finally identified, Albert Nettleton was arrested.

Everyone who had been acquainted with Ivy, knew what a jealous and malicious woman she had been, but even they were surprised when it was revealed at the trial that she had made Albert sign a document she had written and which she called 'The Seventeen Point Charter'.

Amongst other things she demanded that he should do everything she said, that all her decisions must be unquestioned, he was forbidden to make new friends without her consent and he must never look at another woman for the rest of his life.

There were gasps of disbelief from the court as this was read out and all eyes were on Albert.

He listened to the evidence with a bowed head, but gave his own in a clear voice, standing straight and erect with military precision. He told all the truth and denied nothing.

The judge and jury were impressed by his honesty and realised just what a hell his life had been. Summing up, the judge said it was a case of a man tormented for years by a nagging wife, who had finally snapped and smashed her head in with a flat iron.

He was found not guilty of murder, but guilty of manslaughter, and sent to prison for five years. The sentence was shortened by his good behaviour, he was an exemplary prisoner.

An interesting but sad epilogue to this tragic tale was told to me by Mrs Kitchen, who lives at Sea-Garth.

'Some years ago,' said Mrs Kitchen, 'I met a man, the owner of an engineering works, who had been impressed by the honesty of

Albert Nettleton when he applied for a job, after being released from prison.

He was a very quiet man, and a good worker, but sadly, after working there for twelve months, he had committed suicide, unable to forget what he had done.'

So is it the ghost of Ivy Nettleton who is sometimes seen drifting along the sand, near the spot where she was buried?

NOTE:

While researching this story, I discussed it with my friend, Mr Roberts. A local man, he told me that if Nettleton had buried his wife's body a few yards further on, it would probably have never been discovered, as that place is deep quicksand.

Jack Longman's stories

The woman in the well

Jack tells this story:

Tony, a friend of mind, a neighbour now, moved to the Island from Birmingham about thirty years ago, to work here and looked around for rented accommodation. He found somewhere for himself, and then his sister wanted to come too. There was a farm near to the Power Station (Wylfa) which was up for rent and that is the one she took.

Tony said she hadn't been there long when he went up to visit her. As he crossed the farmyard, he looked up at the house and saw a woman passing and re-passing the bedroom window and thought it was his sister.

He went up to the front door and knocked. No one answered, so he knocked again, louder this time. No one came, so he tried the door and found it locked. He thought that was a bit funny with his sister at home, so he knocked again, but still no joy. He cupped his eyes with his hands and looked through the kitchen window, but he couldn't see anyone. He hung about for a little while, then walked back home.

As he was going through Cemaes, he was surprised to see his sister doing her shopping.

'Jenny,' he said, 'who's in your house? They've locked themselves in and won't answer the door.'

Jenny looked at him with a puzzled frown and said: 'Nobody answered the door because nobody's in.'

But Tony knew she was going back then and, he decided to go with her, in case someone had broken in, then locked the door.

When they got back to the house, Jenny unlocked the door, it wasn't locked from the inside and Tony went in and searched the house. It was empty, nothing stolen and nothing had been disturbed – but he still insisted that he had seen a woman in the bedroom.

Now this old farmhouse has been renovated since and it has a little blacksmith's smithy in the yard, which had a tiny window at the back. Through this window you can see the field at the side of the farm.

Dave Gold, who once had the fish and chip shop in Cemaes, bought the farm and the fields, and tidied up the little smithy – he decorated it to make it into a holiday cottage. While he was busy in there one day, he looked out of the little back window and saw a woman walking down the field from the direction of the farm and, she was walking slowly and looked troubled. Now, you don't see many people around there, so Dave went out to pass the time of day with her, but when he got outside, there was no one anywhere in sight and nowhere the woman could have gone.

Dave told me about her because he was so mystified and I remembered what Tony had said all those years ago about seeing a woman in the upstairs window of the farm when his sister said there was no one in. So I asked around and, quite a few people had seen this sad woman walking, but she had always vanished when she got near Morelias.

Now Morelias is a house just on the left of the entrance to the Power Station, not a very old house, definitely post war. A lady I knew moved into it and she used to phone me when she wanted odd jobs doing, like mending her washer and things. One day she told me that she always felt uneasy when she was alone in the house, as if there was someone there, always watching her.

Every room in that house had a plate rack running around the walls, about the height of a picture rail – people used to put their fancy dishes on them for show – and this lady had put little teddy-bears all around the one in the smallest bedroom. She was expecting a baby and had many ideas for making this room into a little nursery. So all the teddies sat around facing into the room.

She went in one morning to finish off the curtains and the teddies were all the right way round, but when she went in again in the afternoon, all their backs were turned and they were facing the wall. She had been alone all day in the house.

'It's as if someone doesn't want me to make it into a nursery,' she said. 'I got that feeling about it very strongly.'

Later that month she phoned me to say all her drains were blocked and could I come and clear them please? So, I went over with my drain rods and rodded hard, until suddenly everything disappeared and they were free again. After I had run some clean water down, I wondered if the septic tank needed emptying. I asked her where the tank was; she hadn't got a clue, so I went out and searched the ground.

I couldn't find it where I thought it would be, down a slope, so I walked back around the house and, just outside the lounge window, I saw a concrete manhole cover, half hidden in the grass and moss. When that cleaned away, it showed a big cover, about six feet in diameter. I remember thinking that must be the septic tank and what a funny place to put it.

But when I levered the top off, I had a shock.

Instead of a septic tank, it was a well. An old well, very big, at least six feet in diameter, like I said, stone built, completely circular, you could tell it had been made in the olden days by a stonemason who knew his job. I could see the water about twenty feet down, don't know how deep the water was, must have been capped off years ago.

That set me thinking, I looked around at the cottages and farms, some quite nearby and I realised that it would have been a communal well that had served them all before everyone had mains water in the 1950's. I knew from other wells still in use that it would have had a low stone wall built around it and a wooden structure to support the winch and bucket that they lowered to the water.

I thought about all the people who had come for water, staggering back with full buckets and gossiping with their neighbours at the well. The field would be empty then; it was long before Morelias was built.

I never did find the septic tank, but I asked some of the local old people and they could remember the well being used.

One old man said,

'Oh yes, I know about the well, did you know a woman drowned herself in it?'

He didn't know any details and I couldn't find out anything about her.

I told the lady at Morelias about it and she wondered whether the feeling in the house that someone was always there and the incident regarding the teddy bears had anything to do with the woman and the well, which was just outside her house, very close.

And the field down which the woman is still sometimes seen walking is opposite the well. She is always seen coming towards it from the direction of the farm where Tony saw the woman in the bedroom window when his sister swore there was no one in.

As I said, Morelias is a fairly modern house, which happened to be built close to the old well.

So – is the ghost the lady who was in the farm bedroom?

And is it the same one walking down the field to throw herself into the well? I wonder what she felt when she hit the icy water and saw the circle of light high above her – there was no way out – was she terrified before she died?

Did she influence the moving of the teddy bears – and the feeling of someone in the house so close to the well?

The last *known* sighting of the woman in the field was on a January day in 1998 – and, as far as I know, nothing has happened at Morelias lately – maybe it has faded forever from the house itself.

I would be grateful if anyone could throw more light on this story, who the woman was – why she did it and a rough date of the event.

And, of course, any more hauntings in the area please.

The unbeliever

This is another of Jack's stories:

One evening, I was decorating an old farmhouse near Cemaes. A farmer and his wife had bought it, had it all stripped down and were gradually renovating it. He was farming the land but until the farmhouse was finished they were living in a static caravan near the old house and, he was working on the construction of Wylfa Power Station, to help them pay for the restoration.

To begin with, they had completely stripped the farmhouse, taken out the doors and windows, frames and all, so that it was just an empty shell, four walls and a roof. Gradually it began to take shape and, when it had been all done, including plastering and central heating, electricity and so on, he asked me if I would come and decorate the kitchen ceiling. It was evening when I got there – they were still living in the caravan and I had almost finished when, all of a sudden, all the lights went out.

I thought it was a power cut, but when I looked outside, all the houses in the area had full electricity on – I couldn't understand it, but I wanted to finish the job, so I had a good idea – I brought the van right up to the kitchen window – and did it with the headlights of the van shining in from outside.

Just as I was packing up, the farmer came in and I said jokingly:

'This house must be haunted – the ghost has switched the power off.'

It was only a joke, but he got very angry when I said it and he glared at me.

'I've worked here lambing at all hours of the day and night – and nothing's ever happened – I don't believe in ghosts – that's rubbish – something's gone wrong – a short or something.'

He was so annoyed it surprised me – he just shrugged it off; nothing – forgotten.

He obviously was a sceptic – but why so angry? It made me think.

Anyway, at a later date, I went back, he wanted the walls, hall, landing and attics doing and I went there to give him an estimate.

I said to him,

'You'll have to take the radiator off the hall wall here, so I can do behind it.'

'That's not a problem,' he said, 'just let me know when you're coming and I'll take it off.'

'Well, it'll be about three weeks.'

'That's alright; it'll give me plenty of time to take it off.'

You see, to take a radiator off a wall, you have to close the valve on the water pipe which carries the water into the radiator, loosen the nut that connects the radiator to the valve, then drain all the water out of it and move it away. Anyway, I went there now with Kevin, my nephew – this was daytime now – and we put our sheets down in the hall, on the stairs and the landing and, of course, we start on the landing and work down to the front door and out, which is the way to work.

Anyway, we were working away, lunchtime now and, in the afternoon we were coming down the stairs, and Kevin says to me now, because we had a ladder on the stairs and a plank as we were working down the walls,

'Oh Jack, the radiator valve is starting to drip.'

The farmer had taken the radiator off and put it in the front room, Kevin could see the valve on the wall was dripping.

'Oh yeah, don't worry about it Kevin, it's only a tiny drip.'

Then it started getting more and more, so we got a little ice-cream box now and put it under the valve against the wall, but it came quicker and quicker and I said:

'That's strange, for it to start dripping now – we've been here all this time, I wonder why it has started now – and so quickly. Anyway, it got worse and worse, we had to get a washing-up bowl and, as fast as we emptied it, it filled up again, so I went to the caravan and said to the lady:

'Has your husband got a mole-wrench or something so that we can turn the valve a bit tighter?'

He was at work at Wylfa then.

Well, we tried with this and it didn't work. By the time we got to the hallway, it was so bad we had to put the valve back on the radiator and leave it on its back in the hall.

When we showed it to the farmer he said,

'Oh, it's either you or the lad who's knocked the valve.'

But I knew it couldn't have been either of us, because we hadn't started work on the lower part of the walls up to then and, we were always very careful not to damage anything, it was a wide enough old hall to pass without touching the walls.

Then he said:

'Oh – perhaps you tried to tighten it too much.'

But I had served my apprenticeship as a plumber, so I know how much pressure to put on. So I said to him that if it was leaking, if it was a faulty valve, it would have leaked all the time it was off – since he had taken the radiator off the wall. Why should it start now – and why should the water flow increase without anyone touching it? Before I'd tried to tighten it? Anyway I told him it had got so bad before he came, we had had to put the radiator back on it, before we'd done the wall.

We managed to finish and, when we got down to the hall, he held it against his legs so we could work behind the radiator and, when we'd finished, we just pinched it back on.

When we had been changing the bowls before, and emptying them when they were full, the farmer's wife had come into the hall behind us and, when I looked round she was standing there with her arms wrapped around herself and staring at the valve, shaking her head slowly. I wondered if she was all right, because she kept turning round as if she was looking for someone and gazing upstairs. She looked scared somehow.

Anyway, I put the empty bowl under the valve and I was going to say something to her, but when I looked at her, she just shivered as if she was cold and went out again.

I thought it was a bit queer, but I didn't say anything to the farmer. He didn't seem to think the valve leaking like that was strange – I asked him and he just shrugged it off – and that was that.

So we cleaned up, tidied up the job and that, and his wife said she had made a cup of tea and it was in the kitchen. So Kevin and I went into the kitchen and the farmer and his wife were both there.

Now, having a cup of tea with them, I just remembered the time I was decorating in the kitchen and all the lights went out, even though the other houses were brightly lit – I was just saying how strange it was that the radiator valve suddenly started to pour out water, even though it was turned off and I said to him, jokingly:

'Oh, it's probably that ghost again – perhaps it's because he/she doesn't want us to work here I'm sure. Yeah?'

'It's trying to tell us something I'm sure.'

Well, his wife looked at me and went quite pale and she said to me:

'Oh! Don't say that.'

Honestly now – her husband's face got very angry and he said sharp like:

'Oh woman – don't be silly now – there's nothing in this house, absolutely nothing, I've told you before!'

I could tell she knew something, by her face, so I said:

'What makes you say that?'

Her husband glared at her as if he was telling her to say nothing, but she wanted to talk about it so, in spite of him, she told me what had happened when they first bought the farmhouse.

The house was just a shell and her husband was working at Wylfa, like I told you, to pay for the renovations, and she said that like women do, even though the house was completely gutted, no windows or doors, just the roof and walls, she used to wander round the house thinking to herself, oh, this is going to be my kitchen and this is going to be my lounge and I'll have my settee there and my cupboard here. Yeah?

And she used to do this in the evening too, just as it was getting dusk, she would walk around and dream that one day it was going to be her home.

One evening, she walked into the hall and looked into what was going to be the lounge and, there in the opening where the old fireplace had been, just in front of it and to the side, she saw something – which stopped her dead.

There was an old man sitting in a rocking chair. He was wearing old-fashioned clothes and he was just rocking slowly to and fro. He seemed to be looking into the fire and he looked happy and contented. For what seemed ages, she couldn't move, she just stared at him and then, gradually he just faded away, until it was an empty room again.

Well, as she told me, I could tell it was the truth and it made goose bumps come up on my arms. But it just made her husband

140

angrier than ever and, he just said, 'Don't be ridiculous – I've told Jack I've been here at all hours – I've never seen a thing – *I keep telling you* there's nothing here.'

Well, I could tell the way they looked at each other that there had been other arguments before. I felt sorry for her and I tried to explain to her husband that some people are more sensitive to things like that than others, they act like catalysts.

He wasn't convinced though – all he would say was: 'What a load of rubbish – there's no such thing as ghosts – it's just ridiculous!' But I could tell by the way he spoke and, how adamant he was, that a lot of it was bluster – because underneath it all he was afraid.

But she was telling the truth, I could I tell, she stuck to her guns and, I wondered if he'd seen anything and was frightened. Anyway, he just grunted and slammed his mug down and went out.

So I asked her if she had any knowledge about the people who had lived there before and she said she had wanted to, but her husband had forbidden her to enquire.

I know it seems an old-fashioned thing to say, but he ruled her really, the influence he had over her was very strong.

I asked Jack if anything else had happened, but he said he had asked her, but she had just looked at her husband and shook her head, because obviously he didn't want her to talk about it.

So, said Jack, I can only tell you what happened while I was there.

As for the husband, *said Jack*, I'm sure he'd seen something too, but if he had, he would have tried to rationalise it or deny it completely, say to himself it was just a shadow or something. He would never admit even to himself that there are ghosts of people around, not doing any harm, because he couldn't bear the fact that he had been proved wrong, he was that sort of stubborn man who only believes in reality. You know – in things he can touch with his hands – yeah? I got the feeling that many things had happened since they bought the house that they couldn't explain. I can only tell you the things that happened while I was there, all the lights going out and the valve on the wall leaking faster and faster even when it was turned off. She would have told me eventually probably when she was on her own, but not while her husband was there. I never did find out and I'm no wiser now.

The Bull Hotel, Llangefni

Standing on its original medieval site, the Bull has grown over the centuries, from lowly tavern to a thriving eighteenth century coaching inn and thence to a very imposing stone-built hotel in the town centre. Samuel Johnson dined there when his horse cast a shoe as the good Doctor was travelling to Holyhead, on one of his many visits to his beloved Dublin.

I first stayed there over thirty years ago and, it was then I discovered it was haunted. My husband, Walt, was a young engineer, I was a young teacher and, when February half-term holiday coincided with one of his business trips visiting construction sites in Wales, I jumped at the chance to go with him and stop on Anglesey.

We booked in at the Bull and were delighted to be shown an ancient four-poster bed which was to be ours for the night, then we had an excellent dinner. One of our fellow diners was a very pleasant man, who turned out to be the landlord from the Railway Inn just up the road. Tanned and fit, he had just returned from a holiday in the Far East – and he invited us to pop back with him to see a few of the films he had taken of (what were then) exotic and barely known countries.

Which we did. Oh dear! His enthusiasm knew no bounds (and his films no ends) and we sat and watched, happily at first, while he and his wife gave a running commentary on the people in places that either appeared and disappeared rapidly on the film or froze with idiotic grins on their faces for minutes at a time. Each scene was greeted by the landlord and his wife with glad cries of 'Oh – do you remember this?' or 'Oh, now this is where' – and so on and oh so very so on!

Anyway, what seemed like hours later, we rose, stiff and glassy-eyed, said our thanks and goodbyes and stumbled out into the dark.

Dark? The night was thick with fog, so thick that the few street lights gave forth a dim orange glow, invisible until we reached them. The Bull was only a short distance down the hill, but we had to grope our way along the walls to reach it. By now it was nearly midnight and the whole town was silent, every one snug, warm and asleep in their beds. Finally, the Bull rose before us, shrouded in darkness, the door firmly closed and locked.

Shivering in the cold, wet fog, we stood on the wide doorstep and knocked politely. Five minutes later, still shivering, our knocking became less polite as desperation set in, but the Bull remained dark and silent.

Walt stepped backwards and looked up.

'Oh, thank heavens for that,' he said in relief, 'a light at last!'

I followed his pointing finger. Right at the top of the building, a small light had flared into life and, even as I watched, another one joined it.

'Thank goodness, I was beginning to think we'd have to sleep in the car,' I muttered, teeth chattering with cold.

We watched with our faces pressed to the porch window, as the lights came on down the attic stairs, along the corridor and finally down the main staircase to the hall.

'Come on, come on,' Walt said impatiently.

Bolts, top and bottom of the massive door were pulled back, the key turned and, finally the door opened slowly. Framed in the narrow aperture were two small, elderly ladies, alike as two peas, peering anxiously out at us. Their grey heads, bristling with curlers, were shrouded in boudoir caps and they were in all-concealing heavy nightwear.

They gave audible sighs of relief when we explained who we were. They were the resident chambermaids who we hadn't seen before, and the Manager had forgotten to tell them we were out. He had gone to the mainland and was not expected back until the early morning, and he always let himself in at the back door. We apologised for rousing them, explaining we had no intention of being so late, but we'd really had no option.

Half an hour later, we had examined all the fine old furniture in our very comfortable room and, we were snuggled down, half buried in the deep feather mattress, waiting for sleep to overcome us. I was thinking about the bed we were lying in and about all the other people who had used it before us. It was very old; the Manager had showed us all the ornate carvings and the hidden sliding panel in the headboard, used as a hiding place for jewellery and pistols in troubled times.

I turned on my back, trying to see the top of the bed-canopy in the gloom. As I peered, a small regular movement of light caught my eyes in the darkness and I stared harder before I nudged my dozing husband.

'Walt,' I said, 'What's that?'

He turned over slowly, muttering about going to sleep.

'What's what?' he asked grumpily.

'That,' I said shortly.

He propped himself up on one elbow and looked.

On the right hand post at the bottom of the bed (on Walt's side) we both saw something very odd.

A globular orange light, about the size and shape of a tennis ball, was moving slowly and steadily up and down the carved wood.

There was a silence, then Walt said,

'Reflection.'

'From what?'

'Street light,' said Walt and got out of bed.

He padded down to the bottom of the bed, and said:

'I'll just show you – watch it shine on my hand, instead of the wood.'

He spread his hand to cover the moving light and I watched closely to see his hand light up and the wood remain dark as the light was deflected.

Instead, the reverse happened, it never appeared on the back of his hand – because, try as he would, his hand *blotted out* the orange ball, as if the illumination was coming from *inside* the wood. It was very eerie and, in the darkness and the silence, watching that unearthly light moving up and down, I felt my scalp tighten and realised that fright really does make your hair stand on end.

It didn't change pace or direction, moving steadily from the top canopy and back to the bed foot.

Walt was puzzled.

'Can't be reflection,' he said, 'there are no gaps in these thick curtains and, anyway the fog is too thick for it to be street lights.'

He walked around the room, checking for chinks in the curtains and bumping into furniture in the dark, before he came back and examined the post closely. I just wished he'd get back into bed and

I lay there, eyes as big as saucers and scared stiff.

'I'll be *damned* if I know what it is!' he said in exasperation, then half in earnest:

'The bed must be haunted!'

This – from my practical engineering husband, who could explain away most of my imaginary fears – made me go cold.

'Ooh Walt!' I said shiveringly, and vanished under the bedclothes – I was nearly smothered, but I wouldn't have put my head out again for love or money!

Walt lay for a long time with his arms propped behind his head, watching the light.

I lay stiff as a log, sleepless beside him, until I heard him say:

'It's growing dimmer.'

Then a few minutes later,

'It's gone.'

He slid down in bed and I clung like a frightened limpet for the rest of the night.

And, for my cynical friends, the strongest drink we had that night had been coffee!

* * *

Many years later, when we had come to live on Anglesey and I had started this book, we returned to the Bull to see if we could find out anything more about the haunted bed.

Alas! Memories of a comfortable, warm and friendly hotel were banished the moment we pushed open the front door. Instead of the thick carpets, polished wood and great open fires in the warm, cosy rooms, we were confronted with a place which we hardly recognised.

Stained, cheap pub tables, and bentwood chairs, threadbare dirty carpets and peeling wallpaper was all it now contained. Dirty glasses, full ashtrays and a clientele of unwashed, unshaven men made the smoke-filled air raucous and sour.

We left without even approaching the bar.

Last year, we were told it was under new management and was being completely refurbished in its old style, so I telephoned the Manager, Mr Roberts (who has since left) and asked him if he would kindly let us take photographs of the haunted room. He agreed willingly and, when we arrived, he filled us in on the interim years since our last and very brief, visit.

The Bull was bought from the Brewery in 1997 and is in the process of being carefully and lovingly restored. It had declined greatly in the 1980's, eventually ending up as accommodation for DHSS clients.

Over the years, all the antique furniture, fine china and valuable sporting prints had been sold, until nothing remained of its former glory. Any furniture that was in the hotel was cheap and nasty and evidence of the DHSS occupants were shattered windows, kicked in doors and tattered curtains. The only clientele left when Mr Roberts took over were mainly drunks and drug addicts. Rubbish and 'trashed' rooms were all that the once fine hotel contained.

'It was the biggest challenge of my life,' said Mr Roberts, 'it was either the druggies or me – so I had to get rid of them for a start.'

Asked if there had been any fights, muscular Mr Roberts said briefly:

'Well, they didn't go peacefully.'

Now, after much careful and expert buying, the place is furnished with many antiques – fireplaces and heavy oak furniture – all sought for and bought in many antique shops throughout Britain, pleasing and graceful china pieces, and has become again a warm and very comfortable hotel.

Mr Roberts very kindly gave us a complete tour of the hotel.

First we went to the spotlessly clean, modern kitchen, where the chefs were preparing lunch, then down to the cellars which were equipped like modern laboratories, the only clue that their prime function was to dispense drinks were the many casks stacked in orderly rows, everything was in exquisite order, and I saw Walt's eyes gleam as we peeped into the wine cellar.

There is an ancient water well beneath the cellars, with a massive hand pump on the wall, which is still usable today – or would be if Manweb hadn't installed a smart new junction box so close to the handle that it is now unusable, despite the yards of bare wall on each side of it.

The cellars are arched with stone or brick, some parts very old, the others early Victorian, and Mr Roberts led us into a very old one that had two mullioned windows which had been blocked in many years ago.

'In this room,' he said, 'we are standing ten feet below the level of the car park which is above this cellar. Those windows must have looked out on a yard or garden at one time – but why was it filled in – and when?'

He also showed us the beginning of a downward sloping arched ceiling where, at one time, the steps went down again, but have been floored over.

'There are cellars beneath these cellars,' he said, 'and one day, when I have time, I'm going to have a look. One of the staff absolutely refuses to enter this cellar at all, as he has often heard someone laughing in the corner where the arched ceiling slopes down.

'I've heard it four or five times now, when I know I've been alone down there, and it isn't a nice laugh. Very low it is, more of a snigger, as if someone was watching me on the sly,' he said, 'you wouldn't get me in there again for a gold clock!'

Mr Roberts went before us at a spanking pace. So many different levels, flights of stone steps, twisting corridors and, fool that I was – I was wearing high heels.

Some of the arched corridors were exceedingly low and, as Mr Roberts flung open a door, leading down worn stone steps he plunged onwards telling us to mind our heads on the low stone roof. I followed as fast as I could, ripping the epaulette off my trench coat as I cannoned into the wall. No time to pick it up – Walt and Mr Roberts were disappearing in the gloom, as I gingerly tottered down the worn steps.

We were shown where alterations had been made in the cellars and, after retracing our steps and me retrieving my epaulette and ramming it in my pocket, Mr Roberts took us back to the ground floor again.

I was longing for a sit down and a drink – but it was not to be. He leapt up the main staircase, Walt with him and me toiling along in the rear, trying to listen as he kindly explained how the restorations were progressing.

Bemused, I saw where walls had been taken down, transforming poky rooms into very comfortable en-suite bedrooms, and sadly, where the yobos had smashed the small square window panes, with their irreplaceable thin old glass, which have been renewed with modern glass and frames.

Eventually, we ended up in the corner bedroom, on the first floor, to the right of the main entrance, where Walt and I had our weird experience.

We wouldn't have known it as the same room, apart from the position of the windows, as the refurbishments had not yet reached here. Gone was the fine old four-poster bed, gone the antique furniture and the thick carpets. All it now contained was a couple of upright chairs and a cheap wardrobe, remnants of the last DHSS occupants.

'These rooms are the next to be decorated and furnished,' said Mr Roberts. He had been very interested in our story (previously told over the phone) and he had made enquiries for us. All he knew, from local talk, was that this room had been very unpopular with the DHSS clients, none of whom would occupy it for long.

As far as the bed was concerned it, along with all the other fine furnishings, had been sold over the years when the Bull fell on hard times.

'This isn't the only room that's weird,' he said, 'I'll take you to the places where things have been heard and seen.'

He led us out onto the wide spacious landing and pointed to a large window at the end.

'See that,' he said. 'Well, most of my staff believe that spot is haunted. I've got a young waiter here and, one day, he came up to go to his room on the next floor. He came whistling upstairs, and waved to the girl on the bar. Next minute, he came flying down again, as white as a sheet. He could hardly speak and hung onto a chair back, as if his legs wouldn't hold him up.

Finally, he told her that he had just turned the corner to go up the next flight, when he glanced along the landing. There, looking out of the window, sat an old lady in a rocking chair. She was side-on to him, rocking gently and looking absolutely solid and real. Then she turned her head and looked at him and, as she did, slowly she became more and more transparent until both she and the chair had faded away completely.

When he could talk about it properly, he said she had a black dress on, a long one, and a white lace collar with an oval brooch at the neck. Her hair was grey and dressed with a bun at the top of her head. He thought she looked Victorian.

Up to that time, he didn't believe in ghosts, but he does now! It took him a long time to get over the shock. I've no idea who the old lady was; no one seems to know about her.'

Finally, we climbed right up to the attics under the roof, some parts of which are medieval, some altered in Victorian times.

One aspect of these attics, which are also reputed to be haunted, is their utter silence. Although the unseen road below was thronged with traffic and, the hotel itself full of Market Day customers, there was not the slightest noise in the attics.

As we stood in the cobwebby dust, listening to the wind sighing amongst the tall chimneys above us, it was very easy to imagine the workmen of hundreds of years ago, busy setting up the massive lead-lined oaken valley gutter which runs through the attics, about four feet above the floors. This gutter runs straight from the front of the hotel to the rear, carrying away all the rainwater from the roof.

The attics are the domain of a ghost dog, frequently seen, a small brown and white terrier, so real-looking that the staff and building workers are sure, at first sight, that it is a live dog. Apparently, it appears in the corner of the attics, trots forward to look at the visitor, and after a pause, it scampers through the attic, before disappearing in the far wall. One of the builders who is doing the renovating was so sure it was real, he spent minutes calling and searching for the little creature.

Puzzled, he went down to ask the staff, many of whom have seen the dog. Although they were shocked at first, the staff have become quite used to him, no one is afraid, it is so friendly. As usual, with most animal hauntings, nothing is known about it or why it should haunt the old attics.

Many people have told me that there are more ghosts at the Bull and, the authority on them is Mr Owen Ivor Jones, but I have been unable to contact him, a great pity.

When Walt had finished taking photographs of the attics, we made our way downstairs and I fell thankfully into a comfortable armchair.

The local lads were very interested in what we were doing and had stories of their own to tell.

One of them, Clayton, told me that a few of the regulars were in the bar early one Halloween and the talk got round to ghosts. Clayton told me that one of the men there said he knew for a fact that the Bull was haunted, but would not say how he knew, just stubbornly sticking to his statement.

Of course he got ribbed unmercifully, told that it was just a lot of old wives tales. One of the group picked up his pint declaring that there were no such things as ghosts.

Hardly had the words left his lips when a heavy mirror, which was hanging above the handsome slate fireplace, was projected off the wall with such force that it cleared the table beneath it and hit the floor about six feet away from the wall, shattering into thousands of pieces and smashing its gilt frame.

Everyone who saw it was stunned into silence and the disbelievers were heard no more.

I know there is a lot more to learn about the Ghosts of the Bull and I would be most grateful for any more information.

Melin Esgob (Llandyfrydog)

Melin Esgob, an old mill now converted into a house, stands at Llandyfrydog, and once belonged to John Hughes, the famous bonesetter, a kind and considerate man, who many times worked for nothing when his patients were too poor to pay. He was also one of the best millers in Anglesey and employed a young man at the mill, one Hugh Jones.

One morning, Hugh went to work as usual, first opening the floodgates to start the mill, then going inside to the power room. As he went in, he shouted greetings to a group of farm workers in the nearby field, who heard the mill start up, showing that Hugh had set the control.

It was nearly dinnertime before one of the men noticed that the mill was turning empty. He called and pointed to the others, then walked over to the mill to see what was wrong. A minute later he came flying out of the door, sick and white and collapsed on the grass. The others ran in then, after realising he was in shock, but halted suddenly at the scene that met their eyes.

When Hugh set the control, which he had done hundreds of times before, his open jacket caught in the power drive wheel and, in a trice, he was whipped into the air, whirling round and round with the revolving wheel. His head was smashed against the wall with each turn and his body was still being whirled around.

This happened in the late 1890's and, for many years after the mill had finished working, people walking past at night would hear the mill start up, a short high scream and regular thudding noise, even though the mill was dark and empty.

A gentleman from Rhos-y-bol told me his grandfather had heard it as a young man, walking past the mill with his sweetheart, starting up suddenly one moonlit night and, they had been so frightened that he grabbed her hand and they ran all the way back to her home.

The sounds were heard many times in the years after Hugh Jones' terrible death, but gradually grew more infrequent as time passed and ceased altogether after the conversion.

The arm of comfort

Joyce Piggin of Church Bay, told me this happy little story.

About ten years ago, Mr and Mrs Piggin bought a small-holding, Tyddyn Uchaf in picturesque Church Bay, which they decided would be their dream home.

Originally it belonged to a farmer, Mr John Evans, who built it as a home for himself and his new bride. He lived in it happily until his death about fifteen years ago, when it passed into other hands. Mr and Mrs Piggin declared their intention of buying it and were delighted when the surveyor told them there were very few faults with the building. The sale went through and, during the time of the transaction, they spent happy hours planning the house and garden.

Eventually, they moved in, and put their plans into operation. One of the first priorities, of course, was a bathroom, for which they would need an extension. The surveyor they called in was Mr Robert Davies, an excellent local man, who came and spent a long time giving the house a close and thorough inspection. He went carefully into every crevice, from the roof space to the floor joists and, finally, came back to them looking very grave.

Mr Davies asked them to sit down and, from his manner they thought something must be very wrong, but they certainly weren't prepared for what he had to tell them. In short, without beating about the bush, he told them that he had found eighty two major building faults, most of which he was familiar with, but some of which he had never heard. He said he wished he had a film company to show how many flaws could exist in one building and informed them, as gently as he could, that the farmhouse was so ramshackle it was completely unsafe to live in and the only thing they could do was pull it down.

They were both speechless with shock and Mr Davies pointed out, that if they wanted to stay on the land they owned, they would have to build a new house. They were stunned.

'I think it was the most traumatic time in our lives,' Joyce told me. 'We had spent so much money buying the place, it had made such a big hole in our savings and it turned out to be worthless.'

Neither of them could sleep much that night, they were in despair and, next day, as Mrs Piggin went through the motions of getting breakfast, she stopped for a moment, as depression overwhelmed her and stood by the kitchen sink, gazing unseeingly out of the window.

It was then that she felt the pressure of a strong, comforting arm laid across her shoulders. Thinking it was her husband, she turned gratefully to embrace him, only to find she was alone. She gazed about her in surprise – and it was then she became aware of a slow change in the room's atmosphere.

'The whole place became permeated by a deep sense of peace and reassurance, such a lovely warm feeling, it made me feel so much better,' Joyce said.

After many discussions, Mr and Mrs Piggin decided that as they loved the place so much, and wanted to stay there, there was nothing else for it but to have a new house built. So they went ahead and, during the next few hectic months, as the financial outlay rose, Joyce spent many hours in doubt and near despair, wondering whether they were doing the right thing.

It was always when she was at her most depressed that someone seemed to be there, the comforting arm about her shoulders and the sense of tranquillity, instilling hopefulness.

'It was as if someone was there who knew exactly how I felt,' she said, 'and it really kept me going through the worst time.'

She said nothing about it to her husband and, it was only much later, when the nightmare was over and they had at last, settled down in their new house, built in front of the old farm that the subject was brought up.

One evening, they were sitting cosily in their warm lounge, able to smile now about all the crises and dilemmas it had taken to reach their final triumph, when her husband turned to her and said diffidently:

'Joyce, when things were really bad and you kept wondering if we were doing the right thing – did you ever feel as if someone had put their arm about your shoulders?'

Joyce looked at him in amazement, then smiled and nodded delightedly.

'Oh yes!' she said, 'many, many times, but I didn't know *you* had!'

He nodded slowly.

'Oh yes, at least half-a-dozen times – I wonder who it was?'

They were both silent then, staring thoughtfully into the fire.

Puzzled as to the identity of their gentle ghost, Mrs Piggin told her neighbour exactly what had happened – and wondered who it could be. Her response was immediate.

'I know who *that* was!' she said, 'that would be old John Evans, he lived there for many years and he loved the place. He was the kindest, most thoughtful man I have ever known!' She nodded emphatically. 'He knew what you were going through and it would distress him to know how troubled you were. That's why he came to comfort you.' Pressing Joyce's hand she went on: 'He must know you are the right sort of people to live in his place,' she said. 'Don't you worry Joyce bach – he'll look after you, you'll be happy at Tyddyn Uchaf.'

And so they have been.

Melody from the past

The small village of Bryngwran lies on the main road that runs between Gwalchmai and Valley and, at a turning in the village, leading north, stands the farm of Mr Owen Thomas Jones, named Tŷ Hen.

A few years ago, Mr Jones's friend, Geraint Evans, had cows and calves grazing in a field that lay lower down the valley. One early autumn day Geraint came to tell him that one of his calves was off colour, would he come and look at it.

Owen agreed at once, got his coat, and the two men walked down to the field.

It was late afternoon, the mist rising from the grass and, by the time they reached the animals, 'only their heads were sticking up above it', as Owen told me.

Owen examined the calf thoroughly and decided there was nothing seriously wrong, so they started back. The autumn afternoon was one of those still, melancholy days, when no birds sing and all is silence.

Suddenly, as they walked, Owen said that a woman's voice started to sing softly, from very close by. He stopped dead, and looked about to see where it was coming from, as the singing grew stronger. As he said, he thought it was a radio, but he couldn't see anyone about. No one for miles.

It was so unearthly, it made him shiver. Geraint had stopped when he did and looked at him enquiringly.

'Where's that music coming from?' Owen asked.

Geraint looked puzzled.

'What music?' he asked, 'I can't hear anything.'

The singing had swelled and when Owen realised he was the only one that could hear it, he knew it was something uncanny. A deep unease gripped him and when Geraint saw the expression on his face, he felt it too, and without another word they 'took to their heels and ran', as Owen told me.

When they burst into the farm kitchen, Mrs Jones was shocked.

'What on earth's wrong?' she asked. 'You're as white as a sheet; you look as if you've seen a ghost!'

Owen was badly shaken and sank into a chair.

'No – I haven't *seen* one, I've *heard* one!' he said.

When I asked Mr Jones what the singing was like – he told me that it was a woman's voice, unaccompanied and singing in an unknown language, neither Welsh nor English – he didn't recognise it at all.

This happened a few years ago and Owen had almost forgotten it, until one day he was talking to an old friend, a retired policeman, also called Owen Jones. He said, as they were talking about the area:

'I remember having an awful fright down there once, when I was a kid. I must have been about twelve or thirteen, and I was bird-nesting that spring, the way lads do.

'I was looking into a hedge down there, no one about but me when, all of a sudden I heard this singing, as close to me as I am to you. It was a woman's voice, beautiful it was, just as if she was standing next to me. Then it seemed to rise in the air and it was coming from above and all around me – but I couldn't *see* anyone.

'Gave me the fright of my life it did!

'I shot out of there as if I had wings on my feet – and I didn't go back again, I can tell you.'

Now Mr Owen Thomas Jones knew he wasn't hearing things and he's learnt since that David Kelsall, Ffynnon Mab, has also heard it.

I was very intrigued with this story. A woman's beautiful disembodied voice singing in the middle of nowhere? So I asked Mr Owen Jones what the area was like. He told me that next to his land was a well made track on land belonging to Parc farm.

This was no ordinary muddy lane, like most of them are, but had a solid foundation and, even lay-bys for traffic to pass, as it had obviously been a busy thoroughfare.

When I asked, Owen told me that it led to what looked like the ruins of a building, there were a lot of big flat stones, almost hidden and overgrown.

My curiosity aroused, I phoned my friend Clare Meade, who is a neighbour of Mr Owen Thomas Jones, and bless her! she contacted him and, after that, talked to Mr Andrew Davidson, the well-known archaeologist. Mr Davidson, although an extremely busy man, kindly spared the time to go with Owen for a brief look.

He said, in his opinion, that without inspecting the ruins thoroughly, that the stones marked the site of a settlement, which from what he could see, was thriving in the late medieval period.

Also, the invaluable Clare sought the advice of a distant relative of hers, Professor David Crystal, the worldwide authority on linguistics, and described the location and unknown language of the woman who was singing.

Professor Crystal declared that the language could possibly have been Irish, as there were Irish settlements known on the Island at that time, but in his opinion it was probably early Welsh, which would be about as unrecognisable in the present day, as would medieval English.

So, unless and until the day when the ruins are excavated (and maybe not even then!) our singer's origins will remain unknown.

I don't suppose we will ever find out why she is still heard.

Old lady of Dwyran

The first story I received after I wrote to The Anglesey Mail *appealing for any ghosts known on the Island (seen, heard or passed down in families) came from a charming young couple who then lived at Dwyran, but have since moved to Pen Mynydd.*

It was written by Emyr Williams, a young organic farmer, and is as mysterious as it is brief. Here is what he wrote.

On the 3rd of February, 1996 (a cold, quiet day), my girlfriend Nia and I were out in the late afternoon walking my dogs. We were going downhill towards the Menai Strait and we had passed a lodge called 'Erw Goch', just outside the village of Dwyran.

Then Nia mentioned that there was someone coming towards us up the hill, but she couldn't see the figure clearly as it was getting dark. Seconds later, a car approached from behind us and I looked back up the road and I kept into the side with the dogs, because I thought it was going to go past, but it turned into a driveway before it reached us.

Nia didn't turn around, as she was only a few feet away from the approaching figure, and didn't want to bump into it, as we were all on the same side of the road. So she saw, lit up by the bright headlights of the car behind us, a very detailed image.

Her description has never varied. She insists she saw a small old lady wearing plain brown clothing and carrying, what she thought looked like, a white plastic carrier bag. The lady had a very kind expression on her face, but Nia was uncertain whether she had noticed our presence at all.

The dogs, by the way, had run ahead of us, and their behaviour was normal. We walked on a little way, then Nia stopped and looked around.

'Where did she go?' she asked in bewilderment.

'Who?' I said.

'That little old lady,' said Nia, 'she was just about to pass us, now she's gone!'

I was just as surprised as Nia – the road we were on is a country road, no pavements and the walls and hedges on either side are unbroken.

Another car came down the hill, and we could see by the lights that the road was completely empty, except for the dogs and us. Nia was astonished and couldn't get over the fact that the old lady had completely disappeared. This was her first visit to my house and she certainly didn't know of any local ghost stories, but I already knew the road was haunted, and I knew Nia was speaking the truth.

I believed her even more when I mentioned the sighting to my neighbours and they confirmed that Nia's description of the old lady matched others that they had been told.

I didn't see the ghost, just heard Nia say that someone was coming up the hill towards us and, of course, when it drew close, I was looking behind at the car, so I missed it, but I often wonder if I would have seen it anyway?

Some people can – and some can't and I don't know (yet!) which group I belong to.

The waller of Capel Coch

On a lovely spring day, with larks climbing in the blue sky and daffodils in full bloom, Mr Thomas Brown, of Beeston, Notts., was walking with his wife, Mary, along the road from Treysgawen to Capel Coch.

They were on an early holiday on Anglesey, thoroughly enjoying the warm sunshine and country views. Apart from the animals in the fields, the only other sign of life was a young man sitting comfortably on top of a five-barred gate ahead of them.

He looked as real as you or me, *said Mr Brown*, and as we got nearer I could see he was wearing working trousers, with what looked like sacking tied around below the knee and held up by braces. He had on a flannel shirt without a collar.

He was looking at us with interest, and seemed friendly enough, and I smiled at him and was just going to say good morning, *when he started to disappear*.

I don't mean just vanish or anything sudden, but first his face and head became sort of wavy, like a reflection on water, rippling like, then it slowly disappeared, and his shoulders, and all down his body to his feet. His muddy boots were the last thing to go – I can remember how weird it all looked – just the two feet resting on a bar and nothing else above them.

We stood there, I think we were frozen with shock, you just can't believe something like that, you know.

We stared at that empty gate for a minute, then I grabbed Mary's hand and we ran back the way we came. Must have run for about a mile. I didn't believe in ghosts 'til then, I know it wasn't very brave to turn and run, but it shook me to the core, because you think about ghosts being in old houses in the night, and thunderstorms, not in broad daylight, on a country road.

This happened ten years ago and Mr Brown told me that when they made enquiries locally, an old man who had lived on a farm near Treysgawen when he was young, was very interested in the fact that they had seen the ghost, because he knew the story about it.

Apparently, a young farm labourer named Hugh Williams had been sent by his master to repair a gap in the field wall, which had been caused by heavy rain, so that he could put in his ewes and lambs. It was no easy task, as Anglesey walls are about two feet thick at the base, a double wall, filled with rubble in the middle. The top coping stones are usually laid on a bed of cement which anchors the stones firmly. When a wall comes down, the waller has to sort out the stones, making heaps of the smaller stones and rubble and laying out the large stones along the side of the gap.

This is what Hugh was doing when his wife brought his dinner to him. She was walking and talking with old Mair Clogs, an old lady known and feared for her acid tongue and 'seeing eyes'. As usual she was hobbling along in her old clogs, leaning heavily on a stick.

Hugh, as a young boy, along with other village children, had annoyed old Mair by following her and jeering, so she had little liking for him, although she was fond of his gentle wife.

Ann stopped by Hugh and, as the old woman shuffled past, Hugh grinned at her cheekily. She scowled and walked on, then suddenly turned and pointed her stick at him, as she looked at Ann.

'He won't finish building that wall,' she said sadly to Ann, and then went on her way, slowly shaking her head.

Hugh was unperturbed. Screwing his finger into the side of his head, he muttered something rude about the old woman, then took the dinner basket that Ann proffered and sat down in the grass to enjoy his sandwiches, but Ann stared after the old woman, feeling dismayed.

Teatime came and went, but Hugh didn't come home. Ann took her little daughter and they strolled slowly back to where he was working, picking flowers in the warm sunshine.

Ann could see no sign of him, until she looked over the wall. He lay at the end of the gap, his head half buried under a length of heavy coping stones, which had projected out of the end of the gap. As Hugh had bent low to fill in the first layer of rubble, the old mortar had given way, causing the length of coping to break off and this piece had crashed down on his head like an eggshell, killing him instantly.

He never did finish the wall.

After his funeral, if the weather stayed calm, people nearby heard the chip-chip of his hammer, as he fashioned the stones to fit, exactly as if he'd still been alive. So persistent and regular was the sound that no waller or farm labourer could be persuaded to finish the wall, and a wooden fence was hastily erected to keep the sheep in.

Many people have heard the stone tapping, others have seen Hugh sitting on the gate – but no one has yet been near enough to communicate and, as one lady said who had seen him,

'I think you are supposed to ask a ghost if you can somehow help it, but how can you speak to it, if it disappears before you open your mouth?'

Hugh has been seen as recently as the 1990's, but like all good ghost stories – it leaves a question, if not two. The first is, how did old Mair Clogs know he wouldn't finish the wall? And does Hugh haunt the spot because he was rude to the old lady or because of the unfinished gap? We will never know.

Haunting at Llannerch-y-medd

Years ago, in Bridge Street, stood a bright little confectioner's shop, belonging to Mr Hugh Jones, a cheerful and jolly man, who was famous all over the Island and far beyond, for his 'Number 8, Llangefni Rock'. Both Hugh and his mother ran the shop together and, on Thursdays and Saturdays, Hugh could always be seen at his stall in Llangefni market, immaculate in his starched white coat and hat. His mother also wore a spotless white apron in the shop and was just as pleasant as her son.

Some of the popular rock was sent by train to Welsh seaside resorts on the mainland and, the demand was such that the stock which he took to the markets was completely sold out by 10.00 a.m. People who have sampled the rock say it was absolutely delicious, but alas! no one has been able to re-create the recipe since. Some people have sworn to me that Hugh took the recipe with him to the grave – others that he bequeathed it to his niece. Whichever tale is true – the rock has never been eaten since and, the little shop, when last I saw it, was empty and boarded up.

A far more unpleasant and sinister reputation enshrouds a small cottage further along Bridge Street, which is the site of a bad haunting.

Years ago, before the haunting started, a Mr and Mrs Hughes lived there for many happy years. Mr Hughes worked on the railway for most of his blameless life and died peacefully in his eighties.

I haven't been able to find out who lived in it subsequently, but the cottage became haunted after a tragic suicide in the kitchen, by the occupant.

For a time, the cottage stood empty until a lady and her family came to live there.

Mr Roberts, of Bryn Teg, gave me most of the following story.

The family had not been living there for long, when the ghost made itself felt in a most unpleasant manner.

I shall call the lady Mrs W. and this is her story.

We hadn't had the house for long and I was on my own for a great deal of the time, when I began to realise that very often it would grow intensely cold in the room where I was sitting even though I had a big fire. The strange thing was, the coldness only lasted about half an hour and, during that time, it was as if someone else was in the room with me, and I felt an atmosphere of terrible despair. Sometimes it was so strong, I got goose pimples on my arms.

At first I thought I was imagining things or I'd caught a chill or something, but it got steadily worse.

To begin with, the cold always started to form about eight o'clock and I would feel whomever it was in the room with me, filling the place with this awful feeling of depression. Then it would sort of seep away after a time and I felt very relieved.

But one night, when it had started, it became very insistent. I daren't look round because I had a strong feeling that someone was standing behind me, just near the door. I was so scared; I just stared into the fire without even looking over my shoulder. It seemed to last for ages, then gradually it went less cold and the oppressive feeling started to clear and I knew the ghost had gone.

I was just beginning to relax, my muscles had been so tense, when I heard the noises for the first time.

They were the sounds of heavy footsteps crossing the room above my head. It sounded as if they were thumping on a wooden floor, yet the bedroom was carpeted. They crossed and re-crossed several times, and then they seemed to stop at the window.

I had locked and bolted the doors; I knew no one was in the house but me. I never moved out of that chair all night, I was afraid to go to bed and, after that first night, they were heard during the day also.

My family was away most of the time; I was on my own quite a lot, so I was very glad when one of my friends came to stay with me, whilst on holiday on Anglesey. I didn't say much about the haunting, I didn't want to frighten her.

One day we had a trip to Bangor and we got back just before 8.00 p.m. No sooner had we got in the front door when it happened. My friend went in first and, I had just turned round to shut the door, when the cold hit us. It was a warm summer's day and we weren't wearing our coats, but it was like walking into a freezer. Then as we stood there, Betty grabbed my arm and pointed to the staircase.

I couldn't see anything to begin with, I thought there must be someone there – and then I saw it, when I looked down. The stairs had a new thick carpet on and, when I stared, I saw the pile of the carpet being flattened by an imprint. It was the shape of a shoe, going slowly upstairs, squashing the pile down on each step, which sprang back up again when whatever it was had passed.

We watched it go upstairs as far as we could see, then we both shot into the nearest room and slammed the door. As we stood staring at each other, we heard the heavy footsteps crossing the bedroom overhead.

It was a long time after they had stopped before we could speak. We sank down into the chairs, I don't know about Betty but my legs seemed too weak to hold me up.

Then Betty asked me about the noises and everything and, when I told her all about them, she said I must leave – I mustn't stay in that atmosphere any longer.

So I took her advice and went back home with her. I put the house on the market and told my family why.

Up until then, they hadn't heard or seen anything but when they went to pack up all the furniture, they told me had seen the footprints form on the stairs every night. I went back a few times to help them, but I never stayed there another night. I didn't have the nerve. I know ghosts never harm people, but some of them are too frightening to live with. I think so anyway, that's why I left.

Apparently, the story got around and a little party of would-be-ghost-hunters, students from Bangor University, arranged to spend a weekend in the now empty cottage. Equipped with food, flashlights, sleeping bags and assorted ghost-detecting equipment, they were seen entering the house in the dusk of an October evening.

Their vigil wasn't a long one; however, for at dawn the next day, they were in the Square, pale and tired, trying to hitch-hike back to Bangor, never to be seen by the villagers again. No one knows what frightened them so badly.

Mr Roberts (Bryn Teg) tells me that the haunting was seen by a party of people who stood together at the bottom of the stairs, to see the eerie pressing down of the carpet as if someone was climbing the stairs, which sprang back up again as the invisible weight was removed onto the next stair tread.

Mrs Roberts, of McKillop Brothers (now sadly closed), very

kindly made enquiries about the cottage and told me that there was a big fire which raged in the empty house about four years ago, the cause unknown. Apparently, the suicide of a young woman started the haunting and the fire brought them to an end, as there have been no reports of any ghostly happenings since then.

Amlwch windmill (Melin-y-Borth)

The windmill between Amlwch and Porth Amlwch, Mona Mill or Melin-y-Borth, which stands close to the former 'Octel' works, now 'Great Lakes', is now only a stump, plain to see, even though the cap and sails are long gone. Built in 1816, it was the tallest mill on Anglesey, its seven storeys towering sixty feet high, and it worked ceaselessly through the 1800's, the boom time for Amlwch.

Mr William Jones was the miller here during the 1890's and his son, also William, worked with him in the mill. William Bach was a cheerful, hardworking young man, about eighteen, popular with everyone because of his good-natured friendly manner. He lived with his mother and father in Queen Street, Amlwch.

One November day in the early 1890's, Mr Jones, Senior, had left the mill for a brief time, leaving his son working alone. It was a most unseasonable day for November, the air was warm and sultry, with heavy cumulous clouds massing over the sea, and thunder growled in the distance, coming steadily nearer. Young Will, sweating, threw off his jacket, he was unable to hear the rumbling thunder in the racket of the working mill.

The air became loaded with static electricity, it was very still and the clouds became low and menacing as the storm moved in. Suddenly, there was a blinding flash, followed immediately by a violent crack of thunder, as the lightning streaked down to earth.

Mona Mill was the highest building around and the lightning struck it, rushed down the inside of the tower to earth itself, in the process electrocuting young Will, who was handling the iron machinery and killing him outright. His father returned to find his son's blackened body on the mill floor.

The shock was so great that Mr Jones never really recovered, he lost heart in the job and, also, the hey-day of the windmills was drawing to a close. He gave up his tenure of the mill in the middle 1890's, not long after that it was closed and gradually fell into ruin.

It was shortly after the closure that local people reported seeing the figure of a young man, standing in the doorway of the mill, who only appeared during thunderstorms.

Even recently, says Mrs Starkie of Amlwch, many people have seen a young man in nineteenth century work-clothes illuminated in the lightning flashes.

I have been told that the last sighting was in the summer of 1998, when he was seen by a gang of boys running past the mill, heading for home out of the rain.

Makes one wonder if he also appears when there is no one near to see him?

Mynydd Bodafon

This is a taped telephone interview with a lady who wishes to be known only as Mrs Jones, which, I think is all I can say without disclosing her address or place of work.

She begins thus:

A few years ago, my daughter and I went for a walk to Mynydd Bodafon. It was a lovely warm afternoon in summer and we intended to walk up as far as the plantation that the Forestry Commission has grown. We were approaching that and chatting to each other when I noticed a man in a small field on my left. He was standing there with his hands on an old-fashioned plough – you know the kind you have to hold onto the wooden handles?

Well, knowing most people on the mountain, I thought – well, who could this old soldier be? But nevertheless, I thought perhaps they've still got some old-fashioned farming methods around here. I didn't think – you know.

So I said 'Good afternoon', but he only seemed to stare vaguely at me. My daughter looked and smiled at him too, but he only stood there staring. He had working clothes on, a sort of granddad shirt and trousers, and he looked middle-aged. I had a good look at him, because he was only about five yards away over the low wall.

We walked a few paces on and, I said in a low voice to my daughter, 'Funny he didn't answer us, did he? He could at least have said 'Good afternoon'. My daughter must have found something strange, because she slowed down and said,

'I think I'll go home.'

We'd only gone on a few feet, and I wasn't really listening to her, I said 'Funny – he didn't have a horse to draw that thing.'

So she said, 'I'm going home' – and she stopped walking.

'But why?' I said, 'it's a lovely afternoon, let's walk as far as the plantation.' Then I realised she'd stopped – so I turned around – and he wasn't there.

I pointed to where we'd seen him – and she turned and looked.

'Gosh,' I said, 'he's made a quick exit!' Because he would have had to cross the field to the gate or take the plough somewhere – but there wasn't a sign of him or the plough.

170

We wondered where he had gone, but it didn't seem very important to me – although my daughter hurried back down the path off the mountain and back home. She was very quiet all the way back.

My daughter and the little girl next door were great friends, her Dad was called David, and he is a bit psychic, and my daughter ran round next door when we got home, and said to him:

'Mam and I saw this funny man in Mynydd Bodafon and he was ploughing without a horse!'

Then she went on to describe the incident to him and he listened carefully, and when she'd finished he said to her:

'Tell your Mam she's seen a ghost!'

And when she came back and told me, it sort of clicked – that is probably what he had to be.

When I asked her how long the sighting had lasted, Mrs Jones said:

Oh, just as we drew near and then passed him, he was five, perhaps six feet away at the most and we had only walked on a few feet when I looked back and he had gone.

She was silent for a moment, as if she was thinking back, then said,

I used to be on the Parish Council and, one night I was there, and you know how people chat before the meeting begins? Well, one man who had just come in said hello to the Councillor I was talking to – then he said:

'Are they still ploughing in Mynydd Bodafon?'

And the Councillor grinned at him and said:

'They're *always* ploughing in Mynydd Bodafon!'

At the time I thought what an odd thing to say, and then later when I got home it clicked!

So I *had* seen a ghost – and, what is more, other people had seen it too!

This seems to me to be a very odd sighting indeed – I wonder why the farm worker and the plough had materialised, but not the horse?

171

Getting to my house now, my children were quite small when we came to live here, and I was talking to the neighbour from down the road one day, my children were with me, and my neighbour looked up at the house and she said a very strange thing.

'Why do you choose to live in that house?' she asked, and I was very puzzled and I said,

'Well – why not?'

Then she looked down at the children and didn't say any more. Well, we hadn't been there long, my husband was at work in Bangor, the children were at school and I was working in the back garden, I looked down the side of the house and saw a young man in the front garden going to the door.

So I got up off my knees and went in and through the house and opened the front door, but there was no one there, and no one at all in the road, it was empty.

Another time my children and I were standing in the road, we were going for a walk, and my son was bending down to tie his shoelace, while we waited.

Then both my daughter and I saw a youngish man disappearing round the corner of the house to the back door which hardly anybody uses, we all use the front. No one had passed us; we were all alone on the road, so we were surprised. And my daughter said:

'Who's that going to our back door?'

My son was standing up now, and he looked blank and said:

'I didn't see anyone.'

'Go and see what he wants,' I said.

So he went through the front garden, down the side of the house and around to the back door, but he came back shrugging.

'There's no one there – I told you I hadn't seen anyone.'

But both my daughter and I had seen him, and we stared at each other.'

I then asked Mrs Jones if she could remember what the man wore. She hesitated and then –

'Well, I didn't really notice – I mean I would have seen if they'd been very old-fashioned, and he wasn't dressed up, otherwise I would have been curious. They were just sort of everyday clothes, working man's clothes.

A short time later, one night my husband and I couldn't sleep, so we decided to get up and make a cup of tea – I suppose it was about 2.00 or 3.00 a.m. and we went down to the kitchen.

I was standing at the sink in my nightie, filling the kettle, and I happened to look up at the little window over the sink. There, standing looking in at me was an old man. I can't remember whether he had a beard, but he had a crop of curly white hair and he was staring in with his nose squashed against the window pane.

He gave me an awful shock, I nearly dropped the kettle, and I said to Glyn:

'Look! There's somebody in the window!'

As soon as I said that, the face was pulled away and I thought he had gone on his way along the road. Glyn hadn't seen him, but he jumped up and went out to check. I thought it must be a tramp, because you don't expect to see anyone about at that time of night.

Although he didn't really look like a tramp.

Glyn came back and said there was no one about anywhere.

Many times at night I imagine there is someone standing at the door, I could swear he is standing by the glass panel. But I'm always too afraid to go and see. On those nights the dog barks and barks.

I remember when we first came to this house – my elderly parents lived with us then, at the other end of the house – and my mother said to my father:

'You know Dad, in the middle of the night, there was a man outside standing on the tarmac, gazing up at the house.'

Dad laughed it off and said,

'No-no, it was only someone passing.'

I know now that he knew what it was alright – he just didn't want to frighten us.'

Another night now, my husband had strolled down to the farm for a chat and a cup of tea, my parents were in the other end of the house, and my daughter and I were in the living room. She was looking out of the window, when she suddenly said:

'There's a man standing by our tree!'

I went to look and I said:

'Where?'

'Standing by the tree, he's still there – look!' And she pointed.

'I can't see a man there,' I said.

'He's moving now, he's going to the wall.'

My eyesight isn't too great, so I thought she must see him, and my eyes must be failing, 'cause I couldn't see anyone at all.

'He's staring at the house and I don't like it, Mam,' she said.

Well, a man in our garden was a prowler, as far as I was concerned, and I was still trying to see him, when my daughter ran in to my father and told him there was a strange man in our garden, staring at our house.

But Dad said to her:

'Oh, don't look at him, don't take any notice,' and he went on reading his paper. So my daughter came back to me, and said:

'Get Dad, ring him up and tell him to come home.

So I did, and asked for Glyn to come at once as we had a prowler in the back garden. He came back at once, and searched all over the place, but again he found nobody.

There is definitely something here – I've never seen anything in the house thank goodness – I'd be frightened to death!

But many people have seen something outside. I knew a lady who lives down in Hebron, her son and his friend often used to go for a drink at the California Inn and, when they came back, they had to walk by our house and they used to yell and shout to frighten off whatever it was that stood outside at night. She told me that her son's friend would never walk past on his own.

My father died about a month ago and he told me before he died that an old man called John Jones had lived here with his son. They were very close and, when the son was killed in an accident when he was coming back from Llannerch-y-medd, the old man was distraught.

He never recovered from the shock and died soon afterwards. So I don't know, we've seen the youngish man, and the old man, so perhaps that's who they were.

I wonder if these were the ghosts of devoted father and son, who were separated by the violent death of the young man.

174

They seem to be looking for each other – I wonder why they weren't reunited when the old man died?

Huw Jones Martha

Our good friend, Councillor Gwyn Roberts of Pen-y-sarn, called in one day with an authentic little story, full of local colour, which I enjoyed immensely. Councillor Roberts is known locally as a very good storyteller, and I shall put it down exactly as he told it.

Firstly, to explain about the Neave family, who had a large estate on the north-east coast of Anglesey. This was the family of Airie Neave, MP, who died so tragically in the 1980's when his car was blown up by a bomb attached to it by the IRA as he was leaving the underground car park at the Houses of Parliament. They were Lords of the Manor of Llys Dulas.

But to Councillor Roberts' story.

Owen Jones was a gamekeeper at Llys Dulas estate for the Neave family. He was generally called Owen Jones Fawr, not that he was all that big, but bigger than his mate who was also called Owen Jones and a gamekeeper as well.

Owen Jones Fawr lived at a tied cottage called Tynrhos Bach, at the edge of the estate woodland known as Nant-y-Bleddyn, a very depressing and lonely place. To help out with the money, his wife was a washerwoman at Llys Dulas, because it was hard to live on Owen Jones's wages – although a brace of pheasants was not unusual Sunday dinner for them, but on the quiet of course.

Owen was a very keen gamekeeper, his name known with dismay and respect by poachers. Poachers were a very familiar sight at the Magistrates Court in Amlwch, and Owen Jones was responsible for his fair share of 'the catch'.

One muggy evening in November, Owen decided he would go early to bed, as it was his night to watch for poachers, so after tea he decided he would walk to Nebo to get his weekly allowance of tobacco from the little general shop and then home and bed.

He stopped and had a chat in Nebo with one or two of his friends, exchanging local news and gossip. One, in particular he spoke to, was Huw Jones Martha – in the old days it was the mother's name that came after the surname. Huw lived with his widowed mother in a cottage at Nebo. He worked as a casual labourer here and there on farms. He didn't seem to like a lot of work but he was not in good health and the bit of money that he earned went on doctor's fees and medicine.

After he bought his tobacco, Owen Jones Fawr returned home and went straight to bed. Sleep didn't come easy, he was under pressure from the Lord of the Manor who had guests coming for a big shoot that weekend and he had to save all the game for the shoot.

About 2.30 a.m. he got up, made himself a cup of tea, went to fetch his gun and set off. He did not follow the road along the woodland of Nant-y-Bleddyn, in case someone saw him, but with all the natural born caution of a good gamekeeper, he went quietly through the fields towards Graigwen.

It was a wild night, the wind blowing hard from the east, the moon shining intermittently between the scudding clouds. When he approached the road leading from Nebo to Llys Dulas, he decided to have a breather and, crouching down under the road wall out of the wind, he had a chew of tobacco and listened intently to the night sounds.

After a little while, his ears detected a new noise. The creak of wood, harnesses jingling and horses hooves approaching. Very curious, he raised himself quietly to his feet and stood silently watching with his head just over the top of the wall. There, passing Twrllachiad·farm, clearly to be seen in the moonlight, and coming down from Nebo on the road to Dulas church, he could clearly see two beautifully groomed black horses drawing a hearse.

Shivers ran like cold water down his back as he watched, for there in the hearse, as it passed him, was an open coffin and in it lay Huw Jones Martha. Owen Jones could not move, he had to hang on to the wall as his legs gave way and he stared until the hearse went out of sight. It was almost half an hour before his strength returned, then he made for home in a state of deep shock and told his wife what he had seen. She gave him a cup of tea and sent him to bed to rest, he was so shaken and distressed.

The next day a farm hand from Nebo brought the news that Huw Jones Martha was dead.

Not long after Owen Jones left him at Nebo that evening, Huw was taken ill and he only lasted a few hours before he died.

Miss Jarvis

To the east of the village of Nebo, which lies above Pen-y-sarn, stands a grand mansion called Bryn-y-Môr. This was originally built for the Llys Dulas family, but after passing through the hands of different owners, is now a home for the elderly.

Sometime between 1900 and 1910, one Mrs Jarvis bought the house, and her unmarried daughter. Miss Jarvis was a pretty girl, in her late twenties, accomplished with her needle, her watercolour paintings and played the piano very well.

Mrs Jarvis was not without money, she employed a good staff of both indoor and outdoor servants and, although she always dined well, she never entertained and refused all invitations from people who wanted to welcome the newcomers. The fact that Mrs Jarvis was so aloof and no one knew of their background, their previous history or where they came from, gave rise to a lot of speculation and, as is usual in any village, they were viewed with friendly curiosity, but being good employers, looked upon with loyalty and respect.

One or two of the older female staff noted that Miss Jarvis seemed to be putting on weight – and as the weeks passed it became evident that she was pregnant.

Imagine the gossip that flared up and went around the village like wild fire. She had obviously been in the first stages of pregnancy when they moved to Bryn-y-Môr – there wasn't a man in sight, either a husband or even a fiancé – and she didn't even pretend to be married, by wearing a ring or calling herself Mrs. This, in the early 1900's, was a great scandal and, as her pregnant condition became more obvious, she became more of a recluse, spending hours in the house or walking in the wooded grounds of the estate with her two beloved large white dogs.

After a few months, she was delivered of a baby boy. It was not an easy birth, labour being long and difficult, and the child itself was weak and sickly.

He only lived until he was three years old, spending much of his short life with his nurse. Whether his mother was too frail to look after him or whether, in truth, she had no love for him is not recorded, but his death gave rise to much talk in the village. Some said he had been smothered with a pillow and, one of the most lurid stories was, that his mother had injected an orange with poison and fed it to him.

Far-fetched as some of the stories were, it was finally brought to the notice of the police, who made enquiries amongst the staff and neighbours, even questioning Miss Jarvis herself and her doctor, before deciding there was no truth in the rumours and they sternly scotched all surmise.

Poor Miss Jarvis! Whatever had happened before in her life was unknown to anyone, but the shame of bearing an illegitimate child, then his sudden death in infancy must have been very hard to bear. What her Mother's attitude was will never be known, but she must have known about the local gossip.

Never strong after the birth, lonely and sad, her health gradually declined and she died before she was thirty-five. Her mother sold the house and left, presumably returning to her former location, wherever that may have been.

She hadn't been dead for many months, when stories began to circulate that the figure of a woman had been seen by local people, moving amongst the trees on the estate of Bryn-y-Môr. Infrequently over weeks, the form seen drifting about was observed by at least six people and identified as Miss Jarvis, as whoever (or whatever) it was, always had a couple of white dogs walking beside it.

Gradually, the sightings were seen less and less often and finally stopped altogether. Over the years, people forgot and the sad tale died, until many years later, when this happened:

John Owen was a farm labourer who lived with his family in a cottage called Pen Bonc, on the west side of Mynydd Llaneilian. He worked at Bryn Fuches, a farm close to the mansion of Llys Dulas, and about a mile away from his cottage as the crow flies. He was 55 years old and, like every other farm labourer in those days, he worked very hard, from 6.00 a.m. to 8.00 p.m., seven days a week, even more at harvesting.

One summer morning John awoke from a sound sleep and looked at his bedside clock. It had stopped at 3.00 a.m., but being June, it was light and sunny. He slid quietly out of bed, not waking his wife, and took his pocket watch out of his waistcoat. It too had stopped at 3.00 a.m., which seemed an odd coincidence, but as he didn't want to be late, he tiptoed downstairs and looked at the grandfather clock.

He stood and stared at the silent clock, the pendulum still and the fingers pointing to – three o'clock.

John frowned – what was going on? Outside the sun was well up. He tiptoed upstairs, careful not to wake his sleeping family and got ready for work. A breakfast of tea and bread and butter, and he was away, with no idea of the time.

From Pen Bonc, up the lane to the main track, then on to the footpath called Trydd Bryn-y-Môr, hoping all the time that he was not late for work. The footpath leads to a stile at the end of the Trydd on the main road and, nearby, stands the large white gates of Bryn-y-Môr.

John was climbing the stile when he heard the clock at Llys Dulas chiming, so he paused and counted the strokes. 5.00 a.m. Thank goodness, he was early, plenty of time to walk the half a mile up to the farm and work. He settled down on the top of the stile and relaxed. Birds were singing, the morning sun shone warmly and he was at peace with the world. He took out his tobacco pouch and clasp knife and opened the pouch wherein he kept his chewing tobacco. Cutting off a sizeable plug, he popped it into his mouth and sat back contentedly, knowing he had minutes to spare.

The main gates to Bryn-y-Môr were only about six yards away, in full view and, suddenly, out of the corner of his eye, John saw a movement. Looking towards the gates, his jaw dropped and he froze. Coming towards him were two large white dogs. Their claws made no sound on the gravel and, although they were looking in his direction, they didn't seem to see him as they drew nearer.

Behind them on the drive, a young woman paced slowly along. Her dress was floor-length, high-necked and long sleeved, in the long-gone Edwardian style. She was tall, elegant, her hair was beautifully dressed, but her pretty face was terribly sad and she wore an air of deep desolation as she continued her lonely walk. Seemingly unaware of him, she turned off the drive and, with the dogs at her side, disappeared into the woods.

To John, sitting transfixed on the stile, the morning air seemed to have become colder. He knew, from all the descriptions he had heard, that he had just seen the ghost of Miss Jarvis and her two beloved dogs, walking in the grounds of Bryn-y-Môr, as she had done nearly every day of her brief life.

John was deeply shocked. All ideas of work had left him and he got up and rushed back home like a drunken man. Back at the house, he saw that all the clocks were going again and on time.

It took him three days to get over the shock. He never used that path again.

Councillor Roberts (Pen-y-sarn), who typed this story for me, says that John Owen told him this story many times, it had affected him deeply and never varied one iota in the telling, which convinces Councillor Roberts that John spoke the truth.

*'He was very reluctant to pass the large white gates of Bryn-y-Môr even in the daytime and, when he did, he kept his gaze firmly on the road before him,' says Gwyn Roberts, 'he has quite a few grandchildren living in the area, but he never told this story to any of them, perhaps he didn't want **them** to be scared of passing Bryn-y-Môr.'*

The patch of blackness

One afternoon last winter, Councillor Roberts of Pen-y-sarn, kindly found the time to visit me and be interviewed on tape. He had a most interesting story to tell, which had been handed down to him from his grandmother, to whom the following frightening event happened. After we had a panad, Councillor Roberts settled back in his chair, I switched on the tape recorder, and he began.

My grandmother lost her mother when she was about twelve years old. They lived then at the Grand Lodge in Llys Dulas with her father and her younger sister. She stayed at home for a couple of years to look after her sister, then she got appointed as a maid at Tyddyn Mawr near Bryn-y-Môr. In those days, maids would live and sleep at the place of their employment and were allowed one day off a week, when they went home to their families. It wasn't really a day off, as they used the time to do their washing and collect their clean clothes and aprons for next week's work. But they were with their family and enjoyed passing on news and gossip.

And that is what my grandmother did. She was coming back one sunny evening in summer, a Sunday evening it was, so she could start work early on Monday morning. Well, as I said, it was full daylight, and quite warm and sunny, and she was just approaching the big gates at Bryn-y-Môr when, all of a sudden, everything went black.

It wasn't like the darkness of night time, when you can sense the things around you and, perhaps, feel the slightest stir of air. It was total blackness, like being shut away in a closed box – totally devoid of light.

The girl was completely paralysed, unable to move any part of her body and she felt as if her feet had been glued to the ground. She felt as if all normal life had stopped, everything was silent and still, as if she was in a pitch-black void.

The shock and fright were so great, she cried out, but heard nothing but her own voice for what seemed an interminable time, but was actually about two minutes. Frozen to the spot, unable to move, try as she might, she called frantically for help.

Eventually, when she stopped screaming to draw breath, she heard a voice – it was the voice of her master you see, from Tyddyn Mawr.

And he was saying 'Suzannah – Suzannah – are you there?'

She was so glad to hear his voice and she shouted back: 'Yes, yes – I'm here – come and help me – I'm here!

'Where?' he asked, 'Where are you – I can't see you!' And he was looking around everywhere.

'It's all dark,' she shouted, 'I don't know where I am!'

He couldn't see her, he couldn't even see the black patch. Then, all of a sudden it was gone, disappearing as quickly as it came, and she could see Bryn-y-Môr gate and her master standing not far away.

To him, one minute the whole area was empty and the next his little maid appeared as if by magic, in a spot that one second before was an empty stretch of countryside.

Distressed and frightened, she ran to meet him.

Afterwards, her mistress was very hard to convince, when they tried to explain to her. First, she thought the girl had been hiding somewhere, next that they were both trying to play a silly trick – but they were both so adamant and perplexed she finally realised it was true, however farfetched it sounded.

Master stood on the hearth rug looking completely baffled.

'I could see – I could see everything all around, the fields and the footpath were completely empty, I couldn't see **any** blackness anywhere – the sun was shining everywhere. I could hear the girl shouting and crying so close – so close – her voice was only a few yards away yet *there was no one there!*'

He thumped his fist into his palm to emphasize his words –

'Then all of a sudden – there she was! She just appeared in the place I was looking at. One minute – emptiness – then, there she was!'

He sank into his chair, hands dangling between his knees and shook his head dazedly – there was silence as they all tried to work out an explanation. There was none.

I interrupted here:
*'You mean he could see **through** the place where she was standing?'*

Councillor Roberts nodded.

'Yes, he could see – he could see everything. One second he could see where he thought her voice was coming from – and he couldn't see her – the next second there she was!'

Then I asked, 'as if she was in another dimension?'

Councillor Roberts said thoughtfully, 'Yes – yes, that was it – another dimension. It was never explained and it never happened again, but it is still a mystery.'

* * *

After I had transcribed this story, I was telling one of my friends about it. She had just returned from a visit to her sister, who lived in the mid-west of America. She was quite excited about it, and told me that her sister had heard a very curious story from her American mother-in-law.

Apparently, in the early nineteen-thirties, a young farmer who lived locally was strolling through one of his fields with his wife and two young children. The children were picking flowers, their mother had hung back with them and their father was walking ahead in full view of them all.

As in Councillor Roberts's story, it was a warm summer day and there was no one else or any animals nearby.

Suddenly, the man cried out his wife's name.

'Where are you,' he cried, 'I can't see anything, everything's gone dark!'

His wife and family looked up and he was nowhere in sight. At first, the children thought he was hiding and ran towards the spot with whoops of delight, but he wasn't lying in the grass, and he went on shouting, his voice sounding more terrified with each moment.

They all passed and repassed the spot where his voice came from, but encountered nothing solid. His wife became very afraid and sent the eldest child back home to fetch his grandfather. He came running with a neighbour, but they couldn't find the man anywhere.

Eventually, most of the people from the neighbourhood turned out and made a chain by holding hands across the width of the field. Darkness came and, by now, his family was frantic, he was still calling and his voice was getting hoarser. He didn't seem able to hear them, although they could hear him. Someone stayed at the spot, never leaving it alone, but time passed, his voice became weaker and weaker, until after five days it finally faded out.

He has never been seen since.

Tyddyn Mawr

Mr Gwyn Roberts had another story to tell about the strange events around Tyddyn Mawr.

Another evening now, my grandmother was still working there, it was very late at night, they we all just about to go to bed, when there came a knock at the door and they all looked at each other.

The knock came again, louder now, and the farmer got out of his chair to go into the hall. As he did, the knocking became louder and the farmer called, 'Who's there?'

But there was no answer, just the knocking, thunderous it was and so hard it made the door shake.

The front door of Tyddyn Mawr farmhouse was quite low, with a glass above it, a fanlight, and anyone tall, the tops of their heads anyway, could be seen in this glass.

So the farmer walked back a bit from the door and looked through the fanlight. He saw a policeman's helmet in the glass and he thought it looked old fashioned, but as it was a policeman, he knew it was safe to open the door, and he also thought the policeman needed help and that was why he was knocking so loud and urgently.

As he turned the big key, and shot back the bolt, the knocking still went on.

'Hold on – hold on – I'm coming!' he shouted as he opened the door. As soon as the door started to open, the knocking instantly stopped.

He flung the door wide.

There was no one there.

My grandmother said her master looked all over the yard, but there was no one about and when they talked about it afterwards, they wondered if it had anything to do with the trouble there had been about Miss Jarvis, when she was alive, and if it was connected to that. By that time, of course, she was long dead.

Hen Felin

Roughly two miles before reaching Amlwch on the Bangor road, a signpost to Llaneilian is the start of a pleasant winding road that leads down to the village, its historical ancient church and tiny sheltered cove. 'Hen Felin' or the 'Old Mill' stands at the top of a steep, rocky outcrop about a quarter of a mile down here. In actual fact, the old mill itself lies beyond the present whitewashed house that bears its name and its ruinous foundations can be seen further along the bridle path near the stream.

Though little trace of the building can be seen today, in the eighteenth century it was a thriving corn mill and, about 1786, a young man named William Roberts lived there with his mother and father and younger sister. They had moved to Hen Felin from Llanfechell when William was about five years old. The whole family – uncles, aunts, cousins etc. who still lived at Llanfechell were devout chapel goers, in fact William's cousin, John Elias, grew up to be a famous Revivalist preacher.

Working class people in the eighteenth century didn't usually go to school, but those who were determined to better themselves picked up an education where and if they could. When William's father was young, he wanted to learn to read before he started working – so he approached a local man of letters and asked to be taught. Being honest and poor, he told the man that he had no money to pay for lessons; the only thing he had of any value was his bed, a sturdy piece of furniture he had made and carved himself.

The bargain was struck and, once young Roberts could read fluently – he handed over his bed. History has no record of how he slept after that!

At that time, religion was very strong on the island and chapel was by far the most important influence on most people's lives, so Roberts senior must have wondered how on earth he had fathered such a Godless-seeming lad as William, who had grown up to be a 'rowing boy' (as they called him then) despite the flawless behaviour of his parents.

He wasn't bad, just wild and high-spirited, and his style of living caused raised eyebrows and pursed lips amongst the neighbours. A cheerful, hardworking young man, he had a great sense of fun, loved to flirt, go around with his own sort and go drinking on Saturday and Sunday nights.

Who could blame him? He worked hard all week at the copper mines on Mynydd Parys. Conditions were abominable. Lowered in metal buckets on ropes to the various mine levels which honeycombed the open sides of the mountain's centre, they were exposed to driving icy rain in winter, soaked by the water trickling from the mine roof, usually working in wet clothes in the freezing cold galleries.

Life was cheap, death from accidents and injuries run of the mill and terminal lung complaints from poisonous sulphur fumes quite usual. The life span of a miner was not a long one.

William was popular amongst his own age group. Intelligent, quick and a real daredevil, some of his lively ways made him a lot of enemies.

Such a one was a very grumpy old woman who lived in a low cottage just across the main Bangor road from the Llaneilian lane which William travelled every day to work. She always stood by her gate to watch for William on his way past. She called him many names, declaring he was heathen and a son of the Devil – and foretelling of the terrible fate which would overtake him if he didn't mend his ways.

One Spring day, very early, William and a couple of work mates were going past – no sign of the old woman, but thick smoke coming out showed she had just lit her fire. William stopped the lads with one hand, putting a finger to his lips and picked up a large flat slate which was leaning against the wall. With a wink, he quietly climbed onto the low roof and laid the slate squarely across the top of the chimney.

Smoke poured down on the old lady just as she was putting the kettle on for a cup of tea. The lads outside heard a great coughing and spluttering – and she burst out of the smoke-filled cottage just in time to see William vaulting over the garden wall, and he and the others legged it up the road to the mine, weak with laughing.

He knew the slate was easy to remove by pushing her clothes prop up the short chimney and dislodging it, but his father's anger wasn't so easy to push aside. William got the full force of it when he got home to hear how the furious old woman had descended on Hen Felin, telling Mr Roberts he should have more control over his son.

Poor William, his greatest sin was his appetite for a full and joyous life; he could never embrace the narrow, constricting rules of his family.

So every Sunday evening, although the family all left Hen Felin at the same time, their ways parted when they had all walked down to Tŷ Croes crossroads. Father, Mother and sister turned left to go soberly to chapel in the Port, but William always turned right to go to Tŷ Siôn Rowland, the house of Rowland, which was a little pub frequented by William and some like-minded others. Not a house of sin, by any means, just a jolly place with cheerful people, laughter, song and a drink or two.

Anyhow, on a pleasant sunlit Sunday evening, the little family split up at the crossroads, as usual William turned right to go to Tŷ Siôn Rowland, waving a cheerful farewell, and blandly ignoring his parents' disapproving faces. He started to whistle happily as he strode along, looking forward to the evening.

The family hadn't gone far when they heard a ghastly piercing scream, followed by another, hoarser and deeper, coming from the direction of the church along the road that William had just taken.

They all stopped and stared at each other in horror.

'Will!' his father said, and without another word turned and ran back along the road, closely followed by his womenfolk holding up their heavy, cumbersome skirts.

William had left them only seconds before, but the road was empty. They ran on nearly to the church, which he could not possibly have reached, then back to the crossroads.

No one.

Frantic now, they started back again to Tŷ Siôn Rowland, when they heard a terrible retching noise in the field at the side of the field. There in the field, yards away from the road, William lay sprawled, face upwards. He was semi-conscious and fighting for breath. His family scrambled over the wall and ran to him. His face was suffused and purple – encircling his neck was a belt of angry looking red weals already beginning to turn blue and swelling rapidly. Roberts senior lifted him to a sitting position against his leg and tried to fan air into his tortured lungs with his hat.

As he came round and looked at them in a daze, he tried to speak and winced with pain. When he was able, he staggered weakly to his feet and they supported him back to Hen Felin. No chapel for them tonight.

The hot tea his Mother made to revive him, he could not swallow, but later, in a hoarse voice, he told them what had happened.

Soon after he had left them, he said, he was walking along the deserted road, when he was stopped dead.

'There was nothing I could do,' he said wonderingly. 'I couldn't move – neither my feet nor arms, I had one foot raised to take a step forward – but I just *stuck* – I froze. Then something huge seemed to grip my throat – it was all around my neck, like a giant clamp – then it lifted me into the air, I thought it was going to tear my head off. It was so tight I couldn't breathe; I was being choked to death. Everything was going dark – I tried to grab it and pull it off, but there was nothing to get hold of Dad – *there was nothing there!*'

He must have passed out then, because he had no knowledge of how he came to be lying in the field, yards away from the road. His father listened gravely. Whatever William had encountered, it seemed to have had the strength to lift him, a tall, strong young man, off his feet and toss him over the wall into the field like a bag of chaff, with great ease.

When William had fallen into a troubled doze on the sofa, his father went back to the place where they had found William. He examined the field and road carefully, but there was no sign of any struggle that might have taken place and the quiet road was as peaceful as ever.

All week poor Will seemed to be in shock. He was quiet and abstracted and very, very thoughtful. On Saturday, usually the highlight of the week at Rowlands, he never mentioned going out that night at all and, on Sunday, he timidly asked his father if he could join them at chapel that evening.

To Mr Roberts' delight, William became a regular chapelgoer. His character seemed to change completely, and he was serious and earnest, where before he had always seemed reckless and frivolous. He wanted to learn to read properly and, when he told his father, Mr Rowlands made arrangements for him to have lessons with his cousin, John Elias, already a minister.

John Elias and his father were excellent businessmen, making superb carpets for wealthy people in the district. They carpeted Mona Lodge, in Amlwch. They still lived in Llanfechell. John Elias was only too pleased to teach his young cousin to read and William tramped all the way to Llanfechell three or four times a week, after work.

His days were very full. Up early every morning to help prepare the day's work at Hen Felin for his father, then tramp to Mynydd Parys to his job there. When that was finished, he would walk to Llanfechell for his reading session. He was so assiduous in his studies that he worked until the small hours, then snatch a couple of hours' sleep there before walking back home, help his father, eat his breakfast and back to the mine.

At Llanfechell, the family house boasted a fine library and, as William's reading widened, he spent many hours in it, lost in religious books and tracts. John Elias was impressed by his commitment and intelligence, and readily taught William how to preach when he was asked. So William became a good preacher.

Cousin John and his father thought the young man was steady and reliable and decided to give him a chance in business. He took a small shop in Amlwch, which in those days was a boom town. John Elias and his father helped initially with the financing and much to his delight, William started to prosper. The recklessness of his youth had not been entirely smothered by time however and the horrible supernatural experience, which had led him to give up his earlier way of life, was now just a memory. John Elias chided him many times on his lack of caution in business deals, but Will took little heed.

Clothing, furniture and other household goods were his stock in trade, which, when his shop was full, he stored in a small warehouse nearby.

He started to travel to Liverpool and buy his goods there and, one of his business associates, put him in the way of a 'good thing', a stock of goods which were to be sold the following week by a firm who was giving up trading, which he could have if he could find the purchasing price.

William knew he was on to a good thing and came back to Amlwch to meet John Elias and his father. William could raise some of the cash, but not enough, and asked if they would lend him the outstanding sum needed.

He was not encouraged by his family. They knew now that he had hardly any business acumen, likeable chap that he was otherwise, and did their best to dissuade him. That made him all the more stubborn and he told them he would go through with the transaction without their help, even if it meant selling the shirt off his back.

William, saved, begged and borrowed the money, and took the coach from Bangor to Liverpool where he bought the goods.

Next, he hired an old barge, it was cheap to hire, but it took nearly all the money he had left. He oversaw the loading and gave the Captain instructions to land at Traeth Dulas – Dulas Beach – where the goods would be unloaded into two carts which he would have waiting there.

Until now, dame Fortune had smiled on William Roberts and, journeying home, he thought gleefully about how he would still stand to make a good profit, even after paying back all his debts.

Alas! Within sight of the Anglesey coast, a sudden vicious storm blew up and raged around the leaky old barge. Loaded and wallowing, it slowly sank, the crew were saved, but the boat and all its cargo were lost.

Thus, William Roberts became a penniless bankrupt and, after a furious row with his relatives, who had warned him of the folly of putting all his eggs in one basket, John Elias and his father severed all connections with William, who after this seems to have fallen into obscurity.

Cadi Randall (Catherine Randall)

Amongst the hundreds of poor immigrant workers who were employed in the great copper mines on Mynydd Parys in the middle of the eighteenth century was one John Randall, who, with his wife and two daughters, Catherine and Ellen, came to live at Parc Bach, near Glanrafon. The records show that he lived there and worked at the mine between 1755 and 1761, but there is no trace of him after that.

Ellen was a quiet, gentle girl, who eventually got married and moved away, but Catherine was headstrong and coarse, with wilful ways.

Amlwch's mining and shipping industries were in full spate at that time; it had become a boomtown and was now a drunken, riotous place.

Cadi was drawn to its lively licentiousness and, very soon, added to its notoriety. Her name as a prostitute was heard in many ports, she was always drunk and her foul language outmatched the most hardened miner.

'Swearing like Cadi Randall' became a phrase used daily as a damning reproach.

The proceeds of prostitution paid for her drink and she staggered blearily from pub to pub. Gin inflamed her always smouldering temper and, heaven help whoever crossed her, she cursed them loudly enough to be heard streets away.

Her attractions were slight, but even these faded with age and the ravages of drink and, in 1788, for the first time in her life, she tottered into chapel in the middle of a service. The congregation's heads swivelled in disbelief, the minister's voice faltered, but he managed to give a welcoming smile before he carried on.

Cadi sat at the back, staring hard at the walls, the minister and the people. Should anyone turn their heads to glance her way, they were met by Cadi's cold glare. She clattered out noisily before the service had ended.

The first time, but not the last. By now, Cadi was 45, her way of life was becoming harder – younger and prettier girls had taken her place and her customers were becoming fewer. She lived alone in a filthy little hovel at the foot of the great tip on Mynydd Parys, for which she paid two shillings per year to the Marquis of Anglesey.

Her visits to the chapel became more frequent, but still irregular and at odd times, she came and went and spoke to no one, ignoring the smiles and greetings with a hard stare.

The elders of the chapel were nonplussed and, as perplexed as much as the congregation, but it was discussed at the next meeting. Why was she coming? Why repulse the overtures of the people? Was it really that she was coming to them for help and didn't know how to declare it?

But the elders were kindly people, and they decided to send a small deputation to Cadi's cottage to show her they were willing to assist her.

So they did, asking if she would come to chapel regularly and, telling her, that if she changed her ways, they would do their best to find her honest work.

It took more than one visit, but seeing the meagre furnishing in the cottage and how little food she had, each time they went, they took small gifts, a homemade cake, maybe a blanket, or a warm skirt.

Gradually though, she came to chapel more regularly and people who welcomed her were rewarded with a nod.

At last, Cadi started domestic work, mainly scrubbing and cleaning, but her positions were many and short-lived, as her furious temper still flared frequently and, in her rage, she would smash the furniture at the slightest provocation.

She owed it to the perseverance of the patient chapel elders, who encouraged people to employ her and very, very gradually Cadi calmed down.

But she was ageing, early debauchery had taken its toll and the hard work became too much for her, as her health began to fail. Then she found a new, much lighter trade as a feather dresser. She went from house to house, sorting feathers according to their suitability, for pillows and mattresses. Soft breast feathers were used to fill the pillows she made and the coarser back and wing feathers for mattresses.

She was in great demand at farms and houses, as most people in those days dressed their own poultry and saved the feathers.

Cadi followed this trade for years – there are no records existing as to where she learned her craft, but she did become expert and went to most houses in the district, where she always had a meal and was paid a small sum.

At the age of sixty, she consented to become a convert at Capel Mwd, but it didn't change her much – she was grumpy and short-tempered and would, occasionally, still become violent if she was criticised, leading the people to be very wary of her and, some even wondered if she had become converted because the influential chapel elders looked after her well-being, making sure she had enough food and work.

The winter of 1828 was long and cruel and, on a cold February day, Cadi died aged 85, in her tiny cottage. Her funeral procession was huge; hundreds of people followed her coffin, because Cadi Randall had become a legend all over the district.

Catherine Randall was laid to rest in St Eleth's church at Amlwch and her body lay at peace.

But not, apparently, her spirit.

On a dark, windy night, two weeks later, two mine workers were on their way home from Mynydd Parys, their heads bent against the cold east wind. One, glancing up, suddenly grasped his companion's arm and stopped dead, outside the empty cottage.

'Cadi Randall!' he muttered.

There, outlined strangely in the dark, the figure of an old woman was standing in the open doorway. She neither moved nor spoke, but seemed to be looking right through them.

The other man was struck dumb – it was indeed Cadi. They averted their gaze, looking down and the first man shoved the other forward with his shoulder. As they set off again, their steps became quicker and quicker, until, not daring to look behind them, they broke into a panic-stricken run and fled all the way to Amlwch, falling gratefully into the noise and light of the first pub they came to.

Of course, everyone scoffed at their story, but they knew what they had seen and stubbornly stuck to the fact that they had seen Cadi Randall at her door.

As time went by, more and more people saw Cadi always at night.

Sometimes she was seen walking over the mountain, sometimes near her cottage and everyone who saw the figure swore it was Cadi Randall, recognising her apron, her long thick skirts and her boots. She always looked solid and life-like, her familiar shuffling steps could be heard, but she seemed completely unaware of living people and passed through stonewalls and closed gates as if they weren't there.

No one could be persuaded to live in her cottage and people hated even passing it. Gradually it became a ruin and, unlike other places, it wasn't cannibalised for its stones, to mend walls and such, everyone avoided the area of the big tip where she had lived.

Cadi Randall died in 1828, but she is still seen, mainly picked out by the headlights of cars going over Mynydd Parys at night.

Amlwch people say that Cadi still walks. Is it possible that her conversion wasn't wholly sincere, otherwise why is her spirit so restless?

Cannwyll Corff on Mynydd Parys

Mrs Mair Williams, whose family can be traced back on the Island for many generations, also had a very interesting tale about her great-grandfather, Mr John Davies.

As a young boy, he started work at the Parys mine as a labourer. By dint of his intelligence and very hard work he, eventually, became a mine agent, a very important position. Also, as doctors were few, far-between and expensive, and the mine accidents were numerous, he taught himself the rudiments of first aid and medicine, and became very well-known for his skills with leeches for 'bleeding' people.

Safety precautions at the mine were elementary and many men died where they worked at the face.

One winter's night, walking home from work over the mountain, he noticed a glow of light moving before him along the path. At first Mr Davies thought it was a fellow miner going home, but the light was an eerie greeny-blue, which did not flicker and jerk as a hand held light would, but floated smoothly along a couple of feet above the ground.

He could not catch up with it, hurry as he might, and he just reached the foot of the mountain when the light came to a halt, hovered for a full minute and then vanished. Mr Davies also stopped, puzzled as to where the light had gone, snuffing out like it did and leaving no trace.

Suddenly, realising what he had seen, he went cold.

He knew now, it was the Cannwyll Corff (Corpse Candle) which always foretold a death.

His wife, Elizabeth, greeted him cheerfully when he got home but her smile faded when she saw his expression.

He told her his story as she helped him off with his boots and, by the time he had finished, her face wore a grave frown. They both knew what it meant to see the Cannwyll Corff and its location was of special interest. Nothing was amiss with any of their families, and the Cannwyll Corff had been on the mountain, so they wondered if that was where the death would take place.

Next day, John Davies had not been at work for very long,

when he heard shouting outside his office and the sound of running feet. As he went out to look, he saw a silent group of miners coming into the yard from the mine, carrying a lifeless body. It was a young boy of sixteen, who had been killed by a roof collapse. His body was placed on a cart and taken slowly down the mountain back to the home he had left only hours before.

John Davies accompanied the grim-faced miner who was leading the horse, who had the unenviable task of breaking the news to the boy's mother and, as the sad little procession wended its way down the mountain, John realised that the corpse candle had gone out just above the place in the mine where the roof had collapsed, burying the young lad.

*   *   *

John Davies led a very interesting life, both as mine agent and 'surgeon' as they were called and, one day (around 1878), Sir Arundel Neave lay dying at Llys Dulas, the Neave family mansion, the coachman was sent post-haste to fetch John Davies. Sir Arundel's mother sent instructions for him to come at once, and bring his leeches. The coachman was commanded to make all speed and John just had time to grab his precious leeches and coat before he was bundled into the coach.

Although they went so fast that 'sparks were flying from the horses hooves' they arrived too late.

John Davies pronounced Sir Arundel to be dead, but his frantic mother wouldn't believe it, and commanded John to apply the leeches. He shook his head, knowing it was useless, but she pleaded so much, in the end he gave in, and placed the leeches on the body. But the blood was dead, and this was fatal for the leeches. One after another, they curled up and died, so John lost all his leeches.

Ghost with a message

Mrs Mair Williams, of Pengorffwysfa, is an author and lecturer and, amongst her other talents, is an authority on Welsh legends and traditional Welsh handicrafts. She is the owner of a beautiful handmade Welsh shawl and gives talks on how it was made and the lifestyles of people at that time. Mair intersperses her lectures with true stories and old folklore tales.

One night she was telling an old story about a haunted farm.

On one of the slopes of Mynydd Parys, below the vast spoil heaps of the old copper mines, stands Trysglwyn farm, nestled in green meadows.

The farm tenant of Trysglwyn, early in the last century, was a very honest, hardworking man. One winter's night, he was going round checking his stock as usual, when he saw the tall figure of a man, watching him from the shadow of the barn. When the moon swam out from behind the scudding clouds, it lit up the figure, showing it to be dressed in old-fashioned clothes and wearing a tall 'stove-pipe' hat.

They stared at each other for a long moment and then, to the farmer's disbelief, the figure started to become indistinct, fading slowly, until it vanished altogether. The farmer suddenly realised he had seen a ghost, rushed back indoors and gabbled out the story to his wife.

This was only the first appearance. The ghost returned very often and always at night when the farmer was doing his rounds. He became frightened of venturing out in the dark, knowing that if he looked round, he would see the tall, silent man behind him.

He became morose and nervous, until in desperation his wife asked him to seek the help of the Methodist minister, who, far from scoffing at the story, gravely told him to gather his friends and relatives at the farm for a prayer meeting.

This was arranged and the house was crowded with these good folk when the minister arrived. Surrounded by everyone who wished him well, the farmer felt reassured and earnestly joined in the solemn prayers.

After the meeting was over, the minister had a private meeting with the farmer, and told him that he felt sure the ghost wanted to tell him something, and advised him not to be afraid, but the next time the ghost appeared, he must ask it what it wanted, as a ghost could not speak unless it was addressed first.

The next night, as he was crossing the yard, he saw the ghost standing silently, a few feet away. His legs promptly turned to jelly and, with a mouth so dry he could hardly speak, he summoned up all his courage and finally managed to ask the spectre what it wanted.

The ghost, in a slow, deep, voice, requested him to get a spade and pointing to a spot near the well, told him to dig, then waited patiently for the farmer as he fumbled with the stable door and found his 'mucking out' shovel, which was quite unsuitable for digging. Finally, with his sharpest spade in his hands, he weakly started work, watched all the time by the silent, eerie figure.

As he worked, he found his strength coming back and dug mightily until his spade rang on metal. He freed the object, with great difficulty from the ground and exposed a heavy cauldron and, even as he lifted it from its burial place, the moon glinted on the golden guineas that filled it.

'Take it into the house,' said the ghost, 'now it is yours, but do not look back.'

So the farmer did, and became rich.

Mair said she always told this story with her tongue in her cheek – a ghost story – or a fairy tale?

One night, about six years ago she told this story to a meeting of ladies – at this point she always grinned at her audience, who chuckled at the unexpected ending.

But, on this night, one old lady frowned sternly at her and said severely –

'Don't laugh at this story. It is true. My great grandfather was at the prayer meeting and, later on, he saw the cauldron of golden guineas. Then the minister asked all the same people to attend a special service to give rest and peace to the ghost. It was never seen again.'

'Also,' said the old lady, clinching the story with a final point, 'much later on, my mother became kitchen maid at the farm and told us that a black cauldron hung from a beam in the kitchen and no one must touch it.'

'Apparently, this gave every one food for thought,' Mair said, and her smile vanished, as did everyone else's!

The miller and the ghost in the tree

In the last half of the eighteenth century, at Rhos Fawr, a few miles inland from Benllech, stood a thriving corn mill, Melin Rhos Fawr, now a ruin.

The flour was taken daily to Amlwch by horse and cart, winter and summer, by the oldest mill hand. He used the old tortuous winding road, full of potholes and ruts. Passing Bodafon farm was an 'S' bend in those days, but now the farm stands well back from the modern road, which slices straight across between Bodafon and the Pilot Boat Inn. In the late years of the 1700's, old trees stood thickly on both sides of the road between the farm and the pub, their thick branches darkening the patch of road on which they stood.

One cold, dark January morning, the cart was trundling its creaky way to Amlwch, with the old man hunched on the front, fingers blue with cold. As he entered the trees, the old man glanced up. There, directly above him, sat a figure, motionless on a bough, staring intently down at him. Although it was pitch-dark, he could see it clearly in the dim glow that surrounded it.

The old man stared in horror and tried to hurry the horse out of the trees, but of course it wouldn't, just plodded along at its own speed, with the old man peering terrified back over his shoulder. The figure never moved.

He arrived at Amlwch pale and shaken and blurted out to the group of men waiting for him that he had seen a ghost.

They greeted his story with jeers and general derision, telling him he had been drinking too much ale the night before but he stuck doggedly to his story, vehemently declaring that he had seen the eerie figure of a man, sitting in the branches of one of the trees at Bodafon looking down at him.

Finally, he relapsed into silence when he realised they didn't believe him, and sat huddled in a corner, not even helping them to unload. Glancing at him and, realising that something had definitely frightened him, they gradually stopped scoffing and asked for more details.

'What did it look like then – this ghost of yours?' one asked. The old man frowned as he thought.

'I couldn't see him properly,' he said slowly, 'he was hidden by the boughs, I just know he looked like a man, I could see his trousers and boots dangling, in a sort of glowing light.'

The men were all interested now. The youngest looked at him curiously.

'Did he speak to you, Wil?' he asked, hefting the last bag of flour onto his shoulder.

The old man shook his head.

'No, he didn't say anything and he didn't move, he just held the twigs apart and stared down at me.'

The cart was empty now and Huw, the foreman, decided the old miller was too upset to be acting.

'Don't worry Wil,' he said kindly, 'just a trick of the light on the tree, that's all.'

The miller looked up at him worriedly.

'No trick of the light, Huw,' he said, 'it's still dark at 6 o'clock.'

'Well, how could you see him in the dark?' Huw asked cheerfully.

Wil climbed stiffly back onto the cart and stared fearfully down.

'He had a sort of dim glow around him, so I could see him against the tree; he just sat there and stared at me.'

Shaking his head slowly, he gathered the reins in his hands and muttered,

'I don't like it, Huw, I don't like it.'

Raising his hand in farewell, he set off back to Melin Rhos.

Poor haunted Wil, every morning that week he saw the ghost. Each time he drew near to the spot, he kept his head sunk between his shoulders, staring hard down at the reins and the horse's rump as he entered the deep darkness under the trees, but try as he might, *something* made him cast a furtive glance upwards, and always the figure would be there.

He was voluble about it for the first day or two, telling everyone who would listen, until it came to the ears of a local man who was in his early nineties. He declared that when he was a child, a well-known sea robber had been way-laid at that very spot by the local farmers and had been summarily hung.

Learning this, Wil became even more depressed and moved morosely about his work. He asked if he could take someone with him on the dark mornings, but his employer was not inclined to pay for two for one man's work, so Wil travelled alone.

Not everyone believed his story, certainly not the two young apprentices, who between them hatched a harmless prank. One of them sneaked out of the house one morning with his mother's best nightdress stuffed under his jacket and passed it quietly to his mate at the mill.

They waited impatiently for an opportunity until everyone was busy then, the other lad, with a grin, melted away into the blackness of the rainy morning and pelted along the road to Bodafon Farm. Here he shinned up the biggest tree and sat athwart a branch shrouded in the nightie, all ready to flap his arms and utter blood-curdling moans when the old man appeared.

He sat and shivered in the cold dark of the January morning, listening to the rain pattering around him. Staring along the wet road, he strained his ears to hear the slow thump of the horse's hooves and the creak of the cart as it appeared.

The silence and the darkness were uncanny, a weird feeling began to make the boy uneasy and the hair started to prickle at the back of his head. At last, he heard the horse, and the cart appeared, moving towards him with painful slowness. He watched it and, at the last moment, just as it was passing under the oak he was perched in, he stretched out his nightie clad arms and gave an unearthly groan.

Wil was hunched over the reins, head tucked into his neck, but gave a great start as he looked up.

Then he gave a yell of horror.

'Oh my God – there's two of you today!'

So saying, he whipped up the startled horse – and they galloped to Amlwch at a rattling pace.

The terrified apprentice also gave a yell of fear – fell headlong out of the tree, gathered up his muddied nightie in his fists, and made a beeline back to the mill.

The story ends with two terrified people bolting in opposite directions, leaving that dark and haunted spot to the ghost!

Massacre at Dulas

Looking down from Snowdonia in summer, the Isle of Anglesey resembles a beautiful green jewel, lying in the sunshine, surrounded by the glittering sea.

It has been green and fertile for many centuries, since the first farmers cut down the thick woods and ploughed the land to plant grain. So much was grown, the Island became known as Môn, Mam Cymru – Mother of Wales.

Cattle were bred too, and the Island was flourishing and rich. Fat and ripe for plunder. Which it was, again and again, by sailing ships bearing Irish, English and Scottish men. Even from Rome – they travelled, and before them, the fearless Vikings came to rob and rape. The coastal settlements and farms were prime targets, houses were sacked, animals were stolen and the inhabitants killed.

Many battles took place around the shallow bays and inlets, where it was easy to land. Such a place was the small sheltered bay at Dulas on the north-east coast, where for years the long-suffering farmers tried to protect their own. Eventually, they started to place lookouts on the cliffs when the weather was fair, the wind favourable and the tide right, for it was then that the sea-robbers were most likely to appear.

One battle which took place so long ago that details have been lost, and the actuality of the event has fallen into folk lore, occurred on the deep winding lane that leads from Dulas to the sea and has been used throughout time by the fishermen.

A lookout man, posted at dawn on the hill above Dulas, sighted a sailing-ship bearing down from the north-east which he recognised as a known raider. He raised the alarm and every able-bodied local man hurried to Dulas, knowing it would take time for the vessel to arrive.

The plan had been in place for a long time and, every man knew what he had to do and where he had to be. With all the stealth and silence of countrymen who know their own patch, they moved into position. Making their way unseen by the sides of the meadows, they reached the deep cleft of the lane, the high banks and thick undergrowth on each side made it an ideal place for an ambush. They took their places and waited in absolute silence.

No highly trained fighting men these, just a band of honest locals sickened by the countless raids. Their weapons were their everyday tools – scythes, sickles, pitchforks and skinning knives. What they lacked in experience they made up for in cold anger – and they waited.

Before long, they heard the stealthy sound of oars, then the crunch of men's feet on the shingle, as they dragged a boat up out of reach of the tide. Through the screen of trees, the waiting farmers could see the sea-robbers, intent on surprise, armed to the teeth, moving quietly up the beach and into the lane. Straight into the trap.

With blood-curdling yells, the local men swarmed down the banks on each side, and fell on the hapless raiders, who were taken completely by surprise. In panic, some tried to run back to the boat, some tried to press on and there was chaos, they were barred both front and back.

The sickles and scythes flashed and fell, and the air was full of the screams of mortally wounded men, who were literally hacked to pieces.

I knew nothing of the massacre when we strolled down the lane on a hot August day, but the heavy brooding atmosphere which hung over it made such a deep impression on me that I asked around to see if there were any old stories about the place.

I was told that a local lady, as a child, had a grandmother who frequently warned her to avoid the lane, as *her* grandmother knew people who had heard screams and groans coming from the area, usually early in the mornings.

When questioned, she said that she didn't know anyone who had heard the noises recently, at least no one had mentioned them, which made me wonder whether they still occur when no one is in hearing distance or, as in some hauntings, the sounds have faded out with the passage of time.

My indomitable friend, Mair Williams, told me about the actual battle and that the lane is known as Nant-y-Perfedd. The name can be understood as 'the brook through the middle of the country', but also it could mean 'the brook/valley of the entrails'.

Most likely the bodies of the raiders were unceremoniously

thrown into shallow graves, like the bodies of the Viking mercenaries found a few years ago at Llanbedr-goch, when the ground was being prepared for the Anglesey Eisteddfod.

This would probably explain the eerie feeling one gets going down the lane, if the remains of violently killed men are still nearby.

My thanks to Mair for giving me this tiny cameo of Anglesey's troubled past.

Owie's tales – Nell

Mr Owie Jones, of Pen-y-sarn, is a storyteller in the old tradition and should really have been born a century ago, when families and friends would gather around a crackling log fire on winter nights and listen round-eyed to stories, which had been finely honed and polished by the telling and retelling.

Here is the first of the stories he told me.

Farmer Cyril had a toothless old ewe affectionately known as Nell. Always apart from the rest of the small flock, she had ingeniously contrived a way in and out of the churchyard next door, where she found the juicy weed stalks much easier to munch than the short grass back home.

Some nights, Nell would not bother going home at all, but would lie in the shelter of a tombstone till dawn.

It was on one such occasion that Tom Evans and his friend, Edwin, over from Flint for the weekend, decided on an evening stroll to the shore, calling in at the churchyard on their way back, to visit Edwin's family grave.

It was starting to get dark when they returned and, unknown to them, Nell had already made her bed for the night and was fast asleep. The two young men talking as they approached woke her with a start and (as sheep will) she gave a deep nervous cough before scuttling away towards her gap and home.

Hearing what they thought was a throaty voice and seeing the greyish fleeing form flitting away between the tombstones, was enough to instantly convince the pair of them that they had seen a ghost – and their exit from the graveyard was rapid if not dignified.

To this day, no one can convince them that they had not seen an apparition – which, I suppose, is how some ghost stories are born.

Owie's tales – The sheep walk

Still in north-east Anglesey, to the south and west of the Bryn Môr mansion, lies a piece of land known as 'The Elfrid' and along it runs a public footpath known as the 'Sheep Walk'.

My friend, Maggie Hughes, was walking along this path to her home one fine warm evening in the late summer, enjoying the familiar views over the countryside. She was halfway along the path and approaching the old stone stile which she would have to climb over, when she stopped in sudden shock.

Before her, as if guarding the stile, one on each side, were two balls of fire. Just above ground level, and perfectly still, they hovered before her astonished gaze. Perfect spheres, each about one foot across, the flames did not flicker raggedly, but appeared to be contained within them, as if imprisoned within glass, constantly swirling and changing.

Poor Maggie. Her initial feeling of shock and disbelief turned to fear and rooted her to the spot, but the fireballs neither advanced nor disappeared. Eventually Maggie summoned up the courage to move. She started to retreat slowly, not daring to turn around so she would have her back to them, and she stumbled backwards for a long way, her eyes riveted on the two weird balls.

They stayed there for as long as she could see them until, eventually, a bend in the path excluded them from her sight, then she turned and ran for dear life, fear lending wings to her heels. She ran the longer way home and, since then, refuses flatly to take the Sheep Walk path again.

Maggie would never, ever, invent such a tale.

Owie's tales – The knockers

Our district of Llanwenllwyfo Llaneilian was never short of ghostly goings on.

Back in the old days it was to this churchyard that a spectral funeral procession is reputed to be sighted, solemnly and silently making its way not far from Lôn Dywyll crossroads, to be followed by a real funeral procession, a few days later.

The bell ringers' path or 'sexton's walk', through a nearby field leads to an old farmhouse called Plas Uchaf. Barry, a friend of mine, and his wife and children have lived there, but not for very long, as it was haunted.

The children hated to go to bed, insisting that they were terrified of a ghost that always manifested in their bedroom. Barry and his wife never saw anything and, at first, they put it down to nightmares and the children's over-active imagination, but eventually they had to move the children into another bedroom.

Now grown up, the children have never deviated from their original descriptions of the haunting.

They all said that they were afraid to go to sleep, but when they did, they were rudely awakened not long afterwards by a feeling of great tension in the bedroom. They all seemed to be woken simultaneously by a sense of being stared at and, as they all sat up in bed, they saw a patch of grey mist at the side of their bed. It gradually resolved itself into a very tall human shape, from which two long arms emerged, grasped the bedclothes and slowly removed them by pulling them sideways.

The children were terrified, scrambling as far away as possible from the figure, and screaming for their parents, but by the time their mother and father rushed into the room, there was nothing to be seen, only their children tearfully cowering in a jumbled heap at the far side of the bed.

Apparently, as soon as the children started to shriek for their parents, the ghost would gradually fade away as quietly as it came.

The only evidence of it ever having been there were all the bedclothes tangled in a pile on the floor, and the wildly sobbing children. Once they had changed bedrooms, the children were never troubled again, so perhaps this was another instance of a ghost which resented anyone using a bedroom which it still considered its own!

Further along the same pretty, tree-lined lane is Bryn Fuches Lodge, where my wife and I lived shortly after our marriage in 1978.

In previous years, both my wife's relatives and mine had lived in the Lodge at various times, and many of them had been troubled by poltergeists, who seemed to have some sort of affiliation with the house, and whilst they had been a troublesome nuisance, they had never done any actual harm to the living people with whom they had shared their home.

They were always known as 'knockers' and I came across them whilst the house was in the process of being restored.

There were four of us in an upstairs bedroom, where we were replacing the old rotten window frames with new wooden ones, when I became aware of a soft knocking noise, rather as if someone was using a muffled hammer. I looked around, but no one had a hammer in their hands, although the knocking was becoming more noticeable.

'Listen,' I said, holding up my hand for silence: 'What's that?'

Everyone stopped talking and stood listening quietly.

'What's what?' Huw asked, looking puzzled.

'That knocking,' I said. They cocked their ears and looked at me for a time.

'Nothing,' said one.

'I can't hear anything,' said another.

By now, the knocking was very loud, it seemed to be in the room with us, but everyone looked blank. I suddenly realised that I was the only one that could hear it. We knew that there was no one else in the house, but Wil went out onto the landing and stuck his head into the other bedrooms.

'Nothing there,' he shrugged, and walked across the room to the open gap which was waiting for the new frame to be fitted.

The knocking was now thunderous and frantic, it seemed to shake the house and I stood marvelling that no one else was aware of it.

Then my eyes were drawn towards the closed door.

From beneath it appeared two tiny flames, about the size of a newly lit match. They came steadily into the room, growing as they moved into two tongue shaped flames, the size of heads. They moved swiftly across the room and disappeared through the empty window space.

As soon as they vanished, the knocking ceased abruptly.

No one had heard the noises or seen the flames except me.

A few months later, when we had moved into our new home, my cousin Glen and her family were due to visit us and have tea, and look around the house. They were going to arrive about three-thirty and, just before then, I was reading the paper on the sofa under the window, and my wife was putting the finishing touches to the tea, when I heard the expected knock at the door.

'Cousin Glen's here!' I shouted into the kitchen, throwing down the paper and jumping to my feet. My wife appeared, smiling and drying her hands, at the kitchen door. I opened the door to the little hallway and, as I did, the knock sounded again, more demanding and louder this time.

To our surprise, no one could be seen through the glass panel of the front door and I wondered if Glen and the children were hiding against the wall and I threw the front door open with a grin. There was no one in sight nor had there been time for anyone to run away – in fact, the knocking had only stopped as I opened the door.

We learned a little later that Glen had had to postpone her visit. It had been the knocking of the poltergeist that we had both heard – but how did the ghost know the exact time she was expected?

Owie's tales – The cat

Part of Llaneilian is a very pretty valley, sheltered to the north-east by the steep slopes of Mynydd Eilian and overlooked by the wireless station, whose struts and cables shriek eerily in the great gales of winter.

Fairly recently, a young man named Elfed Roberts was driving home from work to the upper slopes of Mount Eilian where he lived. The road was narrow and steep, set deep between its banks, as most ancient roads are and he was driving very carefully.

Just as he was passing the ruins of the house at Cae'r Moch (the field of pigs), in front of him there suddenly appeared an enormous cat. Brown in colour, it was sprawled at ease in the middle of the road, lying on its side and completely blocking his way.

As he drew closer, it raised its head and stared fixedly at him with large yellow eyes and slowly started to lash its thick tail, but made no effort to move.

Elfed's first thought was – 'My God – what a big cat!'

Unable to pass, he hit the horn button – giving a prolonged blast. This had no effect, so with clenched fist he gave a series of short, sharp hoots. The cat, unmoving, stared at him, increasing the lad's irritation, so he leant out of the window and yelled at it to get out of the way. The only reaction from the cat was a more furious lashing of the tail. Muttering to himself, Elfed leapt out of the car to remove it manually. The road was empty.

In the few seconds it had taken him to open the door, the brown cat had vanished. As Elfed said, 'I only looked away for a second and it disappeared. There was nowhere for it to go, even if it had time, the banks were too steep. I was thunderstruck – I even looked under the car, and back down the road, but it had completely gone.'

Mystified, he got back into the car and drove on.

This was not the end of the matter because, later that month, he was driving along at the same spot, when the cat appeared again.

'I don't know where it came from,' said Elfed, 'one minute the road in front of me was empty – the next minute – there was the cat.'

This time, again he stopped, but suddenly felt a sense of great unease and was very reluctant to leave the safety of the car, as he met the chilling stare of those cold yellow eyes. It really was a huge cat, brown in colour and, once again, sprawled unmoving in the centre of the narrow road, lashing its tail slowly.

He put the car in low gear and, inching slowly forward, carefully manoeuvred around the animal, squeezing past with two wheels up on the steep grassy bank, while it's malevolent gaze never moved from him. Once past, and regaining all four wheels on the road, he looked through his rear view mirror at the beast and later said that as his eyes met the cat's stare, he felt 'a weird coldness down his back and, literally, felt his hair stand on end, as he realised the beast was no mortal cat.

This creature has been seen by several motorists at that spot; sometimes it is sitting or lying sometimes standing, but always in the middle of the road. Being unable to move past, the drivers have invariably got out to shoo it away, only to find there is no cat there at all. Those who have seen it, all remark on its huge size, savage eyes and the feeling of cold fear, which besets them when they see it.

Many people who have come across it don't mention it unless it has been confirmed by someone else, because as Elfed said, 'Who'd admit to being frightened of a cat?'

Apparently it is still encountered on that stretch of road, but no one can find a rational explanation for its irregular appearances.

Owie's tales – The headless ghost

Below Nebo, just at the bottom of Tanrallt hill, lies the little valley of Pen-y-sarn, and it was at Glanrafon Farm, Pen-y-sarn, that a young man named Tom Owen was employed many years ago.

In those days, farm labourers used to live at the farms where they were employed and Tom was one of these. He lived at Porth Amlwch, was newly married, and reluctant to leave his pretty wife when weekend was over, so it was fairly late one winter Sunday night when he bade her farewell and set off on his long dark walk to Pen-y-sarn.

He had just passed Tremarfor, on the Llaneilian Road, when he suddenly became aware of someone walking, keeping pace with him. He hadn't heard anyone coming up behind him and turned, in surprise, to see who it was, thinking it was someone like himself, returning to his place of work. True enough, there beside him, dressed in working clothes like himself, was the figure of a man, striding along like he was.

The only difference was, he had no head.

After the first initial shock, Tom took to his heels, flying along the road, his heart pounding with fear. He was convinced the spectre was chasing him, but with a terrified look over his shoulder, he saw the figure standing where he had left it, the body turned towards him.

'If the head had been there,' said Tom 'it would have been staring after me.'

He didn't stop running until he had reached Pen-y-sarn and fell into the door of Glanrafon Farm, white as a sheet, and shaking with fright.

Tom never walked back along that road in the dark again.

Owie's tales – The phantom cyclist of Nebo

The following tale leads Owie to wonder whether some families experience more ghosts than others, because his next story involves Maggie's two sons and a very eerie sighting.

Late one night, about two years ago, the two young men were in their car and had just passed through the sleeping hamlet of Nebo and were going up towards Fron Deg. The road, at that time of night, was completely empty and their bright headlights cut a swathe through the darkness, sweeping along the walls and hedges as the car steadily climbed the hill.

Suddenly, they both saw something just beyond the bonnet going in the same direction as them. At first a formless blur, it materialised rapidly into the figure of a young man on a push-bike, pedalling in front of the car.

Maggie's eldest son, who was driving, was just about to slam on the brakes, but as he took his foot off the accelerator, the bike rider turned his head and looked briefly back at them over his shoulder, then started to pick up speed at such a phenomenal rate that by the time they had travelled about two hundred yards up the hill, the phantom and his bike (for it could be nothing less, says Owie) had reached the brow at Greigwen, a good quarter of a mile ahead.

Although the car driver had increased his speed alarmingly to catch up, the cyclist's tail-light was already disappearing over the crest of the hill.

When the two men in the car reached the top, they gazed down the other side, expecting to see the twinkling tail-light ahead of them, but there was nothing to be seen and the straight descent was quite deserted.

This first sighting was approximately two years ago and, it has happened to them since, in exactly the same manner.

This time, the car driver put his foot down as soon as the apparition appeared in front of the car, shooting up the hill at break-neck speed as they tried to overtake the bike, but once again it surged along, the distance between them never narrowed. Once again the phantom vanished at the top of the hill.

They were most curious and tried to get to the source of the haunting by asking around. To their surprise, other people had seen the cyclist, sometimes people who were walking home at night had been passed by a bike which made no noise at all, making them jump as it soundlessly whizzed by, and other folk had been in a vehicle when they saw it.

No one knows of any accident involving a cyclist and the Hughes boys remain mystified.

Owie's tales – Was it the devil?

Nearby Bryn Fuches Lodge stands Brynia Brain and it used to be a favourite place for poachers, as it was alive with rabbits.

Towards the end of the war, on a bitter cold December night, a really expert poacher, one Will Jones, and his young friend, Stan, who was learning the trade, set out for a night's work.

The intention was to work the south side of the hill by 'long netting'. This entails one man working above the net and stringing it across the width of the field and, when it is all pegged in securely and silently, the other member of the team walks along below the bottom side of the net, clapping his hands sharply like gunfire, to drive the rabbits up the hill and into the net.

Everything went to plan, the net was secured, and Stan set off to drive in the rabbits. The darkness swallowed him up in seconds, but as he began to clap, Will could hear the sharp slap of his hands, getting less loud as the distance between them increased.

A couple of minutes later, Will heard footsteps pounding towards him in the dark and, young Stan, stumbling, falling, and cursing, flew headlong towards him out of the night. He didn't stop but hurtled past Will panting, 'He's coming – he's coming – for God's sake – **RUN!**'

That he was terrified was obvious and Will didn't wait for explanations – the boy's fear was contagious and Will took to his heels as well. They ran all the way back to the road, not stopping until the breath was burning their lungs and they could run no further. They collapsed on the grass verge and, when he was finally able to speak, Will croaked –

'Who was it?' He had a faint idea that it could have been a keeper who had surprised Stan – he knew them ali and surely none of them could inspire such fear. He could hear the breath whistling in Stan's parched lungs – and asked him again, 'Who *was* it?'

'My God – it was the Devil!

'*What?*'

'It was the Devil – I've seen the Devil himself!'

Stan was almost incoherent with fear and trembling with shock.

'In the far hollow,' he muttered, 'he rose up at me out of the ground.'

'*What?*'

There was silence from Stan and Will, who was about to scoff and tell the lad it was probably just a keeper, playing tricks, looked at the lad and it was obvious that something had scared him badly. He kept looking back into the darkness, as if to see if he was being followed. Then he got up and strode rapidly down the road.

'What about the nets?' Will shouted after his retreating figure.

'Damn the nets.'

Will had to run to catch up with him. Stan never spoke again all the way home, and the nets had to stay where they were. The lad wouldn't accompany Will even in full daylight next day to retrieve them.

Much later, he tried to describe what he had seen.

'I was just going down into the hollow,' he said, 'you know what a black night it was – when suddenly this – this *thing!*' he shuddered, 'rose up out of the ground in front of me.'

'Its head came up first, then neck and shoulders – it kept rising and rising in front of me. It was so big and broad – must have been all of seven feet tall – and it didn't make a sound. The awful thing was – I could see right through it and it sort of *glowed* – a really weird light – and when I looked up at its face,' Stan shivered, 'it was *horrible*, it had no eyes. Don't ask me about it ever again Will – I can't sleep properly now, and I won't forget it – not ever.'

Up until then, Will had thought someone had played a trick on him to scare them off, but when he put this to Stan, the boy looked at him long and hard.

'That was no trick, Will, whatever that horrible thing was, it wasn't of this world.'

He never went poaching again.

The mystery of the *Baltimore*

Mr Owie Jones, journalist, of Pen-y-sarn, told me the following story, and Mr Rowlant Williams, Pengorffwysfa, kindly researched the Morris Brothers letters for the details.

In the eighteenth century, the activities of wreckers, smugglers and sea robbers (pirates) were flourishing as never before, with the increase in shipping.

They were in evidence all around the British Isles but the combination of gales in the Irish Sea, the rocky coasts of Wales and the fact that many merchant ships sailing between America and Britain at that time had very little knowledge of the currents and hidden reefs off Anglesey, made it an ideal spot for the wreckers to ply their murderous trade.

Life was hard and cheap and the men were not all ignorant cut-throats and thieves – the local gentry and even men of the cloth were involved. At best, turning a blind eye to the provenance of the goods they received; at worst, some of the wealthy landowners supplied the gangs with their own men, becoming even wealthier in the process.

It was a way of life that was accepted by the majority of people until late in the nineteenth century, when the idea was broached to build a rocket station near Rhosneigr, in order to warn shipping away from the infamous Crigyll Rocks, where countless merchant ships had met their doom.

This news was a bombshell to the wreckers, who objected strongly, telling the authorities that the plan destroyed the source of income of many local families. The local gentry, who were very much involved with the wreckers, were just as dismayed, but could not, of course, voice their own objections, so despite the local furore the plan had created, in the 1880's the rocket station was built. But to return to the eighteenth century.

By what means the *Baltimore,* a fast clipper ship plying between America and Britain (or so I believe) was wrecked is not to be found in any official records that I could discover, but what is known is the fact that not one member of her crew survived.

She was grounded and wrecked off Porth Helygen, not far from the hamlet of Nebo, on the eastern shores of Anglesey. The landowner, one Mr Edwards, claimed her rich cargo at once and the Receiver of Wrecks for the Crown hotly disputed his claim.

Mr Edwards did not give up his prize easily and, in 1750, a court case took place in the timbered seventeenth century courtroom at Beaumaris. Correspondence between the famous Morris brothers, William and Richard, in July of that year, shows Richard's curiosity regarding its outcome. That there something dubious about the case is shown in Richard's comments.

*'It would be interesting when you have the time, to receive a report regarding the law of the **Baltimore** in order to see what the men of Beaumaris made of it.'*

I cannot trace the outcome of the case, but the fact remains that about this time, Edwards suddenly became wealthy and subsequently built a grand house in a sheltered hollow on his land named Tyddyn Mawr so it seems as if the verdict of the case was in his favour. Also, the children of that time made up a song making light of the fact that the Vicar's daughters displayed themselves 'arrayed in certain fineries' which, according to the song, were bought from the proceeds of the *Baltimore*'s cargo.

Mr Edwards lived in his new house in evident prosperity quite happily for the rest of his life, obviously unmoved by the gossip that circulated about him in the social circles to which he now aspired.

Even before he died, the house, although so modern, was beginning to gain the reputation of being haunted. The servants telling of voices heard in empty rooms and lights being seen in the grounds, but Mr Edwards scorned such stories as being old wives tales.

After his death, the house and wealth were inherited by his son, Roland, a down to earth fellow with little imagination, who, like his father, was apparently unaffected by the alleged hauntings, living in the house and dying at the ripe old age of 88, in 1818.

In due course, the estate was inherited by a distant member of the family, a gentleman named Roberts. During his tenancy, the stories and gossip about the ghost lights and sounds in the house grew more widespread, with many more allegations by servants on the estate. That Mr Roberts was aware of them may have been the reason he never stayed long in the house – he was away on business for protracted periods and, as he was a bachelor, the great house stood empty. It was Owie's great-great-grandfather's task to make sure everything was secure and to inspect the house each night and morning. He took his son Owen (Owie's great grandfather) many times when he was a young lad and when *he* grew old, he was fond of telling Owie about the frightening experience he had at Tyddyn Mawr one night.

It was winter, a cold moonless night with an easterly gale roaring through the trees and, as they trudged along, they pulled up their coat collars and bent their heads against the blast.

All was well at the front of the house, the big door was locked and bolted and the row of darkened windows fastened and shuttered. Shivering in the cold night wind, they made their way down the side of the building, turned the corner towards the back door – and stopped dead. There – where everything should have been dark, a pool of bright light shone from the kitchen, lighting up the flagstones of the yard.

Mr Jones put his hand on Owen's shoulder and, as the young lad swivelled his head to look up into his father's face, Mr Jones laid a warning finger to his lips, and moved warily forward, making not a sound.

Slowly, they crept towards the kitchen, keeping well out of the light, ducking down as they got near the window, until they were close enough to raise their heads over the sill and peer into the room.

Sitting around the table and, seemingly deep in conversation (though try as he might, Owen couldn't hear even a murmur of voices through the window) was a group of men. Although they could be seen in detail, there was something odd about them, a blurring of the edges, as if slightly out of focus. They were all dressed in seamen's garb, but Owen, who had lived by the sea all his life, realised the clothes were not the style that British seamen wore, and Owen recognised the pattern and fashions as identical to a picture he had seen, depicting sailors of more than a century earlier. Some had the tarred pigtails, which were common in those days. The weird light surrounding them was very bright, but

Owen could not see from whence it came.

As he stared, it slowly dawned on him that he was looking at men from another country and an earlier age and he began to be engulfed in a wave of terror, which made his skull tighten and his hair stand on end.

He nearly jumped out of his skin with fright when his father laid a hand on his arm and leaned forward to whisper slowly and with awe:

'Come, son, we must leave here, these men are not of our time.'

Owen seemed rooted to the spot, unable to move, until his father pulled him gently away. The two of them melted into the darkness, leaving the phantoms to conduct their unearthly business undisturbed.

Owen was convinced for the rest of his long life that he had that night seen the crew of the *Baltimore*.

Mr Roberts never settled at Tyddyn Mawr and although he always denied he had ever seen the ghosts, he avoided living in the house as much as he could.

Eventually, he got engaged and, this gave him the excuse to build another grand house, Bryn-y-Môr for himself and his intended bride.

Alas! (as Owie says) the marriage never did take place, the lady jilting him at the last moment and the forsaken bridegroom lived there sadly and alone, looked after by a devoted housekeeper until he died in 1916.

The following seven stories were written down for me by Mr Donald Pritchard, Headmaster of Pen-y-sarn School near Amlwch, who grew up in Pentreberw, spending his childhood roaming around his beloved marsh and steeping himself in the fund of stories that have been passed down the generations for hundreds of years.

I gratefully included them in this collection and I hope my readers enjoy them as much as I did.

The son who came home

The Parry's lived peaceful lives during the early years of the last century. A close-knit, loving family who lived at 2 Glan Rafon, Pentreberw.

Jane, the married daughter, lived just up the lane from them at No.2 Trefaes, a couple of hundred yards away from the family home, and there was always much coming and going between the two families, Jane's younger brother especially spending many hours with her and her husband.

Richard was in his early teens when the Great War broke out – and a determined campaign was made by the Government to get able-bodied men to volunteer. Huge placards were pasted onto hoardings, showing General Kitchener's face, complete with bristling moustache and pointing index finger over the slogan: YOUR COUNTRY NEEDS **YOU!**

Welshmen and boys flocked to join the services, patriotic songs were heard everywhere and the newspapers were full of pictures of crowded troop trains, with cheerful young soldiers hanging out the windows, grinning and waving. It all seemed very glamorous and great fun to begin with, they looked as if they were setting forth on a great adventure, none having an inkling of the blood, mud and carnage they were about to see.

Young Richard Parry was greatly taken with the idea of joining up. He learned all the words of the popular war songs, singing 'Keep the Home Fires Burning', 'Goodbye Dolly Gray' and whistling the tunes when he didn't know the words. Eventually, he became of age to join and joyfully enlisted as a private in the Royal Welsh Fusiliers, coming home after his initial training.

He was tall and handsome and bore the uniform proudly, full of excitement as he told his family there was a rumour in his camp that his company were soon going abroad.

When his leave was over, he bade them all a loving farewell but his Mam could see how impatient he was to be back with his Army mates and she waved him off with a heavy heart. He was at the age when fear is unknown, but his Mam was older and wiser.

The house seemed very empty without him, but as the months went by, life settled down into a different rhythm and they infrequently received the printed cards which were the only correspondence the men on active service abroad were allowed to send. These were listed messages which the sender could cross out or leave, the ones they required usually being – 'I am well' or 'Have received your letters'. Short, emotionless sentences which nevertheless reassured their families that at least they were alive.

Jane Williams, Richard's sister, went up to see her Mam every day after doing her chores and, one windy April morning, she wondered whether there would be any more news from Richard. A proud housewife like her Mam, she had washed and dried the breakfast dishes, tidied and swept the kitchen then armed with Brasso and dusters, she attacked the front door knob, letter box and brass key shutter until they sparkled in the sun.

She had a brief chat with her next door neighbour who was poking about with a sweeping brush, looking for non-existent dust in the corners of her spotless doorstep and told her she was just going up to her Mam's for a panad (cup of tea). Two minutes later, soft Welsh shawl about her head and shoulders to keep out the chilly April wind, she walked briskly down the lane.

Usually, when she went into her Mam's house, she found it as neat and tidy as her own, with the kettle singing on the hob, cups and saucers on the table and the fat brown teapot warming beside the crackling fire.

Today, however, the grate was cold and empty, yesterday's ashes still lying in the old ash bucket on the slate hearth, and her Mam sitting so still and silent near the table, gazing at the fireplace with unseeing eyes. A crumpled handkerchief being endlessly pulled through restless fingers was the only sign that she was conscious.

Jane stopped in the doorway and stared at her.

'What's the matter Mam?'

No response.

Alarmed now, Jane tried again.

'Are you alright?'

This time, her Mam seemed to come back from a great distance away and stared back at Jane as if she had never seen her before.

Her face was pale and haggard and her eyes were full of sorrow.

'It's Richard,' she said quietly.

Jane looked around quickly, no kit bag, no army hat and no sign.

She looked again at her Mam.

'What about Richard?'

'Something has happened to him.'

The words, spoken with such conviction, struck ice into Jane's heart. She looked on the table, then on the floor, for a letter or a telegram. Nothing.

'You're imagining things – nothing's happened – it's all in your mind – you just sit there while I light the fire and make you a nice cup of tea.'

Her Mam shook her head.

'No. Something has happened to him.'

She sounded so certain that the comforting words Jane was about to say to draw her Mam out of this weird mood died on her lips.

Her Mam pointed to the hearth.

'I was on my knees and I had just finished putting the ashes into the bucket and, as I turned around to get the aden bobi (goose wing used to sweep the hearth), Richard was standing there in his uniform.'

She pointed to the middle of the room and Jane followed her pointing finger, half expecting to see Richard herself.

For a moment they were both silent, Jane felt a cold shiver down her back. Pulling herself together, she tried to sound brisk.

'Come on now Mam, it's just your imagination, nothing's happened to our Richard,' she reassured her Mam, taking her hand comfortingly, 'It's just a bout of hiraeth (yearning, sadness), come on now, you'll feel better when I've lit the fire and made some tea.'

Jane Williams busied herself with the familiar homely tasks, thinking up little items of gossip which are the currency of a village to distract her Mam, frequently looking sideways at the sad, unresponsive figure lost in thought beside her.

After that day, Mrs Parry was a changed woman. From being the cheerful, bustling body she had always been, she became morose and silent, growing thinner as if her food had lost its flavour.

Jane got into the habit of bringing neighbours in to try and cheer up her Mam and two of them were there having a panad three weeks later, when the morning post arrived. All eyes turned to the official looking brown envelope, which had dropped on the mat. Mrs Parry went rigid.

Jane picked it up and took it across to her, but her Mam made no move to take it, she turned her back stiffly and gazed steadily into the fire. Nonplussed, Jane stood with the unopened envelope in her hands and gazed at her two friends, who nodded and indicated in silence that Jane should deal with it. Also in silence, Jane tore open the envelope and took out the single printed page.

Slowly, she read it aloud in a trembling voice that was choked by tears.

'This is to inform you that Private Richard Parry, RWF, has died in France fighting for King and Country on the 25th April, 1917, aged 19 years.'

There was dead silence in the room, broken by the steady ticking of the wall clock.

The tears overflowed and poured down Jane's cheeks.

'Oh, Mam,' she said piteously, and one of the women started to sob quietly into a hanky.

Mrs Parry looked at Jane with great calmness.

'I knew it,' she said simply, 'Richard came to tell me.'

This story was told by Richard's sister, Jane Williams, in 1954.

(Mr Pritchard writes.) His name is carved on the Memorial Plaque in Capel Berea, Pentreberw, and on the Memorial in Gaerwen.

Even the tiniest village in Anglesey has a Memorial Stone or Plaque, listing the names of the courageous men and boys who responded in their thousands to the call to arms during both World Wars, thereby losing their lives.

Nell Griffiths

My father, Glyn Pritchard, was a deacon at Capel Berw and was always a very truthful man. When he was a young man, he had a very eerie experience, which made a very deep impression on him. His family home was 2 Penrhyn Mawr, Pentreberw.

Pentreberw, like a lot of villages on the Island, did not have electricity until 1948-1949, and road lights were not installed until the early 1950's, so when the following event happened, the only illumination in the village came from oil lamps which glowed in the cottage windows.

My father, one evening in winter, had been to court my mother at Gaerwen, which is a couple of miles away. It was about ten o'clock as he approached Collier Mawr. It was a clear moonlit night, very quiet and with very little traffic as was usual. He was about to cross the main road when he suddenly saw a figure opposite him, sitting on a low wall by Glan y Don.

He stopped and stared and, to his astonishment, he saw that it was a woman, wearing a very old-fashioned bonnet and shawl, with a white apron covering the front of her long dark skirt. She did not look up at his approach (even though she must have heard the tramp of his boots as he drew near) but continued to look down at her hands, which seemed to be working busily.

At that moment a car came up from the direction of the marsh and, as its lights swept the scene, Glyn Pritchard said the woman disappeared and the wall was empty.

He knew then that he was looking at something unearthly, because as the car passed them both, the woman re-appeared, still looking down, and now he could see she was knitting.

He went icy-cold and then broke out into a sweat – he knew he would have to pass her to reach the road to home, but was too afraid.

Then he saw the lights of another car coming up from the marsh. Whilst it was still a little way off, its lights fell upon the seated woman and she immediately vanished.

At once my father ran across the road in front of the car and flew past the spot where she had been sitting. He did not stop to look back when the car had gone by, but ran all the way to

Penrhyn Mawr and literally threw himself into the house, pale, shaking and completely out of breath.

His headlong arrival in the house and the way he slammed and bolted the front door was a great shock to his Mam and Dad, sitting quietly in the kitchen. His appearance was enough to alarm them and it took him quite a while to compose himself. His Mam insisted that he mustn't try to speak until she had made him a strong cup of tea.

When he had recovered somewhat, he told them in detail just what he had seen, the woman's dress, bonnet and shawl, her long full skirt made of some dark cloth, her gleaming white apron and her hands busily knitting as she sat on the low wall.

His parents listened intently while he spoke, saying nothing, but listening with great interest. When he had finished his story, his mother wore an expression of stunned amazement and let out her breath in a great sigh. Then she told him that he had just given a complete description of Nell Griffiths, of Glan y Don, who used to sit upon the wall and knit on fine days.

Nell had died years before my father was born in 1914.

Unseen visitor

Thomas Jones lived at 2 Ty'n Coed, Pentreberw, during the 1920's. It was a time of great hardship on Anglesey and Thomas's way of life was no different, in that he had to pick up employment where he could, to make a meagre living.

So he was a Jack-of-all-trades – the village barber, gardener, hedge-cutter and any other job that would bring in a few pennies. His evenings were spent carefully cobbling the shoes of the villagers taking as much care repairing the clogs and boots of the men as he did with the occasional 'best' shoes of the ladies when they were brought to him.

Thomas was a jolly man, with a great sense of humour and a fund of tales, so he was a popular figure in the village and, although he lived alone, there was always someone in his house, both young and old, having a cup of tea with him or warming themselves at his fire. He was kindness itself.

He had very few relatives; in fact the only one anyone knew about was his niece, Mrs Jane Parry, and her family, of whom he was very fond. Her home was at 1 Bangor Street, Gaerwen, where she and her husband lived with their eight children.

John Parry had been born in Amlwch, at 11 Wesley Street, and worked on a nearby farm. He was a handsome young man, with a steady job, and when he and Jane fell in love and married, his future looked secure, and Uncle Thomas Jones was pleased and happy for the young couple. He was even happier when they moved to Gaerwen, within easy walking distance of Pentreberw, because their family was growing rapidly and they needed a larger house.

But in the 1920's, Anglesey (like many other places) fell upon hard times. There was no money in agriculture, many small farms were abandoned, flour mills were empty and employment was hard to find. So, for the first time in his life, John Parry was out of work.

Thomas Jones often went to see them and helped as much as he could, taking food when he had it to spare, listening sympathetically to their problems and helping with wise advice when it was needed. The only solution of course, was for John to find work. But where?

Anglesey men were being forced to leave the Island, going to the mainland to work in the mines or quarries, and it was with a heavy heart that John Parry joined them – to go to work at Llanberis Quarry, from where he could at least come home at weekends, using the ferry which plied between the Mermaid Inn and Caernarfon, and walking the rest of the way, a journey of many, many miles at each end.

During the week, the quarrymen lived in the Sir Fôn Barracks, a crude barn of a place, where the living conditions were extremely basic. Their beds were bags of straw or chaff; they cooked their own food and slept in most of their working clothes.

The conditions at work were abominable – hard toil at the quarry face, which was streaming with water, when it rained, and frozen solid with ice and snow in winter. The men were hardly ever dry; clothes that were soaked during the day were still wet next morning. Their heaviest coats were used to cover them whilst they were in bed; it was so cold, the men were glad of the coat's weight, wet or dry. The working life of a quarryman was usually fairly short, like their counterparts in the mines. Their health and strength was quickly squandered with hard work, damp clothes and poor diet.

So, six months later, John Parry made his way home from Llanberis, crossing the Straits to the Mermaid Inn, a broken man. At the age of forty, this once hale and hearty man was sweating and shivering with pneumonia and nearly delirious. How he travelled back all the way home in that condition is almost unbelievable.

Jane stared at him in horror and just managed to catch him as he collapsed. She couldn't lift him into bed and sent the eldest child running to fetch Uncle Thomas. When Thomas arrived, he took in the situation at a glance and put John to bed with all the gentleness of a woman.

John was given hot drinks, poultices on his chest and kept very warm. Thomas was aware how desperately ill the man was, but didn't voice his fears to Jane, who was distraught with worry. Instead, he looked after all of them, no mean task with eight lively children, their mother and father. He stayed at their house for nearly two weeks, listening to the hacking cough of the sick man and sitting by his bedside to let Jane rest.

Kindly neighbours rallied round with food and fuel, but there was no money coming into the house and Thomas knew that if he could get back home to tackle the boots and shoes that were waiting to be mended, he could at least bring back a few shillings.

After nine days, John seemed a little better and Jane dared to hope that he had turned the corner; even though the pain in his lungs was still acute and his cough still deep, he managed to smile and speak a little. So Thomas explained to Jane that he was going home to catch up on his work, but that he would be back as soon as he had finished.

As he was going – John thanked him and Thomas did think he looked a little better.

Alas – it was only the brief rallying that comes when the disease has won and the body gives up the fight and has a brief interval of calm. But of course, no one was to know this.

Thomas tramped home through the biting cold of a February afternoon and lit a roaring fire when he entered his little cottage.

Several pairs of boots, clogs and shoes were waiting to be repaired; Thomas knew he would have to work late to catch up. So he stirred the fire into a merry blaze, put his oil lamp on the table where it would make a pool of light for him to work in, then fetched his cobbling tools, collected the pile of footwear and settled down to work. The familiar smell of new leather arose as he spread it on the table, ready to measure and cut it to fit the soles. The silence was only broken by the sound of his work and the occasional fall of a coal in the fire, as he worked on and on.

Suddenly, there was the smart slap of a hand against the back window. Thomas jumped – then groaned.

'Llosg yr Odyn' he muttered. Llosg was an old friend who dropped in most evenings, for a bit of gossip and to sit comfortably by the fire, watching Thomas work. He always announced his arrival by tapping on the back window as he approached, and then let himself in by the front door.

But Thomas was in no mood for chatting tonight – he had a lot to do and it was already after midnight.

'I've no time to waste talking to him tonight,' he said to himself as he plied his heavy cobbler's needle.

But the minutes went by and Llosg didn't appear.

'He must have been on his way home from somewhere and just let me know he was passing.' Thomas thought as he stretched his stiff shoulders and carried on.

His tools lay to hand, in a neat row on the table. Suddenly, the awl, which was in the centre, rolled slowly across the flat wooden surface and dropped to the floor.

Thomas stared down at it in surprise, picked it up and put it back in the middle of the table, then went on sewing the boot sole he was working on.

All of a sudden, the awl started to move again. As the cobbler stared, it rolled along the table to the very edge and, just as he thought it would fall, it rolled back to its original position and stopped. Thomas gasped in surprise and, as he did, the awl rolled rapidly to the edge and fell off.

Thomas Jones stopped work and picked it up. The hair on the back of his neck bristled and he had the uneasy feeling that he was not alone in the room, although when he looked around, everything seemed normal.

He decided that he was imagining things. He was tired and he was ready for bed, so he packed up his tools and, looking carefully around the silent kitchen, picked up the oil lamp, and then remembered to make up the fire so that it would still be alight in the morning. This he did by covering the embers carefully with coal dust.

Armed with the lamp, he walked into his bedroom next door and placed it on the chest of drawers. The room was cold, February frost lay thick outside, so he threw his topcoat over the quilt for added warmth. It didn't take him long to get into bed and snuggle down under the clothes.

Everything was quiet, but Thomas felt wide-awake, some sixth sense telling him that all was not well, this was no normal night.

Suddenly he was brought bolt upright by a loud noise from the kitchen. It was the sound of hob-nailed boots tramping back and forth with measured tread. Thomas listened with dread. He knew the door was locked and bolted and he began to realise with mounting fear that it was no living human being that walked in his house. His heart was thumping heavily and he started to sweat.

Usually a very brave man, his instinct told him that the things that were happening that night had no rational explanation and he dived under the bed-clothes but even here, muffled as they were, the footsteps could be heard.

Then silence.

He lay there stiffly, listening so hard he almost forgot to breathe, wondering fearfully what was about to happen next. The topcoat lying on top of his quilt started to slip sideways off the bed and he grabbed it before it fell off completely and pulled it up over his shoulders. He had hardly let go of it when it was instantly snatched away, he could feel it being pulled down to the foot of the bed.

Now very afraid, poor Thomas sat bolt upright again, leaned towards the chest of drawers and turned up the lamp. The wick flared high and the room became full of light. He stared about, dreading what he might see, but the room was empty. Even so, the atmosphere was thick with expectancy, a sense of urgency, and Thomas was convinced he was not alone and something was going to happen. Alone in the house, he had a great premonition that there was someone in the house with him.

He shot out of bed, shaking so much that his hands fumbled with his clothes, thrusting his feet into his boots and grabbing his great-coat where it lay in a heap on the floor. There was no question of him staying alone in that house – he needed the companionship of people, the warmth of company. Not even waiting to put out the lamp – who knows what would happen when he had blown out the wick and the room became black. He hurriedly left his cottage and made his way to Gaerwen.

There were lights on at 1 Bangor Street; he could see the dim glow of a candle in the bedroom and the light of the oil lamp in the kitchen, even though it was the middle of the night. He only tapped lightly on the door, not wishing to disturb the sick man if he was asleep, but the door was immediately thrown open by his niece, tear stained and sobbing.

Jane gave a gasp of relief when she saw him and flung herself into his arms, incoherent with grief. When she was able to talk, she told him that her beloved husband was dead; he had died just after midnight. She had been sitting by his side, holding his hand and, just before he died, he had opened his eyes and given her a smile that was so full of love. He had squeezed her hand with the last vestige of his strength, then had slipped away.

As Thomas sat by the fire with his sobbing niece, he gazed into the flames, lost in thought.

At that moment, he realised that the presence in his cottage that night had been the spirit of John Parry, who had come to Ty'n Coed to 'send' him to Gaerwen to care and support his grieving widow and children. Thomas made John a silent promise that he would fulfil that which he had been asked.

He stayed with the bereaved family for many weeks after John's funeral and looked after and cared for them for the rest of his life.

Mr Donald Pritchard added a postscript to this tale:

'This story was told by Thomas Jones to John Parry's daughter, who became my mother, Mrs Anne Ellen Pritchard.

Her father, John Parry, died on the 24th February in the bitter winter of 1927, aged 41 years.

He was my grandfather.'

Ghosts at the Collier Mawr Crossroads

At one time Anglesey was almost divided into two islands – one, Sir Fôn Fawr, large Anglesey, and Sir Fôn Bach, small Anglesey. The sea at Malltraeth Bay, in the south west end of the Island, once came up to Malltraeth Beach, and over the marsh, to the village of Pentreberw. Today, old house names in the village still retain memories of those days. Penrhyn Mawr, Penrhyn Bach, Penrhyn Cottage, all point to their origin, Penrhyn meaning promontory, when the people of Pentreberw lived at the edge of the sea.

Then, around the end of the eighteenth century a long embankment or cob, was built from above Pentreberw down to Malltraeth Beach, combining and confining Afon Cefni (Afon Fawr) and narrower rivers (Afon Fain) and carrying them in a straight line down to the sea – thus partially draining the marsh and leaving Pentreberw as an inland village.

In the centre of the marsh lies an ancient man-made mound, which is known as 'Mynwent y Llwyn' – Grove Cemetery. It is believed to be a Celtic or Viking burial ground and is known to have been the haunt, for many hundreds of years, of the Black Bull.

This bull has always been regarded as very evil, a creature of the Devil, and greatly feared by the people. Perhaps rightly so, as it is alleged to have caused the mysterious death of at least one woman. And so to the story.

In the middle of the nineteenth century, coalmining was in its hey-day at Pentreberw and, by 1830, the population of the village had risen to more than a thousand people. The influx of miners who came to work in the Berw Colliery was mainly from towns in Flintshire and Ruabon. Hard-working, hard-drinking men who worked in extremely dangerous conditions and to whom death and serious injuries were no strangers.

In their sparse leisure hours, they needed and demanded the stimulation of alcohol and women to soften the stark brutality of their lives. The local pub in Pentreberw was the aptly named Colliers Arms and the landlady who had moved into the village and taken over the pub when mining was at its peak, was quick to make capital out of the miners.

A very potent brew of ale was made from the wild hops which

grew (and still do) on the Marsh. This was served to the thirsty miners who quaffed it in great quantities, which, while washing the coal-dust down, quickly produced a pleasant euphoria.

Thus, one of their appetites was satisfied, while the other was satiated by the prostitutes who were drawn to the miners' money like moths to flames. So the Colliers Arms became more riotous and noisy as the nights drew on, until the village resounded to their raucous laughter and violent cursing.

The Baptist Chapel stood just across the road from the Colliers and the congregation were scandalised and appalled when the sermons could not be heard for the noise and their hymns were almost drowned out by the miners' bawdy ditties.

The new landlady was looked upon as a 'dynes ddrwg' (an evil woman), shunned by the villagers, who swore she would come to a bad end before long.

Stories about the Black Bull had been passed down the generations for hundreds of years and, as summer died and autumn drew near, the tales were revived again and told to the 'foreign miners' as they sat around the fire in the tavern and drank their pints. Local miners who had seen it swore it was true, telling vivid stories of how it looked and each man confirmed that it was an unearthly creature which always appeared on the night of the full moon in September, at the crossroads.

It was being discussed by a group of miners from Ruabon one day on the day shift and, a local man, William Jones, was listening with a derisive smile. A practical, unimaginative man, who always scoffed at the story.

'Seeing is believing,' was his phlegmatic observation, as miner after miner tried to convince him, and he remained seemingly unmoved. But they were so emphatic in their belief, that secretly he became impressed and wondered whether there was any foundation to the story or whether it was just another myth. He determined to find out for himself. He had no fear of ghosts – he had tramped home from the mine at all hours of the night, in all kinds of weather and seen nothing untoward.

William lived at No.2 Capelulo, on the Collier Mawr Crossroads, just opposite the Colliers Arms, and it was to this crossroads the Bull was reputed to make its way, when it came up from the marsh.

So the September harvest moon (or nine full moons as the locals called it) was just rising above the trees when William Jones tramped down his garden, carrying a ladder. He climbed up it to the top of the wall, to where he had a good view of the crossroads. As he lit his pipe, he gazed around at the peaceful scene, everything still and quiet, the roofs silver in the moonlight. Leaning on his arms, he puffed contentedly and waited. Time passed. He saw the last staggering, singing miner turned out of the tavern and watched him weaving unsteadily homewards as the Colliers pub door was slammed shut and barred.

Time passed, William grew bored and decided to go to bed. Knocking his pipe out on the wall, he was peering into the bowl to see if there were any embers still glowing in it before he put it in his pocket, when a faint sound came to his ears. Hastily putting his pipe away, he clutched at the top rung and listened.

Then he heard it — a booming noise from the depths of the marsh, eerie and distant.

William tensed, straining to listen. There was silence, long enough for him to think he had been mistaken, then it came again. Nearer this time, a roar, echoing across the marsh. It was the unmistakable bellowing of a very angry bull. William peered at the crossroads and the road leading to the marsh and, just before a small cloud drifted across the moon, he saw the body of a huge animal trotting up to the crossroads. The bellowing became louder as it approached and, when the cloud had passed, he saw it.

There it stood, a gigantic black bull, higher than a tall man at its shoulders, small red eyes burning like the fires from hell. A huge beast — sniffing the night wind and snorting through dilated nostrils. William stared in disbelief — it looked murderously real, stamping and raking the ground with a hoof and then bending its massive head down sideways to rip up the hard-packed surface of the road with long cruel-looking horns, all the while uttering snorts of anger.

Unable to move, and stiff with fright, William clung to his ladder, quite certain that if the bull saw him and charged at his garden wall, the stones would fly about like cardboard and, once it was in the garden, he would be instantly impaled on those sharp horns and, within minutes, he would be gored to death, his body flung about like a rag doll.

The bull, across the road from him, outside the Colliers Arms, was swinging its head from side to side, small furious eyes glaring around. Pacing in front of the pub, it stopped, looking up at the windows and bellowed with a deafening roar. Terrified, William Jones recoiled and fell backwards off the ladder into his garden – landing with an almighty thud, unaware that his bowels had given way – and he had soiled his pants.

Shortly after this and, according to some, as a direct result of the bull's appearance, the landlady of the disreputable pub started to feel ill. Most of the good living inhabitants of the village avoided or ignored her, but the maid, pot-man and various people on her staff noticed that she was losing weight and was becoming very tired doing her usual task of running the Colliers. Her lively mood had changed too – she became pensive and more and more depressed. As her depression deepened, they noticed that she had become very nervous, peering into the shadows in dark corners and starting up at any sudden sound.

Came the morning when she was too weak to leave her bed and the life of the pub went on without her. She ordered her maid to sleep in the bedroom adjacent to her own and always to leave the oil lamp burning through the night.

As the disease advanced and many remedies had been tried and failed, she tossed and turned restlessly in her bed, muttering to herself and demanding that someone should always be in the room with her, begging not to be left alone. The staff knew that she was terribly afraid of dying and, one morning, when her maid was leaning over, plumping her pillows and talking cheerfully to her, she suddenly grasped her wrist, looking up with haunted eyes in her thin face and, said urgently:

'Don't let me die – don't let me die – I am on the brink of the black hole – and I'm so frightened.'

Someone was at her side all day, while she muttered and tossed, complaining that her room was too hot and she felt as if she was on fire. So her maid, Nia, opened the window wide, but still the woman complained, throwing the covers off repeatedly. By night-time, Nia was exhausted and, when her mistress fell into a fitful sleep just before midnight, she gladly turned the oil lamp down a little and crept downstairs for something to eat, leaving the window wide open.

The staff had closed the pub, cleaned the bar and were gathered in the kitchen having their supper.

As they looked up at her – she nodded her head.

'She's asleep at last,' she said with a tired sigh and made herself a cheese sandwich before she sank onto a chair.

They talked in low tones, their faces grave. An uneasy atmosphere, gloomy and troubled, lay over the room. Talk became intermittent, gradually everyone became silent, lost in their own thoughts and the ticking of the wall clock became loud.

Suddenly the silence was broken by a heart-stopping scream from above, followed by another and another and a violent hubbub broke out, the sound of smashing crockery, overturned furniture and a heavy thumping like the tread of hooves. All heads snapped up looking at the ceiling, but everyone seemed frozen with horror as the hellish row went on.

Huw, the barman was the first to move. Nia dropped her half-eaten sandwich and ran to the door behind him, the others following. Even as they rushed up the stairs, the last scream ended in a terrible gurgle, and then there was silence.

The scene that met their eyes was unbelievable.

The washstand had been violently overturned, throwing the jug and basin to the floor where they lay in smithereens. The oil lamp still burned on the bedroom table, throwing a dim light on the body of the landlady. She lay across the bed, thrown down like a sack of wheat, her limbs contorted. Blood was everywhere, her nightgown in tatters, her whole body slashed and gored. In her throat was a deep circular wound, from which blood still ran. It was matched by another exactly the same further down her body, which was covered everywhere with murderous wounds.

From the bed, a trail of huge bloodstains led to the window. The flowing lace curtains stirring in the night breeze were bedabbled with long red smears and trails and the room was filled with the strong animal stench of a bull.

Ghost ship

I found this little story most compelling. It was one of the batches that Mr Pritchard gave me and I tell it in practically all his own words. I wonder if perhaps the John Pritchard in the story is a relative of his?

John Pritchard of 1 Ty'n Coed, Pentreberw was weary. He had been out shooting and was going home very late one night, with a couple of rabbits slung over his shoulder. When Pont Barcle came into sight, he decided to rest for a while, after hours spent tramping across the fields.

Thankfully, he dropped the rabbits at his feet, laid his gun carefully on the wide parapet, before scrambling up himself and perched comfortably, tired feet dangling, over the bridge. Fumbling in his inside jacket pocket, he removed his old tobacco pouch and skinning knife. He laid the length of 'Taffy Twist' in his palm, cut off a thick wedge of tobacco and thumbed it into his mouth, between teeth and cheek. Then, chewing slowly, he laid his big hands on his thighs and surveyed the scene.

The moon to the south was full, a harvest moon, and it shone on the slates of Plas Berw roof, the willow shrubs on Morfa Mawr, and turned the cold water of Afon Fawr (Cefni) into a silver ribbon.

He turned his head to face the A5 road. The furnaces of the two lime kilns threw a yellowish glow into the sky and, as he raised his eyes, he could see the dark masses of Penrhyn Mawr and Ty'n Coed outlined against the velvety sky. The water was high in the river, just below the high tide mark on the white wooden marker boards on either side of the bridge. He leaned over and spat a squirt of brownish juice from his tobacco chew into the restless water below.

'The sea must be coming in strongly at Malltraeth,' he thought.

August mist, forming after the warm day, began to rise from the river and lay like a metre-high white blanket across the rough, hummocked grasses of the boggy marsh, toward Morfa Mawr.

His eyes suddenly fell upon a movement in the mist. At first he thought a piece of it had become detached and was moving, but as he stared and the shape became whole, he gave an indrawn hissing breath. He was looking at a long, slender ship. It had a high curved head and a square shaped sail, which was bellied out and taut, as it would be with a strong following wind, but the night was still. There was no creak of timber or sound of the sail, as the ship moved on as silent as a swan, past the old coalmines and over Sand Road, Lôn Dywod. John realised, as he watched, that there was something wrong and eerie about it – it was not floating down the river on its way to the open sea at Malltraeth, but sailing over the rough herbage of the marsh, which had been drained for years.

In the time of the Vikings, it would have been covered in deep water and their longboats would have been a common sight. Gradually, as it faded out of view, mist and boat became one. When it had gone, it began to dawn on John what he had just seen. For a moment, shock kept him rigid, and then he began to shake like a leaf. Like a man in a dream, he automatically picked up his gun and rabbits and made for home.

He never saw the Viking longboat again.

This story was told many times by his son, Robert Pritchard, who was a sniper in the First World War, with the Royal Welsh Fusiliers.

Treasure in the water

In Pentreberw stands a snug, comfortable farmhouse, surrounded and sheltered from the high winds by substantial outbuildings. It has not always looked so prosperous however, because in the early nineteenth century agriculture on Anglesey was in decline and the farm, Llosg yr Odyn, was falling into disrepair.

Huw Prytherch lived there with his family, struggling to make ends meet and, any profits made were swallowed up, paying the wages of essential farm workers and servants.

Huw was a very good carpenter and, when he made up his mind to get a job, he was gladly accepted by the management of Berw Colliery. Although the wages weren't high, Huw and his family could live on them, thus he didn't have to rely on the land to keep him and it helped the farm to stay solvent. Also, his eldest son, Owen, a sensible, level-headed boy managed the day to day running of the farm.

Things worked smoothly for a few years and, when they hit a bad patch, Huw would always cheerfully say that things would get better.

Alas – not so. One day a small deputation of officials arrived at the front door with the dire news that Huw had had a fatal accident whilst he was renewing some timber underground in the mine.

The family was stunned and desolated. What would happen to them now that cheerful Huw and his valuable wages were gone?

Owen thought deeply. He was the eldest and, as such, he would become the head of the family and take on the responsibility of their well being and the management of the farm.

But he had no trade at his fingertips like his father, he worked long hours on the farm and his presence was essential. He would just have to work twice as hard. What else could he do? What assets had he got?

He was tall and very strong. He was also extremely brave, fearing no man. A friend of his father's had taught him how to fight bare-knuckled and he was so good at it, being cool-headed and fighting scientifically, that no one in the district could beat him. So he started taking on professional fighters at the local fairs and earned a few shillings by thrashing them soundly.

He loved his home, had always lived there and, from being a child, he'd heard stories that the farm well, from which they drew all their water, was haunted. Like most children, he hadn't taken much notice and the stories were not discussed in his presence when he was small, in order not to frighten him.

As he grew up, however, he realised that many of the women servants stayed only briefly, leaving because they refused to work somewhere that was haunted. Owen was inclined to scoff at this saying it was just old wives' tales, until something happened which made him believe differently.

A maid servant called Siân lived in at the farm. She was a cheerful, happy girl who always sang as she worked and, one night, as dusk fell, Mrs Prytherch sent her to the well to collect a bucket of water for the dishes. Siân went happily enough, but came flying back again five minutes later, clutching the empty pail and stammering about seeing a ghost at the well.

She refused stoutly to go on working at the farm and said all she wanted to do was go back home to her Mam, she had had such a fright. Mrs Prytherch put the girl to bed and Owen strolled down to the well in the dark, but as he suspected, he saw nothing.

Siân was true to her word, gathered her few belongings together and left the farm next morning, still pale and upset. Owen was taking his work boots off in the hall, coming in for breakfast, when she passed him with the briefest of goodbyes. The rest of the farm workers were in the kitchen with his Mam having their breakfast and he could hear them discussing both the ghost and her abrupt departure when he entered the room. The farm foreman and Mrs Prytherch were counting how many servants had left that twelve month because of the ghost.

Intrigued, Owen sat and listened, where previously he would have laughed, but he had seen how upset Siân was, and he knew her fear was real. So he asked them if any of them had seen the ghost, what was it, when did it appear and what did it do?

They were glad he did not scoff and were only too eager to tell their stories. Those who had seen the ghost told him they would never go near the well in the dark. The pictures he gleaned from them varied. Some said the spectre was just a light patch, others said it was the figure of a man. Who he was and what he wanted they didn't know, they hadn't stayed long enough to find out. Apparently, he just stood there, and no one knew just when he would appear. Everyone, men included, made sure they only visited the well in daylight.

Word had spread around the village that the place was haunted and the Prytherch family was finding it more and more difficult to employ indoor servants and farm workers who were willing to come and work there.

Owen decided there must be some substance to the story – most of his men were steady, unimaginative people, not given to nervous fancies, yet they seemed to be just as convinced as the maid servants.

So, every night from then on, after doing the rounds of his stock, Owen made his way to the well in the field next to the farm and waited patiently in the dark, looking and listening for anything untoward. But all was still, just the usual sounds of the night. For several weeks he made it his last job before going to bed, but as winter set in, he became bored with the routine and cold and tired, so he stopped only briefly by the well.

One chilly moonless night, with a cold wind blowing through his jacket, he went there again and glanced around, not expecting to see anything. All was quiet and still and his warm bed beckoned so he turned to go. A glimmer of light caught the corner of his eye and Owen held his breath and stared. The light became stronger and longer, until it formed a column. It was a long cylinder of light, like a tube of white fluorescent gas, which gradually solidified and took the shape of a man.

Tall, dressed in a dark suit and bowler hat, he appeared to be surrounded by a white glow. When he had fully materialised, he stood still, gazing steadily at Owen. Owen's back went stiff with shock and a thrill of fear ran through him as he stared. Most people would have fled, but Owen stood his ground and, when he could find his voice again he cried out in Welsh:

'Yn enw Duw – be wyt ti eisiau?' ('In the name of God, what do you want?').

He knew that no spirit or ghost could speak unless it was addressed first and he waited with a thumping heart for the reply.

There was no answer from the figure, which was still gazing at him, but it slowly raised its right arm and pointed in the direction of the well. It stood in that position for what seemed an age and, Owen, realising it meant him no harm, summoned up enough courage to ask:

'What's in the well?'

Still no reply, but the ghost moved nearer to the well and pointed down into the water, gazing with great urgency at Owen.

Owen nodded to show he understood and, after staring gravely at him for another minute, the ghost dropped his arm, turned and walked slowly away. The glow around him dimmed and diminished gradually until it had gone out altogether and the apparition had vanished into the darkness. Shaken, but very curious, Owen went to bed, wondering what on earth the ghost had been trying to tell him.

Before breakfast next day, Owen went out to find his foreman who was preparing for the winter ploughing, told him what had occurred and said he was going to examine the well to see if there was anything in it. Together, they walked into the field.

The structure of the well was stone and the water deep but so clear the bottom could easily be seen. Nothing lay there, so the two men began to examine the stonework very carefully. The outer wall was solid, nothing out of place, so they turned their attention to the inside. The foreman leaned over, tapping and gripping the stones. Nothing.

Owen went carefully down the few stone steps, which jutted out of the inner wall and felt around them carefully for any loose ones. He reached the bottom step and had almost given up the idea that there was anything to find, as he had now reached the waterline, when, under the step, in the water, his hand encountered a stone that wobbled when he touched it.

Owen called out to the foreman that he had found something and, with the man behind him holding his belt to stop him overbalancing and pitching into the icy waters, he crouched gingerly down and, by rocking the stone to and fro, he managed to remove it.

This he handed up then bent down again, plunging his hand into the water and groping about the cavity. There was definitely something in there and he grinned up excitedly at the foreman as he searched blindly with his fingertips.

Whatever was in there was smooth, round and hard, and quite a lot of them. He carefully picked out a few and, when he withdrew his hand and opened his fist, they both gave gasps of amazement. Glinting and wet on his palm lay a small heap of golden sovereigns. Carefully he passed them up and searched again. When the hole was finally empty, a substantial pile of sovereigns lay on the coping stone of the well. The dates on them showed they had been hidden there many years ago. Triumphantly, the men carried the gold back to the house and laid it with great ceremony on the table in front of the dumbfounded family and staff, who had just sat down to breakfast.

The money was not wastefully spent. The farm could now be vastly improved. Old buildings were repaired, new ones built and the leaky old thatch covering the roof was ripped off and replaced with slates.

Who the ghost was and why it had returned was the subject of great conjecture for years to come, but its mission was accomplished and it was never seen again.

(As told by Mrs Williams, Llosg yr Odyn, 1956.)
Given to me by Mr Donald Pritchard, Headmaster, Ysgol Pen-y-sarn.

Signs and portents

Mr John Roberts of Bryn Teg, first introduced me to the 'Deryn Corff (Bird of Death) and his version is included elsewhere in this book. Mr Pritchard confirms they are a widespread belief on the Island.

The white owl was looked upon as a messenger of death, flying over the house of a sick person or hooting in the trees.

My friend, Mrs Nan Jones, said that when her husband was lying gravely ill in hospital, she took her two daughters to visit him one winter's evening.

As they were driving across the island in the dark, a large white owl came hurtling out of the night, and smashed against the car windscreen. After the initial shock had worn off, Nan, knowing full well what the sight of the bird portended, sternly warned the girls not to say a word about it to their father. Sadly, he died later.

People in Pentreberw (writes Mr Pritchard) firmly believed the 'Deryn Corff existed. What sort of bird it was, natural or heavenly or hellish they would not say. Nobody had seen it or could describe it, but they knew it was a messenger forecasting the passing of a soul from this world to the next.

Where it came from, no one knew, but it came always at night with its fateful message. The method of delivery was usually made by the tapping of its beak on the window of the room where the dying person lay. Sometimes one slap against the window made by the body of the bird, other times it would thrash its wings wildly against the casement. Another way was for the bird to screech around the house or from the trees nearby.

According to William Jones, Penrhyn Mawr, Pentreberw, during the 1904 Revivalism, the 'Deryn Corff was screeching and screaming in the trees of Greigiau Coed, Pentreberw, for weeks at a time, during the religious meetings in the area.

Another messenger of death was the Death Watch Beetle, which made a noise like a clock tapping out the hours that the sick person had to live.

Dogs howling in the night was a sure sign that death would follow – as was the crow of a cockerel between 8.00 p.m. and midnight.

The story of the Cannwyll Corff (Corpse Candle) is also well known. Sometimes they were called 'Jac y Lantern' and the old miners believed that the yellow and bluish light that flickered along the marsh was a sign that death would befall someone in the family of those who saw it.

The marsh of Pentreberw showed its Cannwyll Corff lights very vividly in the 1960's and, although the young people scoffed and declared it to being methane gas, generated by the decaying vegetable matter in the marsh, the older generation still believed in the old interpretation and were proved right time and time again.

Grey horse cave

Many years ago, I worked on a poultry farm at Rhos-on-Sea and I was told many stories by the farm labourer, a cheerful gentleman named Huw Jones.

One story, about a family called Wynne, who lived at Penrhyn, Cemaes, about two hundred years ago, stuck in my memory.

Mrs Wynne was a wealthy widow, with a prosperous farm, and two sons who had no love for each other. The elder brother could do no wrong in his mother's eyes and, she indulged his every whim, so that he grew lazy and spoilt, leaving the younger one to do the lion's share of the work.

Eventually, the older one persuaded his mother to let him go on the 'Grand Tour', which was fashionable at that time and he took himself off to travel around Europe. Being very selfish, he couldn't be bothered to write home and, when a couple of years went by, with no news of him, his grieving mother assumed that he must be dead.

His younger brother, dedicated to his work, became the natural master of the farm, and was given a free hand by his mother, who had become morose and tearful and had no interest whatsoever in the place, now her favourite son had disappeared. He (the younger son) met and fell in love with a local girl and he told his mother he would like to get married, bring his bride back to the farm and, eventually, raise sons to follow in his footsteps. Mrs Wynne wasn't particularly interested in his plans, but didn't object, so the boy went on to make arrangements for his wedding.

One day in winter, when he had just had a fitting for his marriage suit, the door was thrown open to let in the blustery wind – and his brother, absent for nearly three years. In he strode, looking handsome in a sumptuous cloak, smiling broadly at his dumbfounded family.

His mother, after the first shock, was delighted to see him and threw her arms about him, alternately laughing and crying. The servants swarmed about him – he had gifts for everyone and all were delighted to see him, although he greeted his younger brother very coolly and had no gift for him.

250

The fire was made up and a great feast prepared and, while the hustle and bustle went on around him, he sat toasting his toes, regaling his mother with fascinating stories. His travels were over, he declared, and he was home for good.

When the food was brought in and the family moved from the fireside, the older brother casually sat at the top of the table, the rightful place for the head of the house, which had been occupied by his brother for three years.

The younger son, who was stunned to see the return of the prodigal son, had been sitting silently brooding as the talk and the laughter flowed round him and the sight of his older brother usurping his place at the table was too much for him. No one noticed when he left the room and, snatching his coat and hat from the hall, he went to saddle up his horse, consumed with fury and despair, his plans in ruins.

Mounting, he set his horse into a gallop, spurring it on into the darkness and wind, not caring where he went and making straight for the headland and the edge of the cliff. Full pelt they went and horse and rider plunged to their deaths on the rocks below. His body was never found, but that of his horse was days later and the only evidence of his death was when his hat was found. Both horse and hat were washed into a cave, which has always been since called, Grey Horse Cave.

I had almost forgotten this tale until, whilst compiling this book, Mrs Irene Williams of Park Lodge, Cemaes (which incorporates in its building the Wynne's original farmhouse – once called Cromlech) kindly sent me the following story which, although slightly changed by years of telling, lends credence to the old tale.

Mrs Williams' story:

There is a legend on Park Lodge, namely the Legend of the Blue Mare Cave. It is said that a couple of hundred years or so ago, a man living in Park Lodge was jilted and, in great distress, rode his blue mare over the cliff at a point where the currents swirl and nothing is washed ashore. Except, on that occasion, the body of the blue mare was washed back into the cave along with the rider's hat, but nothing was ever seen again of the rider.

Now to the point that is interesting. A local hotelier asked me if his wife could ride across our land trying out a horse she was proposing to buy. I gave her permission to do so, but later that day, her husband telephoned, saying that the vet had looked at the horse and said she would be unwise to buy it. Therefore, she would not be coming up to Park Lodge.

Sometime much later in the day, my son-in-law, Stephen, came in and said, 'She certainly gave that horse a good gallop, I could hear it clearly thundering across the headland, but strangely enough, I could not see her.'

I then, of course, told him about the phone call – he did not believe me and, to this day, I still wonder whether he does.

After reading this, I was puzzled as to whether the horse was grey or a blue mare – as the two versions of the tale were both strongly rooted and I had difficulty in correlating the two stories. To my great relief, I read a third version – an old one, which described the animal as blue-grey.

Whether horse or mare, I still don't know, but it seems as if Wynne the younger is still re-enacting his ride to death – two hundred years later.

The lady of Park Lodge

Mrs Irene Williams, of Park Lodge, Cemaes Bay, who sent the very interesting story of the Grey Horse Cave to me, also told me of the ghost of a gentle lady who regularly walks through Park Lodge.

Part of the main house and the farmhouse adjoining it, are over three hundred years old, so it is not surprising that such old buildings are haunted.

Mr and Mrs Williams and their late daughter's husband, Stephen, moved into the house in 1987 and were soon aware that odd things were happening.

One day, Mrs Williams' husband, John, and Stephen were chatting in the kitchen, when they both heard the tapping of a woman's high-heeled shoes, moving briskly and lightly along the path outside, approaching the kitchen door, where they stopped. They listened for a moment, but no one knocked, so John got up and opened the door. There was no one there.

As they had both heard the noises distinctly, they stared at each other in bewilderment, and then went out to investigate – each going separate ways, around the house. They found nothing and were completely baffled, as the clicking footsteps had sounded so definite and normal.

Since then, the footsteps have been heard many times, both outside and upstairs and are still a regular occurrence.

Articles are frequently moved also, in particular a beloved framed photograph of Mrs Williams' late daughter which always stood on an occasional table and was never moved.

One morning Mrs Williams went into the room and was puzzled to find the picture standing on the mantelpiece. Everyone denied having touched it, so Mrs Williams put it back on the table.

A few days later, a pretty china windmill went missing from the radiator shelf in the hall, but subsequently it re-appeared on a similar radiator self in the dining room. Once again, no one had handled it and Mrs Williams left it where it was, as the ghost seemed to prefer it in that position!

Park Lodge is now a small holiday complex, consisting of the old farmhouse, self-catering cottages and a camping field.

Mrs Williams goes on:

A couple of years ago, some friends of ours came to stay at the farmhouse, they had a long way to travel and, being tired on their first night, went to bed early.

A visitor on the camping field, after an evening in the bar, was warned not to make a noise as he walked past the adjoining farmhouse, as I didn't want my friends disturbed.

Next morning the camper came to the house and said he was very sorry, assuring me that he had not made any noise going back to camp, but he must have disturbed the lady in the farmhouse because:

'I saw a lady at the window with a type of nightcap on, looking out at me. I nodded and said I was sorry, but there was no reaction from her.'

Mrs Williams was curious and questioning the camper, he told her that as it was a clear moonlit night, he could see the lady clearly. He thought she was in her late twenties, very pretty and the 'nightcap' she was wearing fitted the description of a mob cap worn by ladies in the eighteenth and early nineteenth centuries.

Although I was convinced it could not be our friend in the farmhouse, when I saw her, I asked her if she had slept well, to which she replied:

'I slept like a log from nine o'clock until eight o'clock this morning.'

Last year, other friends of ours were sleeping in the farmhouse and their little boy, aged four, was put to bed at 7.00 p.m. his usual time. The following morning he said to his mother:

'Mummy, I woke up in the night and there was a lovely lady standing at the bottom of the bed with a pretty blue dress on. She smiled at me and I went back to sleep.'

The child was not in any way frightened by this experience.

There is an adjoining door between the farmhouse and the hotel bar and the boy's Mummy said she had many times popped through to the farmhouse to check on him in bed and, each time she had found the adjoining door wide open, when she remembers quite clearly that she had previously closed it.

On another occasion, a small dog was in the lounge opposite

the main staircase. He appeared to be asleep, but to our amazement he suddenly jumped up, trotted to the bottom of the stairs and stood there staring up them. He was wagging his tail furiously and became very excited. Despite all our efforts to distract him, he wouldn't take his eyes off the stairs. After a few minutes, his tail stopped wagging, he became calm, and then eventually he lay down and went to sleep again.

None of us saw a thing!

Mrs Williams and her family feel a great affection for their ghost, calling her their 'lovely lady' and they know when she is near because they smell a beautiful aroma, like lavender or cologne, then a feeling of a presence passing in a waft of air, leaving them with a sense of warmth and comfort.

She goes on to say:

The Lady also has quite a sense of humour. One evening, the house suddenly got very hot and, when I checked the central heating boiler, it had been turned up from low to high. I knew it could not have been any of us; we were all in the same room. This little trick was repeated very often after this, I've got so used to it by now, that when it happens I go straight to the utility room and return it back to its normal setting.

I have tried to trace the origins of this happy lady ghost, but none of us, John, my husband, Stephen, my son-in-law nor I have ever been able to find out anything that may tell of her origins nor have we ever had a sighting of her. Perhaps she is one of those ghosts who still likes to be where they were happy in life. She certainly makes us very aware of her presence and gives us a feeling of being a very kind and gentle person, in no way frightening, but in her life-time she must have been quite a character!'

* * *

Mrs Williams has two self-contained cottages, originally outbuildings of the farm, adjoining the main house. Twelve years ago, when the Williams moved in, they had the old structures rebuilt as cottages. One day, when the work was going on, one of the workmen came to tell her that they had heard footsteps crossing the room above them and, when one went to see who was up there, the room was empty. It happened in both No.1 and No.2 cottages and the men became quite used to it.

One of them, known as old John, said to Mrs Williams,

'Oh, whoever it is is friendly, they're doing no harm, and they're just interested in the work going on!'

'Just last week,' Mrs Williams told me (in September) 'two men stayed in No.2 cottage – they were on a walking holiday and had brought their dog. The second night they were there, the dog had just finished his dinner, when he started to act in a very peculiar way.

First, it stared fixedly at something they couldn't see, then it went stiff and the hairs on its neck bristled. Suddenly, it went berserk, and they had a terrible job calming it.

Another funny thing happened with a dog staying here. We have a very beautiful Oregon pine staircase, which everyone admires. A guest was crossing the hall with his dog, when suddenly it stopped dead, staring at the staircase and growling deep in its throat. We all came out into the hall and gazed at the staircase, but we couldn't see a thing. After a few minutes it stopped growling and turned away, after that it was quite normal.

Not long ago, a couple with a small boy came to stay and they had a bedroom at the rear of the house. In the evening, when the boy had been put to bed, his mother came down looking puzzled.

'Did you ever have a staircase there?' she asked pointing upstairs to the back of the house – I came out of the room and felt I should go down the stairs in front of the bedroom door, but of course there are no stairs there.'

'Perhaps there was a staircase there at one time,' said Mrs Williams, 'the house has been greatly altered over the years perhaps she was a bit psychic.'

It appears to me that Mrs Williams is the fortunate owner of a house where people have lived and worked happily for hundreds of years and have left it with a full and vibrant atmosphere that still lingers.

The road to Point Lynas

The headland, topped by the tall white lighthouse on the NE coast of Anglesey, is known throughout the world by mariners.

'Oh yes, I know Point Lynas,' they say, 'that's where we pick up the Liverpool Pilot.'

It is no surprise to learn that this high granite outcrop, bare and windswept, is haunted.

The lighthouse buildings once housed a master keeper, two assistant keepers and their families, but the only living creatures there now are the sea birds. The walls of the houses, one in the centre and, one on each side, are two feet thick and nestle within a sheltering enclosure. But the light and the foghorn are now automatic and controlled from Liverpool.

It's a very eerie place on a dull day, with the wind shrilling through the struts of the tall radio mast, and the foghorn wailing every sixty seconds when the sea mist rolls in. The road up to it is kept in good repair by the Mersey Docks and Harbour Board. It climbs up straight and narrow from the Pilot's Accommodation building at the bottom. It is dug between earth banks, topped with high walls on each side, which protects anyone on it from the high winds.

A popular walk, dog owners love it, the thin tarmac road is eschewed for the springy turf on side, where their dogs roam freely, no sheep to worry about. Many walkers use the road, but it was deserted when Walt and I went up there about seven o'clock one morning last summer.

We had walked up to the lighthouse, stopped at the locked iron gates as usual, peering in at the enclosed yard, and turned to go back again. The headland was deserted. Not a soul on the road or on either side, we could see both banks clearly, as they rise above the sunken road. When we were halfway down, I looked back up the straight road and saw a tall man just in front of the gates, coming down towards us at a smart pace.

'Someone's behind us,' I said casually to Walt. He looked around and stared at the figure.

'Didn't see him coming up,' he said.

From the top of the point, the headland (which has no trees or bushes) can be scanned for miles. It is possible to see anyone approaching, either on the road or the grass on each side. Short and turfy, no place to hide.

I looked back. The tall man seemed quite solid, but he was wearing a long, dark, old fashioned looking coat and was approaching very quickly, with long strides.

'He's catching up with us, he's walking very fast,' I said. 'Let's move to the side a bit so he can get past.'

We moved aside and strolled on. I was trying to listen for his footsteps, so that as he went by, we could exchange a cheery good-morning and comment on the lovely day.

Time passed, he didn't appear, so I glanced back again to see if he had stopped.

The road behind us was empty.

I stopped. 'He's gone,' I said.

Walt stopped also and looked back.

'Where did he go? He can't have climbed over the wall, no point,' said Walt.

We looked all around, but couldn't see a soul.

'He didn't have a dog, did he?' I asked. 'I wonder if he turned round and went back?'

'Wouldn't have had time to go all the way back up the road without us seeing him,' said Walt.

We had reached the Pilot's Accommodation building at the bottom of the hill and sat down on the low stone walls. There was no sign of anyone about.

'Wonder who he was,' I said, 'he looked real enough didn't he? And yet – did you get the feeling that there was something odd about him?'

'I don't know,' said Walt thoughtfully, 'tall bloke, thinnish, his coat looked a bit old fashioned. Did you see his face?'

I shook my head.

'He was too far away – and when he got nearer I didn't like to turn around and stare. You're right about his coat though, it did look old fashioned. Did you notice the black gaiters and boots?'

Walt nodded. 'He was really striding out – I was waiting for him to pass us, listening for his footsteps.'

We looked at each other.

'That's another thing,' I said, 'He was wearing heavy boots, but I didn't hear any sound – did you?'

'No, I didn't, he seems to have vanished into thin air,' said Walt.

I looked around, even though it was a warm summer morning, I gave a little shiver.

'Come on, let's go home,' I said.

We've been that way many times since, but have never again seen the tall man in the old fashioned clothes.

Weeks later, I was recounting this episode to Mike Jones, the plumber, telling how weird it was that the man had vanished.

Mike looked thoughtful and shook his head.

'It's a funny road, that one,' he said, 'I've heard a few stories about things that have been seen there, that people can't explain. For instance, you know how people go fishing off the rocks there at night?'

I nodded; we had often seen the bright lights of the powerful lamps the fishermen used at nights to lure the fish nearer. The discomfort of the sharp rocks and the cold night winds never seemed to deter the men who sat huddled in the dark.

'Well,' said Mike, 'I know of two lads who were going fishing there a few years ago and they had just got as far as the Pilot's House – they were going down to the jetty where the Pilot Boat comes in. That's just before the road going up to the Point. If you turn off to the right, there's a place there that the fishermen like.

Anyhow, just before they left the road, they shone one of the torches ahead of them, and they saw something that made them stop dead.

Ahead of them were two strange creatures standing side by side, staring at the boys. Apparently, they looked a bit like animals bigger than dogs and about the size of sheep, but white in colour. They didn't have fur or hide; they were covered in skin, like a human, except they were standing on four legs. In the light of the torch, their eyes looked almost human and they stood and stared silently.

They weren't like any creatures the pair had ever seen and, when they started to walk slowly towards the boys, they both turned tail and ran back as fast as they could move. One of them told me they were both convinced that they were being chased, but they were too frightened to look back.

Whatever the things were, they didn't follow them.

The boys couldn't describe them properly, but they were very scared and they never went fishing at Lynas again!'

Poltergeist at Mynydd Mechell

It is often found that places which have been the site of intense emotions, hate, fear, depression, rage etc. seem to retain something of that atmosphere in the very fabric of the building.

Sometimes, even ordinary well-balanced people are thrown off their fulcrum by sudden, unexpected events that cast them into the depths of despair and hopelessness.

This is what happened to a very popular, hard-working couple who ran a business in the pleasant, peaceful village of Mynydd Mechell. Things went smoothly for them for many years, until in the late 1980's, their shop was burgled. A chain of disasters followed, which ultimately destroyed their lives.

After much soul-searching and discussions, they decided to put the business up for sale and buy an old cottage nearby, to retire into.

Moving house is stressful in itself, but the burglary, buying the cottage, and putting the business up for sale, brought many problems which ended the tranquillity of their lives.

They found a buyer and, as the sale was going through Mr and Mrs N. bought the cottage, and started the strenuous task of renovating it, running the shop at the same time.

The sale of the business was not quite completed when Mr N. who had become very unwell, consulted the doctor, who, after tests, diagnosed asbestosis and he learned he had not got long to live.

He died before having a chance to live in the cottage and, the suddenness of his death, the funeral and having to leave the shop immediately so the new owners could take over, must have been a dreadful series of nightmare events for the widowed Mrs N. When she moved into the cottage she was under severe mental strain.

This is where the story becomes somewhat muddled and obscure.

One version is that Mrs N. was so lonely, she decided to take in a lady lodger. One evening, they started to play about with an ouija board (perhaps in the faint hope that they be able to contact Mrs N's husband) or maybe just to while away the long winter evenings.

The other version is that it was the lady lodger who tinkered about with the board, but whoever it was, they managed to raise an elemental – a malignant entity which is easily aroused by someone under great mental stress and is hard to dismiss even by someone initiated and which the two ladies found impossible to control.

Some people say it was a poltergeist – no one really knows. But whatever it was, manifested by knocking on the bed-head, breaking dishes and ornaments in empty rooms, opening and closing the front door and sounds of someone walking up and down the stairs.

The terrified lady lodger was so unnerved by these events, that she packed her bags and left hurriedly, leaving poor Mrs N. all alone.

She was now convinced that the cottage was haunted by evil spirits and she tried to banish them by sprinkling salt in every room and drawing a huge pentacle all around the outside of the cottage, telling people it would keep evil spirits away.

Eventually, Mrs N. broke under the strain, had a mental breakdown, and her daughter, who lived down south, took her mother away to live with her.

Although the manifestations had now ceased, the cottage, now empty, acquired the reputation amongst the village children as a place to be avoided because of the ghosts and every morning the children ran past it as fast as they could on their way to the school bus. It was known locally as 'the haunted house' and was very hard to sell.

So it stood empty for over two years, until a young couple bought it and moved in. It is to Pauline, the lady of the house, that I am indebted for this story, although she tells me that she doesn't know the precise details, as the villagers don't wish to talk about Mrs N., who was very popular.

Pauline said the only thing in the cottage when they moved in was something that Mr N. had made. Apparently, when they were furnishing the cottage, Mr N. had carefully cut out, from a magazine, a picture of a mother and baby (rather resembling the Madonna and Child) which he had carefully glued to a piece of slate. Then he had coated it with transparent varnish and made a nail-hole in the top.

It was during this time that he had become very ill and was morose and depressed. Before he died, he hung the picture in the living room of the cottage and said it must never be moved.

Pauline disliked it and (perhaps wrongly) blamed it for many small accidents that happened when she and her husband were renovating the cottage, which had become damp during the two years it was unoccupied. So she persuaded her husband to take it down and get rid of it, but not to destroy it. He carefully carried it down, and hid it in a wall near the bus stop. When I asked if it was still there, Pauline said it had disappeared from its hiding place. She also told me that the house is indeed haunted, but not in any unhappy way, and she has told me of its history, as far as she knows it.

Apparently, before Mrs N. bought it, an old lady lived there, the cottage had been in her family for generations and she had never lived anywhere else. She never married, but her life-long love was a farmer who lived just down the road, who visited her every evening and sat in an armchair by the fire, comfortably smoking his pipe.

Her garden was full of the flowers she loved and she also had a flourishing herb garden. The farmer friend did all the digging and the heavy work in the vegetable patch, while she tended her beloved flowers. This tranquil and happy life-style continued for many years, until she died aged 84.

The summer before last, Pauline, her family and, a friend from Scotland, were all lazing in the sunshine, when her Scottish friend, who is psychic, asked who the old lady was, standing amidst the flowers at the back of the garden. No one else could see her, even though the friend pointed her out, saying she looked very real and solid. After about two minutes, the old lady just faded away.

Another time, Pauline's Scottish friend was standing in the kitchen, looking through the open door, when she saw the same old lady in the herb garden.

Although neither Pauline or any of her family, have ever seen the old lady or the farmer, the smell of his pipe tobacco is sometimes very strong in the house, particularly in the evenings. Pauline tells me she has smelt it in the kitchen, on the landing and, recently, in the bedroom.

These two seem to be very happy, contented ghosts, she says, and the atmosphere is so friendly she never wants to live anywhere else.

I do apologise if any of these details are wrong, I have only written the story as it was told to me. I should be very interested if anyone has any further information.

The haunted lane

Whilst I was collating stories for this book, Mr Kelvin Sutherland of Llangefni, wrote to me. He starts his most interesting letter by telling me he is a retired electronics engineer of Scottish birth, who has lived most of his life in Wales and the last forty years on Anglesey. He married a Welsh lady, Betty, who was born and bred in Llangefni.
In his own words he writes:

In the mid-1970's we were living in a house which was built on part of the old Tregaian Estate near Llangefni. Tregaian Estate was then owned by Major Lloyd, who loved the place dearly, and was often to be seen strolling around the lanes and fields, stopping often to enjoy the peaceful views.

I had been up to Tregaian Manor many times to pay the princely sum of £1 a year ground rent and to try to negotiate the purchase of my freehold. He was indeed a gentleman of the old school, offering me a glass of wine whilst we talked in front of a huge fire in the library. It was during these conversations that I gathered something of the deep love he had for his home and lands. Whenever I broached my request, he was always very courteous and pleasant as he told me of his reluctance to break up the estate, so sadly I always came away empty-handed.

Then, one day, we heard that Major Lloyd had died and left the estate to his nephew, whom I immediately contacted and purchased my freehold for a mere £200.

During the summer of the same year, on a lovely sunny afternoon, Betty and I took our little dog, Lassie, for a walk. Lassie was a cross between a terrier and a labrador and she was very intelligent.

We strolled along the lane that leads from Rhosmeirch to Capel Coch, then turned back at Ty'n Coed, passing over the little bridge that spans the pretty brook below and, eventually, approached the back gate of Tregaian Estate.

Just as we drew level with the gate, Lassie, who up to then had been happily trotting along before us, sniffing in the grasses on both sides of the lane, abruptly stopped and became rigid. She absolutely froze and we both realised she had suddenly become terrified. The hair rose stiffly on the back of her neck, her ears were flat to her head and she gradually sank down with her belly flattened to the ground.

We were mildly surprised, but wanting to get home I remember saying as we passed her, 'Come on, Lassie, good girl, home now,' but she didn't budge.

It was then that the cold struck us. Bright warm day it might have been, but it was just as if we had walked into an icy freezer. It stopped us in our tracks and we stood there shivering, our scalps crawling and goose bumps rising on our arms. We looked at each other and I wondered if I looked as frightened as Betty did.

'Let's get out of here,' I said, grabbing her hand and preparing to run. Then we remembered Lassie, still crouching on the road, ducking her head in fear. We bent down to her and, coaxing and dragging, we got poor Lassie to her feet again. She was terribly reluctant to move through that area of cold and slunk between us, pressed closely against my leg and looking very, very scared.

Then suddenly we had burst out of it.

It wasn't that it gradually became less cold, it happened between one step and the next. One second we were freezing and, the next, we had walked into the lovely, comforting warmth of an August afternoon. At once, Lassie became her old self again, running along the hedgerows, looking for rabbits, or butterflies, or anything else to chase. She had immediately forgotten her fear, as soon as we had moved out of that uncanny area of cold.

We climbed the short hill to Rhosmeirch and I stopped to look back down the part of the lane we had come through and the fields on either side. They were quite empty, no cows or sheep and, certainly, nothing that could account for what had taken place.

On the way home, both feeling very disturbed, we tried to account for the feeling of deep fear that we had felt during the abnormality of the drop in temperature. Lassie has suffered no lasting ill effects, but I must admit we have never had the courage to go that way again.

When I described our experience to a local friend, he told me that old Major Lloyd loved to walk down his back drive to the gate. Here he would lean and contemplate his favourite view, usually on warm summer days, and often stroll along the lane we had used.

I wonder if that is what he was doing in some other dimension or some region still unknown to us, when we accidentally walked through it that August day?

But I am certain that Major Lloyd would never instigate feelings of fear in anyone – whether he was in this world or the next, so maybe something had taken place in that spot years ago that had left very bad vibrations on the atmosphere.

Nan's Stories

Mrs Ann (Nan) Jones has been a great friend of ours for years and is a regular chapel attender, besides being one of the most truthful and honest ladies I have ever met.

Further along the stretch of the A5025 involved in these three short stories, the spectacle of the 'Burning Mini' occurred.

There are so many reported manifestations of a 'fiery' nature that this area seems particularly haunted and I am currently investigating it more deeply. So, to Nan's first story:

One Saturday afternoon in 1974, my husband and I were returning home from Bangor. It was a lovely sunny August day, about five-thirty pm. Hugh was driving and we were approaching Bryn Refail, when I looked out of the left hand window towards Mynydd Bodafon and saw a horrifying sight.

The land rises gradually uphill here and, about a field and a half away, I saw a large, stone-built house, standing alone with no garden or outbuildings. It was on fire and the interior was blazing fiercely, every window filled with flames.

Hugh saw it almost as soon as I did and slapped the brakes on hard. We expected to see people from the adjacent houses running to help, as the fire had really taken hold and had obviously been burning for many minutes. But there was no one to be seen and Hugh said in horror,

'Let's go – there may be someone trapped in there.'

He put his foot down and drove at break-neck speed to the corner of the road which turns left to Mynydd, to be nearer to the house. We shot up the hill, Hugh pulled up with a screech of brakes and we both tumbled out of the car, ready to race across the field. We were only a few yards away, level with the spot where the burning house was.

But everything had vanished – there was no house, no fire, nothing but the field standing quiet and still in the warm sunlight. We looked around in utter disbelief and stared at each other speechlessly. If only one of us had seen it, we would have thought it was a dream, but both of us had seen exactly the same thing.

Very shocked and shaken, we got back into the car and drove

slowly home in silence.

Discussing it later, we both realised that while the whole house was ablaze, the fire was contained *within* the house, there were no flames shooting out of the windows and absolutely no one in sight – we had taken all this in as we were driving to it. If it had been a natural fire, surely there would have been people running about – either around outside the house or coming to help?

To this day I can't explain it.

Story No. 2

Four or five years later, a friend of my cousin, who lives in Llanfechell, was driving home after shopping in Bangor. Again it was a warm August day and the place was Bryn Refail, the same stretch of the A5025 as in my first story. This was the late seventies when the volume of traffic was much less and the road was deserted as she drove steadily along.

As she drew nearer to Bryn Refail, she was appalled to see a huge barrel trundling towards her on her side of the road. It was on fire and flames were spurting fiercely from each end, as if the wind was fanning them. It was set on a collision course with her car, approaching very rapidly, and she swerved madly to avoid it, running off the road and coming to an abrupt stop.

She leapt out of the car and turned to see what had happened to the rolling barrel. To her amazement, there was nothing there.

'I could hardly believe my eyes,' she said, 'but there wasn't a sign of anything – it was such a shock. I was shaking so much I had to sit in the car for a while, before I was able to start the engine. If only another car or someone walking had come along, I would have stopped them – I know I was in shock.

Whatever you may believe or not, I *did* see a big blazing barrel rolling towards me and, yet when I looked back, the straight road was completely empty, no barrel anywhere.

I have relived it time and time again, but it still makes no sense.

Story No. 3

The partner of a friend of mine was a lorry driver and he was returning from a journey to his home in Amlwch. It was a fine night, about 2.00 a.m., near the end of May in 1993 and he was whistling happily as he drove through the clear starlit night.

As he was approaching Bryn Refail, he suddenly saw, standing motionless in the middle of the road, the figure of a soldier dressed in the uniform of World War One.

I knew it was the First World War uniform, I recognised it from old photographs I'd seen – he was wearing a uniform jacket with brass buttons, flat hat, puttees and webbing. I could see it all very plainly in my headlights.

He was staring straight at me, but he didn't move a muscle – I thought he would leap out of the way, but he didn't, just stood and stared. I remember swearing as I stamped on the brakes – then I prayed I wouldn't hit him.

As I did so, the figure shot vertically straight up into the air and vanished.

One minute he was standing in front of me, only feet away, he looked as stiff as a ramrod, then – *whoosh!* up he went like a rocket – I saw his whole figure, boots and all flash up into the air – and disappear.

He told this story to his partner and it was she who told me about it. She said that when he arrived home he was as white as a sheet and just fell into chair. He was shaking and very scared, and no amount of scoffing or questions would make him deviate one iota from his story. He swore he would never drive along that stretch of road again at night and, as far as I know, he never has.

Things that go thump in the night

Along Llaneilian Road, at Amlwch, standing back on the hill overlooking Porth Amlwch, is a large house which is very haunted. In the very early nineteenth century, one James Treweek, who had moved there from Mona Lodge, Amlwch, owned it. This man was to shape the fortunes of the majority of people, in Amlwch and surrounding districts.

He was a brilliant Cornish miner who had been brought to the Island by the new Mona Mine Company in 1811, as Manager, when they took over the west side of Mynydd Parys. Also, he was the most important figure in the history of the copper mines, second only to Thomas Williams in the history of their development.

By 1833 he was in charge of everything connected to the copper trade and industry in Amlwch. Mining, transport, smelting, shipping and the workforce, all were his concern, and he was known as a fair but firm employer.

The mines employed everyone locally in various jobs and, in 1778, it was estimated that about eight thousand people, including the miners families depended on the copper for their existence.

A very religious man, he was responsible for building the large chapel that stands in Wesley Street and, before that was completed, he held Sunday evening prayer meetings in the fine panelled hall of his home.

Whether the hauntings originated with the Treweek family is not known, the first mention of them that I can find was only about thirty years ago.

After the Treweek family left or died out, the house was bought by successive people, until it came into the possession of the Misses Jones, over half a century ago. They lived there very happily, proud of the house, its conservatory and large gardens, until the elder sister had a stroke and died in Caernarfon and the surviving Miss Jones found the house too large for her, so she sold up and moved into a bungalow.

There were a couple of owners between Miss Jones and the Smiths who live there now and it was Mrs Smith who wrote to me about the hauntings and also kindly gave me a taped interview.

I quote Mrs Smith:

We moved into this house twenty-two years ago and it was virtually derelict when we arrived. We had no water, electric, gas or even floors in the majority of the rooms. After getting the essential services put in, we started the mighty task of restoring the house.

In many of the bedrooms, there was either half a floor or no floor at all, so we had to sleep on a mattress on the bare boards, as there was no place on which to stand a bed. The bedroom floors were one of our first jobs.

One of the bedrooms we call the green room (for obvious reasons) and when it was finished and furnished, my mother-in-law came to stay and that was the first time anything happened.

She got up one morning and complained to me that in the night, the bed had started bouncing up and down (she meant the mattress I presume) but it didn't last long.

The second time it happened was about three nights later. Upstairs, the house is separated into two wings, and I was in the bathroom, right over the other side of the house from her.

She came running to me out of the bedroom, crying she was, going hysterical and she said she had been lying in bed, when suddenly something started to bounce the bed and it wouldn't stop and she sobbed to me that 'the demons were after her'. She absolutely refused to go back into that room, and she has never done so since.

I asked Mrs Smith what she thought it was because, to the best of my knowledge, the Misses Jones had not been troubled.

Oh, I don't know. When the younger Miss Jones lived there alone, she told me she used to hear knocking on the walls at night, they would start at the front door and she thought they were outside, because they went all around the house on the walls and windows. She heard them plainly as she slept downstairs, but she put it down to the village children coming up at night-time and banging around the walls.

When I asked her what the next happening was, she said –

Well, as I told you, much of the woodwork had been removed and, at one time, the hall, which is large and square, was beautifully panelled, but the panelling had been ripped out, so it was sort of raw. Anyhow, we have replaced the panelling as it used to be, although it's still a bit of a mess. Well, it was here that we heard the first noises.

You know when you have a gathering of people all together – you get a sort of murmur? A happy type of murmur as you would get from a group? We used to get that and it was always in the hall, at night, we would be in bed and, at first, when I heard it I used to come down, wondering if we had left the radio on or something.

When I got down to the bottom part of the stairs, I would get a really distinct feeling that a lot of eyes were on me. It would suddenly go very, very silent, as if I had interrupted something and I felt a lot of people were watching me. Just like you do if you go into a roomful of people who stop talking to look at you.

It was such a strong feeling, I said, 'Excuse me,' and turned round and went back upstairs!

I only went down twice – after that if I heard them I just let them get on with it!

*   *   *

Roy doesn't believe in ghosts, he dismisses the whole idea of them and tries to rationalise everything that has happened, but there are a few things that defy explanation.

We hadn't been here very long, we were working very hard and, usually, we fell asleep as we hit the pillow, but one night Roy immediately dropped off and started to snore. It wasn't an ordinary snore, more like someone pretending, a sort of comical snore. I didn't think it was funny, I was tired out and it stopped me from sleeping, so I poked him and pummelled him, but whatever I did, he wouldn't wake up. I kept at it for hours, trying to turn him over, but he just lay there fast asleep, a dead weight.

This went on all night and I hardly got any rest, then he woke up suddenly about half past five and started complaining that he'd never been to sleep at all and felt terrible and he might as well get up.

I said, what are you talking about, you've been snoring your head off all night – it's me that's had no sleep, I've been prodding and poking you and tried to turn you over, it's been a nightmare!

Anyway, he was a bit irritable and he jumped out of bed and

said he was going to shoot crows.

I was half asleep; I turned over and snuggled down again, so I didn't notice anything odd about him.

So out he went and he hadn't been gone five minutes when I heard a shot, then the door opened and slammed shut, and Roy came belting back upstairs, he was white and very upset.

He told me he'd just got outside the house when the rifle was snatched out of his hands by something unseen, sailed through the air in front of him, then turned around, aimed at him and fired. He ducked, the bullet flew over his shoulder and the rifle fell to the ground. Roy raced back into the house and gabbled out what had happened. I remember him saying: 'Whatever is here, doesn't like me shooting!' Incidentally, he's never been shooting since.

Anyway I was staring at him and, I suddenly noticed some scratches on his neck, so I pointed at them and said, 'What's happened – your neck's all scratched?' So he pulled the top of his tee shirt down and I could see there were a lot of scratches that went below his neckline. He pulled his tee-shirt off and looked through the mirror.

What we saw then gave us both a terrible shock, I can tell you. He was covered in scratches. The scratches were in the shape of crosses, every line crossed by another, all interlocking. It was just as if someone had got a sharp pin or a needle and made a scratch about two inches long and then crossed it with another scratch, really deep, they had brought the blood to the surface in tiny beads, but not enough to bleed properly. Through the mirror I could seem them all over his chest, from his neck to his waist and, from the bed, I could see his back was the same.

Apparently, they had been inflicted during his deep and unnatural sleep, but how they had been put on his back when he had lain on it all night, we couldn't imagine. Also, he had never felt a thing, though such numerous scratches must have hurt as they happened, they were so deep they took weeks and weeks to heal.

This happened years ago, but I am still mystified as to their cause.

* * *

We have a downstairs cloakroom and, when we moved in, we had a high level water cistern over the toilet, and one morning we came downstairs to find it had suddenly overflowed for no particular reason and the hall was all flooded to a depth of about two inches. We cleared everything out and mopped up and sent for the plumber. He came and inspected it and could find no fault with it at all.

As soon as he had gone, it overflowed again. It did this so many times we got fed-up with it, had it removed and a low-level one installed.

It had only been in a couple of days and we were sitting in the lounge in the evening watching television, when we heard the new cistern flushing. This was very strange, as the handle was very stiff and there was no way it could move on its own. So I got up to see what was going on and I went along to the cloakroom and quietly pushed the door open.

Just as I did, I saw the cistern handle going down and the toilet flushed. I shouted to Roy:

'I've just seen the toilet handle going down – come and look!'

I was standing in the doorway staring at the toilet and seconds later something unseen passed me, going out of the door. It passed right through my elbow, which I was sticking out and it was a feeling of unbelievable cold. We have a walk-in freezer where we keep the fish (Roy is a fisherman) but it was much colder than that, the sort of cold you cannot describe, it was almost solid.

The toilet had stopped flushing, so I went back to watch TV. I sat down on the settee, and then started to feel very odd. I got a most peculiar feeling, a feeling that I was 'coming out' of myself. Not dizzy or anything like that just this uncomfortable feeling which was very frightening.

I grabbed hold of the arm of the settee and went 'O-o-oh'. The feeling stopped then and I felt myself sort of sliding back. As I sat there wondering what the heck had happened, it started to happen again. This time I went right out of my body, I started to rise upwards and I looked down and could see myself sitting on the settee.

I grabbed the arm again, I can remember that, I couldn't speak – I just groaned 'O-o-o-oh' again, much louder.

This made Roy jump and he looked at me.

I think my face had become different, changed into someone else, I don't I know.

Roy leapt off the settee and grabbed the phone, he never took his eyes off me – he dialled his brother's house and he didn't say 'Hello' or anything, he just blurted out – 'I've seen a ghost – we're coming over!'

Then he grabbed my hand and dragged me off the settee and out to the car. He set off like a bat out of hell, never said a word – just kept staring over at me.

His brother was waiting at the door and Roy just pushed me into the house and said to his brother, 'We're going for a drink' – and off they went, leaving me to explain all about it to his sister-in-law.

Presumably, he told his brother what had happened, but he's never mentioned it from that day to this – he just won't talk about it – I don't know whether he could rationalise that or not!

*   *   *

More recently, Matthew, my son, and his friend, Sam, were in Matthew's bedroom late one night. Sam goes home at all hours. They were messing about with the TV and the computer.

Suddenly, a slow banging started at the other end of the corridor and gradually came along the wall towards his bedroom door, getting louder and louder as it drew near. It became a terrific din, as if a giant fist was thumping along. They thought at first it was either Roy or me banging to tell them they had the TV on too loud, so they turned the TV down and opened the door to say sorry.

As soon as the door opened – there was instant silence, not a sound and the corridor was empty. It was puzzling, but Matthew thought it was his Dad playing tricks, so they went back inside.

The instant the door closed, it started again, getting faster and louder. Matthew grinned at Sam, putting his finger to his lips and they both crept to the door and, as a tremendous blow landed on the door, they flung it wide open.

The corridor was empty and silent as a grave. This time they were really scared. They rushed back inside the room, slamming the door and sat close together on the bed to listen.

Once again, soft measured thumps started, this time on the wall opposite the bedroom door, banging along that wall, turning the corner at the end, getting louder as they came along the near wall, close to his bedroom door. By now they were tremendous thumps, making the whole wall vibrate.

They were too scared to bolt out of the bedroom door. In fact, Sam threw the window open, ready to jump out if anything should come in through the door.

I woke up. The banging was very loud and I lay in bed and listened. To me it seemed to be coming from the front door, as if someone was knocking hard. I thought it was Alan, Sam's father, come to fetch him home because it was so late. Then the noise moved to the conservatory door, so I went downstairs to open it.

As I opened the kitchen door, our two dogs who were fast asleep, woke up and lifted their heads as I came in. At first I thought it was strange they weren't up and barking at the knocking, then I thought it must be someone they knew and weren't bothered about.

The knocking stopped as I got to the door, so I went outside to look for whoever it was and, of course, the dogs followed me out and went down the garden.

I looked down the lane, wandered around the house to each door and found no one. So I waited until the dogs came back and we all went indoors again.

The whole procedure must have taken about fifteen minutes, and as I locked up, I remember thinking how quickly whoever had been knocking moved around the house from the front door to the conservatory, as it is quite a long way.

I stopped to listen in the hall, after putting the dogs back in the kitchen, but there wasn't a sound, the whole house was quiet.

What I didn't know of course was that the boys were listening too and, as the knocking had stopped, this was the moment they had summoned up enough courage to open the door.

I was wearing a long white dressing gown and was climbing softly upstairs, just as the boys peeped out. It must have been a great shock to them to see a tall white figure at the stop of the stairs, lit up by the moon.

Immediately, two things happened. Matthew let out a great yell of horror (which frightened me to death) and Sam bolted back, making for the open window.

I shouted Matthew's name, and was he relieved when he recognised his Mum – then we saw that Sam was halfway out of the window. We flew across the room and just managed to grab him and pull him back in again before he jumped.

But they were both in a state of shock and couldn't get out of the house quick enough to go and stay at Sam's. Neither of them would come back into the house for nearly a week!

What I thought was strange, the banging seemed to me to be *downstairs* on the doors, because to me that was where the noise was coming from, but the boys heard it *upstairs* on the landing walls, while neither of the dogs seemed to hear it at all, as they were both fast asleep in the kitchen.

* * *

I broke in here to tell Marion that in my experience, dogs usually hear things before people, and she said:

Oh yes, that's why I thought it was strange, because usually the dogs do hear. For instance, you remember the green room which my mother-in-law avoids?

Well, that room is just above our lounge and it has thick carpet wall to wall, but very often we hear footsteps in there as if someone is walking on bare boards.

In that room, there is a wash basin on the far wall opposite the window and, sometimes when we are sitting in the lounge below, we hear footsteps above us, crossing the room to the wash bowl, then going over to the window and, sometimes coming back. Quite clear footsteps again as if they are on wood and not the thick carpeting which is in there now.

It's not our imagination, because the dogs hear it too, they look up at the ceiling, their fur bristles and they start to growl and bark. We have a lot of noises in that room and the dogs hear them all. Sometimes it is as if someone is rocking on a rocking chair – you know that squeaky-creaky noise? We go up and stand outside the door and it can be heard quite clearly, but as soon as we open it, the noise stops. The dogs hear that too, which is why it seems so strange that they never heard the knocking, which was so loud.

Nearly all the rooms have noises in them at some time or another, especially when we are working on the house. We are doing all the work ourselves, it's a slow process, but whenever we have finished a room, we will hear noises as if someone walks across the landing or the corridor, it always sounds like walking on wood and goes into the room we've just completed. I think whoever it is, is watching what we are doing and having the feeling that the house approves and wants us to go on.

There is a lovely atmosphere, in some of the rooms, particularly the green room but that is definitely haunted.

We used to accommodate parties of about twelve fishermen, who would stay for bed-and-breakfast and go out with Roy during the day. I remember two of the men stayed in the green room for the first night, went out fishing with Roy next day, but booked themselves into the Kings for the rest of their fishing holiday. I never knew what happened, but the rest of the party wouldn't spread out and go in the green room, even though some were a bit squashed in!

Perhaps whoever still lives in the green room, doesn't like people staying there!

*   *   *

We have a friend, Albert Litherland, who comes to stay with us for about a month every year. He likes the green room; he says it has a lovely peaceful atmosphere. We have a four poster bed in there – a modern one, there used to be an old one there when the Miss Jones's lived here, but it was sold before we came.

Anyhow, in June this year, Albert came to stay, he wasn't very well and, sometimes, stayed in bed quite late. Well, he was sitting up in bed one morning, reading the daily paper, when suddenly he felt a weight plumping down on the side of the bed by his feet, as if someone had sat down.

The covers tightened and he saw the imprint of someone's bottom, the shape of it I mean quite clearly but he couldn't see anybody. After a short time, the imprint disappeared and the covers no longer stretched, as if whoever had been sitting there got up.

His next experience, a few days later, was more frightening. He awoke suddenly in the night, he couldn't explain why, with the feeling he was not alone. Again he felt the same sensation, as of someone plumping down near the foot of the bed and the sudden tightening of the bed clothes over his feet. Then, to his relief, whoever (or whatever) it was got up again, but instead of going away like it did the first time, he felt someone (or something) *lie down on the bed beside him*, full length, moving about a little as if composing themselves for sleep.

He told Marion later:

'I thought – shall I put my hand out and see if there is anyone there – no, better not. My hair was standing on end and I lay there unmoving, as stiff as a plank for ages. My eyes came out on stalks like a crab's, trying to squint sideways without moving my head or any other part of me come to that.

It seemed hours before I saw the faintest streak of grey in the east and I eased myself gently to the side of the bed, away from what was lying there, then I slipped silently out from the side and shot downstairs into the kitchen!'

And when Marion and her husband got up, there he was in his pyjamas, drinking endless cups of coffee!

Answering my question, Marion said he still uses the green room, but always leaves the bedside light on!

*   *   *

When we first moved in, every now and again the house used to be pervaded by a terrible smell, sometimes in a front room that used to be a parlour, I believe, but mostly on the stairs. After a bit, it dawned on me what the smell was like – sweaty socks! I searched and searched at first for dirty socks, but I never found anything. Funnily enough, it came back again this week, but it seems to have gone now.

I couldn't understand it, until about eighteen years ago, when the mystery was solved. One day, an old couple came to the door

280

and said they hoped I wouldn't think they were cheeky, but would I mind if they came in?

Apparently, it was their golden wedding anniversary, they had spent their honeymoon in our house and they just wanted to see it again. So I said, of course, come in and have a cup of tea.

They were very nice people and told us that fifty years ago a man rented the house and farmed the land, and his wife did bed and breakfast. Although they were spotlessly clean the farmer had something wrong with his feet that made them smell horribly sweaty, even though he had clean socks on every day.

He always wore his big clumping boots in the house; he daren't wear slippers because the smell came through them. In fact, in summer, he used to sit in the parlour with his feet out of the window, they smelt so awful! I don't remember his name, I don't think I took much notice even when I was told – but when the smell came back this week, just as strong as ever, I thought to myself, well, that's alright, it's just the old farmer passing through!

Treysgawen Hall, Capel Coch

The original Treysgawen Hall was built in 1802, but sadly burnt down and the present building was erected in 1882 by the wealthy Pritchard-Rayner family, who owned the copper mines on Mynydd Parys, near Amlwch.

Dating back to Roman times, and the largest deposit of copper in Britain, Parys Mines made Porth Amlwch a thriving place in the eighteenth and early nineteenth centuries and built up substantial fortunes for both shipping magnates and mine owners alike. Many of these families advertised their status by building large, elegant houses and Treysgawen is a fine example.

Built of sandstone, it stands in mature and beautiful gardens and the atmosphere is relaxed and tranquil.

Inside, the furnishings and decor are sumptuous and we were admiring the exquisite porcelain ornaments when the assistant manager, Neil Rowlands arrived and welcomed us very cordially as did his friendly, heavyweight black Labrador, Buster. Buster and I developed an immediate rapport and, as we sat down for coffee, Buster ambled over to me, flumped onto the carpet and made sure I couldn't leave by sprawling beside me with his great head resting comfortably on my feet, thereby successfully pinning me down throughout the interview.

Neil watched this with approval, and told me that he valued Buster's opinion of people, because it had been noticed that if Buster barked at any newly arrived guest, the person in question would invariably present some problems during their stay.

I felt quite flattered at Buster's vetting and, at least, Neil knew we weren't going to make off with the silver!

While Neil was dispensing the excellent coffee, we chatted about the Hall which besides being a quiet country hotel, is also the centre for the Sue Rowlands, Psychic and Spiritual Studies, and raises a great deal of money for Children's Charities.

The lofty lounge in which we sat is very elegantly furnished, carefully chosen pieces blend together to make a perfect whole. When I expressed my admiration, Neil said the whole place had been completely refurbished in 1990 by a firm of famous decorators who had come up from London.

Neil, a down-to-earth ex-navy man, who is the son of the manager, has no assumed airs and graces and when I asked him about the *hauntings, he thought for a moment, marshalling his facts.*

Well, the wing you passed on your left as you drove through the second pair of gates used to be the servants quarters when the family lived here. Downstairs was the kitchen, scullery, knife room etc. and the servants' quarters upstairs.

Early in the nineteenth century, one winter's night, the servants had all retired to bed, leaving the fire damped down with slack coal, so that the heat might be retained overnight, when the unfortunate maids had to get up in the freezing darkness next morning.

All water for washing and early morning tea had to be boiled in the kitchens and carried up to the individual members of the family and their guests each day. Coal carried up and bedroom fires lit, so that these favoured people could carry out their morning ablutions in warmth and comfort.

Pity the poor maids, dressing in the icy attic bedrooms, then tiptoeing along dark corridors and down steep stairs to the kitchens.

On this particular night, the butler woke in the small hours to the smell of burning. The landing outside his room was full of smoke and he could hear fire crackling in the kitchen. Raising the alarm, he woke up the staff and half-dressed, half-asleep they tumbled downstairs to find the kitchen ablaze. Every one fled through the kitchen door and, in the chaos no one realised that the little kitchen maid, Mair, was missing, until they heard her terrified screams coming from the bedroom where she was trapped.

By now, the whole wing was going up like a torch, the flames roaring in the strong westerly wind. Attempts to reach the girl were in vain, the men who tried were driven back by the heat – and the shrieks went on and on, until the floor collapsed and the heartrending cries were cut off abruptly.

The story of the girl's horrific death has been told for generations, even after the shell of the ruined wing was demolished. Her small ghost still haunts the room which used to be the old scullery and Neil confirmed one sighting.

One afternoon, not long ago, a member of the staff was working in the room and, turning round, she saw the figure of a young teenaged girl standing by the stove.

Mrs Davies said: 'She was quite small and she had on a dark skirt, a sacking apron and, on her head, was a sort of mob cap that was far too big for her and came down right over her forehead. She stood quite still, with her arms down and her hands clasped together, but it was her eyes that I saw most clearly – they looked at me so piteously and there was such an air of sadness about her. I felt so sorry for her and not a bit afraid. Then she gradually faded away and there I was, just staring at the stove.

Suddenly I realised that I had seen a ghost and I rushed out of the room, and gabbled out my story to the first person I met, who happened to be the housekeeper. I was amazed when she just nodded and smiled. She said I had seen the ghost of young Mair, and she told me the story, which I hadn't heard before, and said not to worry, other members of the staff had seen her and even tried to talk to her, but she just stood there sadly for a few minutes, before fading away.

I was much shaken, because I had never seen a ghost before, but when I thought about it, realised I wasn't frightened at all, I just wanted to help her and everyone who has seen her feels the same.'

In answer to my question, Neil shook his head.

No. I've never seen her, but she doesn't strike me as being menacing, not like the unexplainable thing that happened to me the first summer we were here.

It was May, a beautiful still warm, moonlit night and we had a full hotel. About half-past twelve, I was on my security rounds, I was about halfway along the top corridor when the fire doors at the end just flew open, at an absolutely tremendous speed – and crashed back against the walls.

There was no wind outside whatsoever – I could see the tops of the trees, they were quite still. I felt no draught, as I would if the wind had blown them open.

I stopped dead and realised that the air had become intensely cold – icy in fact.

So – that panicked me a little bit –

I interrupted him:

'I would have been downstairs and gone!'

He grinned.

Well! I did run backwards, I daren't turn around! It's never happened to anyone else to my knowledge, but all the staff have seen people – phantom people I suppose they are, so have I – people going upstairs or coming in the front door and no one is there. What I mean is, they are seen on the staircase, then they just fade away or, if the receptionist sees them coming in, no one arrives at the desk.

Also, the lady you saw on reception is always hearing her name being spoken. She looks up and says 'Yes?' and there is nobody in sight.

I often see people when I'm on my own, but one day two of us saw something at the same time.

The second chef and I were sitting at the end of the hall, at the bottom of the conservatory having a cup of coffee before starting the evening's work at about 6.30 p.m. All of a sudden we saw two guests come down the stairs walk through the hall and straight into the bar.

We both saw them and, we didn't think anything of it. I just hurried a waiter into the bar, to go and serve them, and attend them, and he went in and came straight out again looking puzzled. The bar was completely empty, nobody there he said.

I went to look, because both the chef and I had seen two people go in and there is only one door. He was right, they had vanished.

In answer to my question about how they were dressed, Neil thought deeply for a moment, and then said:

The dress wasn't significant, it must have been modern, because there was nothing about it for me to think it was out of the ordinary, it was just two guests, a man and a woman who had come down, we saw the body rather than the clothes if you know what I mean. If they were dated clothes we would have noticed, so I suppose they must have been modern within reason. This happened a couple of months ago and it was a very clear sighting.

We are forever seeing people walking around the gallery upstairs or going into the guest rooms. It usually happens to me as we are now or perhaps a bit busier. I'll be walking between the restaurant and the bar, and I'll see someone going upstairs or walking along the gallery and, by the time I've stopped, thought and looked again, there's nothing there.

Touch wood – you get feelings you know, you become aware of things around you, something or someone is watching you. At times that is very strong, but apart from the fire door, that was very frightening, nothing bad has ever happened.

Apart from one occasion, last January, when we closed the hotel for renovation. We kept all the staff on full time, taking curtains down, steam cleaning the carpets, deep cleaning the silver, washing crockery etc.

We finished work one night about 9.00 p.m., we were fairly whacked and a group of us had flopped down on the settees and chairs in the hall by reception. There was I, my fiancé, mother and father, the housekeeper and our headwaiter, and we were all fairly quiet because we were so tired.

Suddenly, we heard a noise overhead. It started slowly and gradually grew louder and louder as it crossed the floor above our heads. A slow, massive, dragging noise, just as if someone was dragging a huge kitchen table over bare boards, across the floor above us, even though there is thick carpeting all over the hotel.

We all just froze – staring at the ceiling until it had passed overhead and stopped – then we stared at each other – everyone had the same expression on their faces – what the hell was that? The building was closed down and completely empty – no one else in besides us. Talk about eerie!

It took us a minute or two to find our voices and, when we did, the men decided that we all ought to go and search and the best way to do it was for us to split up into two's.

I was intrigued. 'What did your girlfriend say?' I asked.

Walt grinned. 'He hasn't seen her since!'

Neil laughed and shook his head.

'Well, she didn't really want to go and look, but she said she would if she could go with a man.'

I nodded approval.

So we got into twos and we all took a different part of the hotel – we searched every bit of it. Nothing. Every room was peaceful and in order – nothing disturbed and we still haven't got a clue what the noise was.'

'How strange,' I said, 'and yet, it's got such a lovely friendly atmosphere.'

'It's just a calm, tranquil feeling, particularly in this room.'

Neil agreed. 'As soon as we walked into this place and felt the ambience, we had to have it.'

'As you walk in the front door you get that feeling,' Walt said, 'no doubt about that.'

I put my coffee cup back on the beautiful low table between us. 'Not like the big house we went into last week on the other side of the Island near Llangeinwen,' I said, 'A very beautiful house, but as soon as we stepped inside, the atmosphere was so cold and hostile – you could almost cut it.'

'I can understand that – we have a place like that on the top floor, I'll take you up there when we've finished coffee and see if you feel it.'

He leaned back on the comfortable settee and crossed his legs.

'The top floor used to be the servants' quarters long ago when the family lived here, lots of dark, poky little rooms. The hoteliers we bought it from had torn that floor apart and made big, spacious rooms for their own accommodation.

We don't live here, my father's got a house in Dwyran, I live in Bull Bay, so all we have here is a 'duty' room, so that whoever is on duty sleeps in that room overnight. We had the whole floor completely gutted and redesigned by the architects, so that now there is a lounge and en-suite bedrooms for the staff. It's all completely brand new.

The previous owners complained there was a lot of 'goings on' up there. Doors opening, voices talking which always stopped when someone opened the door of the room, footsteps coming up wooden stairs, voices calling from outside and noises that couldn't be explained.

We wondered if all the alterations may actually trigger off something and, lo and behold, it actually did when I was 'sleeping over' one night in the duty room, which of course is not used by guests.

I had just got into bed and was listening to all the peaceful small noises a big building makes when it is settling down for the night, when all of a sudden the room started to go cold. It went so cold it became icy and all the little noises faded out, there was a dead silence and a horrible feeling of expectancy.

I remember thinking – oh no – something's about to happen and, I had just thought that when I heard an almighty bang from the room behind me – these two rooms have a large pine wardrobe in each and it was just as if the wardrobe in the room behind me had fallen on its face, it was such a crash.

I knew the room was empty, these are not guest rooms, just utility rooms, the walls are very thin, just partition walls.

This frightened the life out of me; I could feel the hairs rising on the back of my neck! The room went even colder and there was a massive **Boom!** all around my bed head, like thunder. I'd never, ever 'til that day understood the saying 'scared stiff'. The hotel was full, people all over the building, but I could *not* physically move my arm out from under the sheets to pick the phone up and call anyone.

I was just paralysed with fright.

I'd left the light on because I'd felt the weird atmosphere when I first went into the room – but I *saw* absolutely nothing.

'How long did it last?' I asked.

'That was it!' he said. 'The whole thing only lasted about thirty seconds max.'

He stared into his coffee cup, as if re-living the feeling of fear.

'I couldn't sleep for the rest of the night and, when I got up, my face was as white as a sheet, my eyes were half-closed and I wasn't fit for anything. When my mother arrived, we both went up to check the rooms; they were all locked as usual and in perfect order. There was no explanation.'

My left foot and Buster were now both fast asleep, I tried gently to pull my foot out, his head seemed to weigh a ton, it was no good, he went on snoring gently and, by now, I'd lost all feeling in my toes. Looking down at him, I asked Neil if Buster had ever reacted to anything.

'Oh, many times,' said Neil, 'he'll look at some point across the room and growl, then walk over and sniff as if someone was there, but we've never seen anything at all.'

Just as we spoke, Buster awoke, looked at the door and gave a short bark. When he lifted his head, I hastily moved my foot and, just then, the telephone rang in reception. A young waiter appeared to tell Neil he was wanted on the phone.

We were discussing the phantom cobbler of Porth Amlwch when he returned and I told him the story.

'I believe that,' Neil said seriously, 'because there is something here in the rooms that I told you about on the very top floor, the ones which were the servants' quarters before the house was bought from the Pritchard-Rayner family. When we first came here, and the renovations were in full swing, the head chef was living in and his wife used to come and visit him at weekends. He had a room in the servants' quarters right at the end and he used to go to bed every night with his light and television on, so that he could either read or watch TV.

Each night before he went to sleep he would switch off the TV by remote control and, lastly, his bedside lamp. He switched it off without fail, but every morning when he woke up, his lamp was on. So when his wife came to stay, he asked her to watch him putting out the light last thing, which she did and he told her it would be on in the morning. It was. The same thing happened as long as he stayed in that room.'

At this juncture, Buster awoke and gave his single bark. The telephone rang. I looked at Neil.

'Did he know?' I asked.

Neil looked from me to Buster. 'Know what?'

'That the telephone was going to ring – does he always bark before it goes off?'

Neil looked at Buster in surprise, and then he looked bewildered. 'Do you know – I've never noticed it before.'

'Well, watch and see if he does it again,' I said, scratching Buster's ears and watching his eyes glaze over with pleasure.

Once more, Neil was summoned to the phone, and when he returned he took us on a tour of the hotel. The rooms were sumptuous, each one had the same high standard of elegance, and we appreciated the soft colour schemes and the large windows which framed beautiful views of the grounds.

We stopped outside room 16, and Neil selected a key from the large bunch he had picked up at the desk.

'As you see,' he said, inserting one in the door, 'we keep all the guest rooms locked and each is thoroughly cleaned after the guests leave, then my father or I inspect them before the next people arrive.

Well, a few weeks ago, Dad was on his tour of inspection, and he unlocked the door of No.16 and went in.'

So did we.

'As he did so, he saw a large, black cat with green eyes standing by the side of the bed. It stared at him for a moment, and then dashed across the room to the dressing table. Naturally, he was most annoyed to think that someone had been careless enough to let a cat get in, so he looked to see if the window was closed, then he shut and re-locked the door thus imprisoning the cat. He went downstairs and brought the head housekeeper up here, asking her what the hell a cat was doing in a guest bedroom.

She was protesting all the way saying:

'I don't know Mr Rowlands, I don't know Mr Rowlands, there shouldn't be – there couldn't be –'

Dad unlocked the door of No.16 saying:

'Well, see for yourself then!' and they both entered the room.

There was no cat. No sign of one anywhere and they searched every inch of the room. My Dad was amazed, and a bit nettled, and tried to convince the housekeeper that he really had seen a big black cat.

Telling us about it afterwards, he said it looked as solid as any other cat and, when we asked, he said shortly that of course it had made no noise running across the thick carpet.

So it remains just another small mystery.'

Our tour now took us into the attics, the original quarters of the servants, then made into the spacious living rooms of the owners prior to the Rowlands and were now very comfortable rooms for the staff, including the bedroom for any member of the management who was sleeping in.

Neil first took us into the room he was occupying when the frightening incident took place that he had described to us.

It was comfortable and modern, and the atmosphere seemed quite normal.

Then, he unlocked the door next to it, from where he had heard the bang.

This was furnished identically and, like all the other rooms, it was comfortable and spotlessly clean. Identical it may have been – but for one very creepy exception.

It was covered in dead flies. The bed, the dressing table and the buff-coloured carpet were all littered with them.

Neil sighed. 'This is a problem we can't get to the bottom of,' he said, 'it only happens in this one room. It was thoroughly vacuum cleaned the day before yesterday – and here they are again. It happens time after time in this room, we've had Rent-a-Kill in more than once, they've had the floorboards up and searched the loft, but they are baffled, they can't find any reason for them.'

We stared around the small, still, room. A thin shaft of watery sunshine came in through the large skylight, the only window in the room. It was securely fastened, no cracks or spaces in the frame, and Neil told us it was only eighteen months old.

'It's not often that Rent-a-Kill are completely baffled,' Neil said, flicking a dead fly off the bed, 'they have gone over everything with a fine tooth-comb, they say there is no explanation, but every time we come in here – there are the dead flies.'

I was looking closely at the flies whilst he was talking, but I couldn't see one live one amongst the corpses, and thought uneasily that I didn't like the atmosphere in that room, something I hadn't felt in all the rooms I had been in. I said so.

'I know what you mean,' said Neil, 'this is where the bang came from, and I think that whatever haunts this floor has its centre here. My mother is a medium and, she says, she feels as if there is a man in this room who is deeply distressed, almost disorientated, and it is he who haunts this wing.'

I wondered if it was all the alterations – perhaps they had disturbed him, we would feel disorientated if we went home and somebody had changed all the rooms round.

'Probably he feels annoyed,' said Walt.

Neil threw up his hands and shrugged.

'Who knows?' he said. 'Whatever it is, it didn't like the disturbance and it certainly isn't friendly.'

I heaved a sigh of relief once we were out of that heavy atmosphere and the door was re-locked.

We started down the servants' back stairs, which were so incredibly steep. I felt dizzy, and hanging on to the banister, I looked around to see how Buster was coping with a flight of stairs that resembled the north face of the Eiger, up to now he had padded happily around with us.

He was missing.

'Where's Buster?' I asked.

Neil grinned. 'Oh, he's not daft, he doesn't like it up here, he won't come up if he can help it and he's probably peeled off somewhere.'

I thought of the maze of corridors and rooms.

'Won't he get trapped?' I asked.

'No,' Neil said over his shoulder, 'there are all sorts of ways around the place, and he knows them all.' He cocked his head back – 'but you'll never find him going in that room.'

He was waiting for us in the hall, his heavy tail gently swinging and, as we said our thanks and goodbyes to Neil, he accompanied us to the car. Being the psychic dog he is, he seemed to know about the small bag of dog biscuits we always carried on the back seat and he stared pointedly at it until I passed it to him.

He returned to Neil who was standing at the open front door, carefully carrying his prize in his huge pink mouth.

A final wave.

'Don't forget to notice if he barks before the phone rings,' I called and we drove away.

The haunted marsh

This story, another of Mr Pritchard's, tells of an apparition which hasn't lost any substance with the passing of time, but has been seen by at least three people and, probably, more that are unknown to us, over the last hundred years.

The first recorded story was about a miner who lived at Capelulo and was in charge of 'landing the basket' at the New Berw Mine in the middle of the nineteenth century.

It was very hard manual work and one time, coming off shift he was tired and looking forward to a good night's sleep. In the early hours of the morning he turned his face towards home, two miles away.

His way took him through the marsh on a cobbled path through the reeds and he was helped along by a young moon shining fitfully through the scudding clouds.

The marsh was a lonely place through which Afon Cefni flowed, crossed by an old humpbacked bridge.

Pyrs' route took him to the junction of the new Telford road (now the A5) and he was deep in thought, counting the weeks until his new potatoes could be lifted and eaten, swimming in golden farm butter. He looked up from the road and was astonished to see a figure coming towards him from the direction of the bridge.

He stopped and waited as the man drew near and the moon sailed clear of the clouds so, that the scene was quite distinct.

The man was immensely tall, nearer to eight feet than seven and dressed in a long, full cloak of a brownish woollen material. His legs were covered in cloth leggings, cross-gartered from foot to knee, and his hair was long and curling on his shoulders and he never took his eyes away from Pyrs' face.

As he drew closer, Pyrs' surprise was replaced by a growing feeling of dread. Something about the man was wrong. The air surrounding him was as cold as ice and a shiver went through Pyrs before he broke out in a sweat of fear.

His mouth was bone dry, but he swallowed and managed to stammer a polite greeting.

'Bore da (good morning),' he muttered. There was no reply. The only thing Pyrs wanted to do now was to put as much distance between them as he could so, he gave a brief nod and turned to walk on, as fast as his trembling legs could carry him.

To his utter dismay, the silent figure fell into step beside him. As they went on Pyrs was quaking with fright. He started to talk, about anything and everything, just to break the heavy silence.

They passed a well.

'Look at that,' Pyrs babbled inanely, pointing at the water, 'that was dug to feed the pumping engines in the two mines at Penrhyn Mawr you know.'

He suddenly thought that this apparition wouldn't have a clue what he was talking about and he stole a glance sideways.

Now, although Pyrs was a strong miner, over six feet tall, he had to tilt his head sharply upwards to see the stranger's face. Towering head and shoulders above Pyrs, he made him seem like a dwarf.

They walked in silence, a strong breeze blowing fitfully into their faces made a hissing sound as it swept across the reedy marsh. It plastered Pyrs' overcoat against his legs and flattened his hair back but, looking sideways he saw that it was not affecting his companion in the least. His full cloak fell straight around him and his long curling hair was untouched by it, staying as still as if it was carved from bronze.

It was as if the man was in an atmosphere of his own and the night wind did not affect him at all.

Poor Pyrs – his teeth were clenched tightly and he was nearly stumbling with fright – what a great relief it was to come up to the Collier Mawr crossroads.

He stopped walking – as did the phantom and pointed to the left fork of the crossroads with a trembling hand,

'I live over there,' he said faintly, 'I'll be leaving you now.'

He turned back to the tall figure.

The road was empty.

He was alone.

* * *

The sighting of the Viking ghost by Pyrs Griffiths took place about 1860.

More than twenty years later, around 1880, it was seen again this time, by Mr Pritchard's great grandfather.

John Jones of 1 Penrhyn Mawr, Pentreberw, worked at one of the two lime kilns in the area. He was a tough quarryman, strong and fit and frightened of no man.

His job was arduous, first he shovelled coal consistently to feed the furnaces burning in the lime kilns then, when the limestone turned to powder and fell, he had to shovel all the hydrated lime from the bottom.

It was hot work and the lime dust parched his throat, making him drink copious amounts of water.

He finished his shift at 2.00 a.m. and, like all the workers in those days, had to walk home.

Pentreberw lies in the centre of a large marsh. At one time, it was surrounded by sea, boats constantly sailed up Afon Cefni carrying commerce but, gradually the river became shallower until it was completely silted up, Pentreberw became landlocked in a marshy waste.

The Vikings knew it well. There is evidence of Viking settlements in many parts of Anglesey – as recently as 2000 A.D. a Viking burial site was discovered at Llanbedr-goch.

A very large, grassy mound lies at the centre of the marsh. One school of thought argues that it could be the grave of Tygai, an old Celtic saint who came to the area around the fourth century A.D. Some people call the mound Mynwent Tygai but, the main legend is that it is a Viking burial mound, containing the relics of an important Viking chief and was probably a boat burial.

It is a very eerie place. The air always seems still and heavy and people passing in twos or threes often fall silent until they have passed it, feeling as if they are in the grip of an unexplainable awe.

Horses were particularly aware of the atmosphere. Many of the workhorses had to be led past it with the cart drivers climbing down and walking at their heads, talking to them in reassuring voices.

As John left work, he turned into the cold night wind, striding through the long reeds on the rough track across the marsh.

In the distance, he could see the glowing furnaces of the other lime kiln near the Telford road and, nearer to hand, the huge grass mound of the ancient Viking burial site.

The usual deep sense of unease gripped him as he passed it, recalling that only last week, a fully loaded lime cart had been wrecked here. A young horse, newly broken into the job, had panicked at that spot. It had stopped dead, like many before it and, when the driver had climbed down and tried to make it walk on, the horse had gone wild with terror, whinnying, rearing and plunging until it had snapped a cart shaft and broken the harness.

As soon as the driver had untangled and freed it, it had careered up the road at full pelt and had, finally, been recaptured, trembling and sweating a couple of miles further on.

In fact, a broken piece of shaft was still lying where it had been kicked into the side of the road. Noting it, John wondered what caused the fear the horses felt at that spot.

He had left the path and was on the new road, the only sound he could hear was the noise of his hobnailed boots on the tarmac.

Ahead of him was the old humpbacked bridge, Pont-y-Gors (Bridge on the Marsh), and, as he drew near, the night wind which had been rising steadily whipped open his overcoat, so he turned his back to the wind and buttoned it up.

When he turned again, he got a great shock.

A minute ago, he was all alone but, in the single instance that he had turned his back, someone else had appeared.

Standing in the middle of the old bridge stood a figure. It looked like a man – but it was gigantic; at least seven and a half feet tall.

John's jaw dropped, he could only stop and stare, rigid with fright.

The man (or whatever it was) was also motionless, his gaze fixed unwaveringly on the quarryman standing before him.

His dress was as unusual as his stature.

A full cape, which hung untouched by the night wind, fell to his knees, below which were leggings bound with leather. His hair was shoulder-length, falling into curls at the bottom.

His appearance and silence unnerved John, whose scalp tightened and the clammy sweat of fear glistened on his forehead.

Swallowing hard he, at last, got his wooden tongue to work,

'Bore da i chi.' (Good morning to you.)

The stranger did not appear to hear him. Instead of the polite words bringing a touch of reality to the scene, they dropped into a deep well of silence.

There was a great feeling of unworldiness around them, a feeling so uncanny and fearful it turned John's legs to jelly.

He had never been so frightened in his life – his one desire was to get out of the place and away from what he now knew to be a phantom.

Gradually, he forced his lifeless legs into action and backed slowly away from the bridge, never taking his eyes off the giant ghost, he continued his backward retreat as fast as he could.

When he had put a gap of twenty or more feet between them, he turned and pelted homeward, turning his head to see if he was being pursued. Each backward glance showed him the form still stood unmoving on the humpbacked bridge.

So great was his fright, he never walked that way at night again; instead he walked along the railway line from Pentreberw towards Llangefni, turning off at the sidings to the lime kiln which then existed.

John Jones, said Mr Pritchard, was my great grandfather and, many years later, when my mother jokingly asked him if he believed in ghosts, he solemnly told her he did, because he had seen one and then related this story.

To bring things more or less up to date, Mr Pritchard said,

'The next thing I heard was when I was a young man in 1962. I was a student then and, during the summer holidays, I got a job as a bus conductor with Crossville buses at Llangefni.

It was an interesting job, travelling around the Island meeting all sorts of interesting people. I had to cycle four miles across the marsh to Llangefni. The only shift I didn't like was the late one, detested by all crews. We departed from Bangor at 10.30 p.m. went through Newborough and arrived at the Llangefni depot just after 11.30 p.m.

One day, I got to the depot in time for the evening shift; it had been raining and I was very wet. I put the kettle on first to make myself a cup of Camp Coffee and was just taking my wet mac off when my driver, Tommy Roberts, looked up from playing cards with the lads at the table and asked –

"Are you still cycling to and fro from Pentreberw across the marsh?"

I nodded.

"Well, sooner you than me," he said, "I wouldn't cycle over that marsh at night for all the tea in China."

Now, I knew about my great grandfather's experience and, I must admit, I always pedalled a bit faster when I drew near the cemetery mound and the humpbacked bridge but, so far I hadn't seen anything spooky.

"Why not?" I asked him.

"Listen," he said. "When I was your age, I was courting a girl who lived and worked at Plas Dinam, Llangaffo. It was a serious affair and we had every intention of getting married.

"I left her very late one night, I think it was about 1.00 a.m. and I started to cycle home from Dinam, Llangaffo, through Pentreberw. It was a lovely night – crisp and clear with a full moon – you could see for miles.

"When I got to the humpbacked bridge, I decided to take a breather so, I stopped on the brow of the bridge, didn't get off the bike, just leaned sideways holding on to the parapet and lit a cigarette.

"It was very peaceful. I could see the outline of Llangaffo where my girl lived then, I turned and looked across the bridge towards Llangefni – and I got the biggest shock of my life.

"Not two yards away from me stood the immense figure of a man. I haven't got a clue where he came from – the bridge was empty when I cycled onto it. Yet, there he stood watching me.

"I'm sure my heart stopped – then it started hammering away like mad. He was so *tall!* More of a giant than a man.

"I just boggled at him – he was so weird! Completely silent and still – the sort of stillness you get in old churches and empty buildings.

"He didn't do anything, nothing to frighten me or that, but he was *wrong* somehow – he just didn't belong to this world.

"He was staring at me, but he never moved a muscle.

"You know when people say their hair stand on end? Well, that night I found that it's quite true, your scalp goes tight and your neck hair bristles.

298

"He was a ghost alright – and I couldn't move, I was petrified. Then, suddenly, I dropped my cigarette, grabbed the handlebars and pedalled like mad to Llangefni. I kept looking over my shoulder to see if he was following me but, he stayed on the bridge.

"I was so frightened; I swore I would never travel through the marsh to Llangaffo at night ever again.

"The trouble was, my girl lived at Llangaffo so, how on earth could I meet her?

"As soon as I got home, I sat down and wrote her a letter, telling her all about it and said wild horses wouldn't drag me across that marsh again at night – so I wondered if she would leave her job at Dinam and come and get a job in Llangefni?

"But, she wrote back and said no – she was very happy at Dinam and she had no intention of leaving. Well, I had no intention of crossing that haunted marsh again either.

"We wrote a lot of letters arguing about it, neither of us would give in so, although I was very, very fond of her, I ended the courtship."

Tommy was silent for a minute, lost in his memories, and then he sighed and said –

"Do you know, if it hadn't been for that ghost on the bridge, I would have married that girl."'

* * *

That was Donald Pritchard's story and it reminded me of a series of hauntings witnessed not long ago in the South of England.

For years, people reported seeing a figure in shining golden armour which always appeared in the vicinity of an ancient mound. When the mound was eventually excavated, it was found to contain the remains of a king or chieftain dressed in golden armour, which substantiated the stories.

I'd love to know what the Grove Mound Cemetery contains.